ENTREPRENEURSHIP
AND
SMALL FIRMS

ENTREPRENEURSHIP
AND
SMALL FIRMS

David Deakins

Professor of Enterprise Development
University of Paisley

The McGraw-Hill Companies
London · New York · St Louis · San Francisco · Auckland
Bogotá · Caracas · Lisbon · Madrid · Mexico
Milan · Montreal · New Delhi · Panama · Paris · San Juan
São Paulo · Singapore · Sydney · Tokyo · Toronto

Published by
McGRAW-HILL Publishing Company
Shoppenhangers Road, Maidenhead, Berkshire, SL6 2QL, England
Telephone 01628 23432
Fax 01628 770224

British Library Cataloguing in Publication Data

Deakins, David
　Entrepreneurship and small firms
　1. Entrepreneurship　2. Small business
　I. Title
　658' .022
　ISBN 0-07-709068-3

Library of Congress Cataloguing-in-publication Data

Deakins, David.
　Entrepreneurship and small firms / David Deakins.
　　p.　cm.
　ISBN 0-07-709068-3 (pbk. : alk. paper)
　1. Entrepreneurship.　2. Small business–Management.　3. Small business–Great Britain.
　4. Entrepreneurship–Great Britan.　5. New business enterprises.
　6. New business enterprises–Great Britain　I. Title.
HB615.D43　1996
228'.04–dc20　　　　　　　　　　　　　　　　　　　　　　　95-50820

McGraw-Hill

*A Division of the **McGraw-Hill** Companies*

　2345　CL 99876

Typeset by Mackreth Media Services, Hemel Hempstead, Herts
Printed and bound in Great Britain by Clays Ltd, St Ives plc

Printed on permanent paper in accordance with ISO Standard 9706.

Dedication

This book is dedicated to the memory of Joe Wilson, a true entrepreneur and visionary—an entrepreneur who through his inspiration was responsible for being involved in some of the research in this book. Joe died, after a courageous battle against leukaemia, as this book was nearing completion in 1995. Much of his visionary and innovative work remains for others to build on. Without his contribution this book, and the research on which it is based, would not have been possible.

Contents

CONTENTS

Acknowledgements

As stated throughout this book, the author is indebted to colleagues that he worked with at UCE, in particular the small group of staff associated with the research centre during the period 1990–4 which included Monder Ram, Guhlum Hussain, John Sparrow, Toby Philpott, and Patrick Bentley. The author is also indebted to entrepreneurs who became involved with the research programme at UCE, especially to Joe Wilson, to whose memory this book is dedicated. The author would also like to acknowledge the contributions of students and participants in seminars who have helped to shape the research programme and he is also grateful to additional staff who have enthusiastically supported curricular developments and innovative teaching methods, notably Mike Cunningham and Chris Martin.

Introduction

This book has arisen for a number of reasons. Firstly, a gap has been perceived in the literature concerning entrepreneurship and small firms, between the more practical start-up guides for small firms and would be entrepreneurs and the more academic literature associated with research with entrepreneurs and small firm owners which has burgeoned with the increased attention paid to the small firms sector in the 1980s and the 1990s. This book seeks to fill this need, which was recognized through the provision of an Enterprise Studies course at Birmingham Polytechnic (now University of Central England—UCE), and later at the University of Paisley, placing the academic and research contributions in the context of the reality that small firm owners/managers and entrepreneurs face in their everyday decisions. Thus this book includes suggested practical assignments and case studies that, if used with students, will develop problem solving skills and competencies in analysis. These assignments are designed to develop 'enterprise skills' in students and to build towards the completion of a feasibility study and business plan for a client organization which should preferably be for an existing small firm or entrepreneur. They can also be adapted to provide students with help for their own start-up business including a feasibility study and business plan.

Secondly, this book has been written for the purely selfish reason of disseminating research findings from research carried out at Birmingham and Paisley. At UCE, a group of staff formed a small business research group in 1990. Later this became the Enterprise Research Centre, before the author left to form the equivalent Paisley Enterprise Research Centre at Paisley. Most of the research reported in this book was carried out by the author with colleagues while at Birmingham. The author is indebted to the small group of staff, mentioned in the Acknowledgements, who made this research possible. Occasionally when people of like minds get together, a programme of innovative ideas develops as was experienced during the period of four years at UCE—a very productive time in terms of research undertaken and results produced. Often this research was applied and underpinned contemporary developments in courses at UCE that were being established in entrepreneurship and small firms.

Although some of this research has been disseminated and appropriate articles published, there is still a considerable amount of research that has not been previously printed, such as the work that we have done with start-up clients of a local enterprise agency in the West Midlands. The results or this research are reported in Chapter 3. Another example includes research on the use of insurance and risk management which is reported in Chapter 1.

Thirdly, there has been considerable course development in polytechnics and the new universities on relatively new 'Enterprise' degree courses that build upon the work of courses in HNC/HND, sometimes offering HND students an opportunity to obtain a degree in one year instead of the normal two year additional period. At the time of writing, there is also considerable development of the curriculum involving courses in entrepreneurship and enterprise in Scotland following concern about low business birth rate in Scotland and a perceived need to encourage greater awareness of enterprise and entrepreneurship. Despite these considerable curricular developments there has been no associated growth in appropriate textbooks and lecturers often have to resort to their own specialized course materials. It is hoped that this book may be adopted as a suitable text for many of the students on these new courses.

In addition, there have also been other curricular developments in Business Studies degree courses and in Business School MBAs which place greater emphasis on small firm business development and business planning. First level courses in MBAs now offer Certificates and Diplomas in Business Development and many MBAs now (rather belatedly) contain small business and entrepreneurship modules or options. Again, although there are specialized academic texts, there has not been the development of texts that combine practical examples of case studies with theory and research. It is hoped that this text will go some way to fill these gaps and the needs of students on these new courses and modules.

Fourthly, as recognized above, it was felt that there was a need to combine theory and research with practical examples through case studies of entrepreneurs and small firms. Sometimes case studies are re-written by academics from material provided by entrepreneurs or from a series of interviews with the entrepreneur. The case studies in this book are presented as written by the entrepreneur and small firm owner, although some interpretation has been added as well as suggested assignments.

One of the aims of the Enterprise Research Centre at the time was to involve entrepreneurs, not only in course and curricular development, but also, in seminars and the discussion of research findings. Some of the material in the book reflects contributions from entrepreneurs and small firm owners who participated in these seminars. This book also reflects other contributions from representatives of the enterprise community that attended and participated in the seminars. Too many seminars are held by academics for academics even on areas of concern in small firms and entrepreneurship. We have tried to avoid this and it is hoped that the book reflects the views of entrepreneurs and the spirit of some of the seminars that were held at Birmingham.

Although the entrepreneurship and small firm literature has begun to burgeon following the growth of small firms and concern with 'enterprise' and the 'enterprise culture' in a number of advanced economies in the 1980s, this literature is still an emergent one. In some areas, such as the finance of small firms, theory is still being developed. Unusually for an emergent academic discipline, evidence has tended to run ahead of theoretical developments. Research has tended to be carried out in an *ad hoc* way without theoretical underpinnings being developed. In addition there has been a tendency to apply theory from large firms that is not always appropriate for the relationships entered into by entrepreneurs and small firm owners. Furthermore, because of the way that much of small firms' research has developed, there are also gaps in our knowledge of entrepreneurs and small firm behaviour. For example, as discussed in Chapter 1, we know little about how entrepreneurs learn and develop entrepreneurial expertise and about the process of entrepreneurship.

There are some views of entrepreneurial and small firm behaviour that are commonly held but have yet to be either underpinned by theoretical developments or are based upon, in some cases, quite limited research. For example, one convention that has recently been challenged is that successful small firm development depends upon the extent to which such small firm owners and entrepreneurs can engage in local economic networks. However, Curran and Blackburn (1) have recently shown that, for the majority of small firm owners, local economic networks are unimportant. They have also commented that because of trends such as globalization, entrepreneurs are more likely to be in, and rely upon, relatively dispersed networks. A further example of a convention that has yet to be adequately challenged is that, to be successful, entrepreneurs need to display certain personality characteristics such as high ambition and a desire to be in control of their environment. These so-called 'entrepreneurial personality characteristics' are discussed in detail in Chapter 1 where we question much of the convention that surrounds such entrepreneurial personality characteristics.

While the small firm and entrepreneurial literature continues to emerge we can expect that there may be a number of these current conventions that will be challenged and eventually disproved or changed. As a result, at the present time we have an imperfect body of knowledge about entrepreneurial and small firm behaviour. The reader will find that the author expresses his own views about current conventions in a number of different areas in this book. Therefore, while acknowledgement is made to the contribution of colleagues at UCE, of entrepreneurs, of other participants in events at UCE and Paisley, and not least of students, this book is also a reflection of the author's own interpretation.

Although the research with entrepreneurs and small firms has grown with the associated literature, much of this research has been quantitative. The result is that, although we now know much about the importance of small firms for the economy, we still know comparatively little about the processes of entrepreneurship and enterprise development. Much of the research has adopted a 'black box' approach to the study of the small firm owner/manager or entrepreneur. It has been concerned with measurable outputs such as the contribution of small firms to changes in employment. Although there are notable exceptions, there has not been the same output of qualitative research which is likely to increase our understanding of processes in entrepreneurship and relationships between institutions with the entrepreneurs and different firms. The emphasis (not exclusively) for research carried out at UCE has been on qualitative research—only by interviewing entrepreneurs can we begin to understand some of the processes involved in entrepreneurship and enterprise development.

The book begins by examining concepts in entrepreneurship. The first chapter questions some of the blinkered pursuit of the entrepreneurial personality. We can draw an analogy between this blinkered approach, which attempts to define the characteristics of the personality of the entrepreneur, and the current concern to identify the characteristics of the growth or 'entrepreneurial' firm. The search for the growth firm is examined later in Chapter 10. In the same way that it is impossible to identify an identikit profile of the successful entrepreneur, so it is proving impossible to identify an identikit picture of the fast-growing or fast-track small firm, despite considerable research effort to do so. We can also say that this focus is undesirable since the potential of many small firms and entrepreneurs is likely to be overlooked and may lead to the rejection of potentially successful entrepreneurs and growth firms.

Chapter 2 examines the importance of small firms for the UK economy, an importance which is now undisputed and well established. This importance is likely to increase in the future due to the increasing pace of change and the greater need for firms to be flexible, to respond to change quickly, and to be specialized. This 'flexible specialization' need and ability of small firms has been well established and will continue to account for their increased importance and contribution to the economy in the future. Chapter 3 examines some start-up issues and introduces the complementary Greenwed case study.

Sources of finance for entrepreneurs and small firms remain an area of study which is of major importance to successful outcomes in the entrepreneur-ship process and enterprise development. We examine some of the emerging theory and research in this important area in Chapter 4. This is followed by the complementary case study of Peters and Co., a business plan written by the entrepreneurs involved.

Participation in entrepreneurship across different groups of society is far from even. This is the case, for example, when we examine the participation of different ethnic minority groups in entrepreneurship and enterprise. Some of our research and some of the special issues in ethnic minority entrepreneurship are examined in Chapter 6.

Some commentators have claimed that there has been such a transformation in society in the UK in the 1980s and 1990s that we now have an 'enterprise culture' to support entrepreneurs and small firm owners. We examine the support infrastructure in Chapter 7. It is noticeable that we do have a unique infrastructure of support in the UK compared to other countries. We compare the UK system of support to that of some European countries which do not have the network of support agencies such as the Training and Enterprise Councils (TECs) or the Local Enterprise Companies (LECs) in Scotland and the enterprise agencies.

There are special issues that affect the process of entrepreneurship when combined with the process of innovation. For example, an entrepreneur concerned with the process of innovation requires seed capital to fund research and development (R&D). Some of these special requirements are examined in Chapter 8 and this chapter is followed by the Eco-Wall case study, again written by the entrepreneur to give a real world example of the different problems faced by entrepreneurs in the process of innovation.

As stated at the beginning of this introduction, this book has been compiled primarily from a course in Entrepreneurship and Enterprise at UCE and later at Paisley. Those courses built towards assignments undertaken on a consultancy basis by students on, firstly, an investigative feasibility study and, secondly, a strategic business plan. For students to undertake such work, it was necessary to be aware of different sources of information and different research methods. These are dealt with in Chapter 11. Finally, we have included a chapter on the design and implementation of the final business plan. It is important to take both of these chapters together since the business plan is meant to build upon the work undertaken for the feasibility study and should be the logical outcome of research undertaken for that study.

Finally, this book has been written with students in mind. Therefore, 'learning outcomes' have been included at the end of each chapter, as well as suggested assignments and recommended reading. For students who undertake the suggested assignments, it is hoped that they can produce a worthwhile document at the end that has practical value and application—the business plan. It has not been possible to list the most valuable learning outcomes that students obtained while working on such assignments. These came from working with small firm owners and entrepreneurs. Like the students, the author remains indebted to all the entrepreneurs that have freely given up their time to help students and to make this book possible.

Learning outcomes

At the end of this introduction you should be able to:

1. Describe the orientation and emphasis of previous research into small firms and entrepreneurship.
2. Identify two areas of misconceptions in the small firm and entrepreneurship literature.
3. Appreciate the need for continuing research into small firms and entrepreneurship.

REFERENCES

1. CURRAN, J. and BLACKBURN, R. (1994) *Small Firms and Local Economic Networks: The Death of the Local Economy?*, Paul Chapman, London.

1 *The Entrepreneur: Concepts and Evidence*

INTRODUCTION

What makes an entrepreneur or small business owner? Is an entrepreneur different from other individuals or can anyone be an entrepreneur given sufficient resources? Can anyone set up in business or do you need to have special skills and characteristics? These are questions which have occupied researchers and theorists for some time; indeed theories on what makes an entrepreneur date from the early Industrial Revolution. We will attempt to answer some of these questions later when we examine factors that can encourage successful new business creation and entrepreneurial success. However, it is useful to review the contribution of the major theorists on entrepreneurship first. It is only when these have been examined that we can understand the characteristics, traits, and factors that researchers have sought to find in the modern entrepreneur. Later we question much of this research effort into the characteristics of the entrepreneur which can be seen as misplaced. It may, for example, be better to concentrate on the management skills that are required of business owners. Developing this theme, we consider some of the author's recent research which examines the concept of risk management and the use of insurance by entrepreneurs.

Developments in entrepreneurship are sometimes seen as stemming from three sources: firstly, from the contributions of economic writers and thinkers on the role of the entrepreneur in economic development and the application of economic theory; secondly, from the psychological trait approach on personality characteristics of the entrepreneur, which is examined critically later; thirdly, a social behavioural approach which stresses the influence of the social environment as well as personality traits. Each approach is considered in this chapter, and it can

D end 9 intro

be claimed that all three approaches have something to contribute to our understanding of the entrepreneurship process. However, it will be seen that the value of psychological and social approaches are more controversial; indeed there is some dispute over whether 'entrepreneurial' characteristics can be identified at all.

There are many economic writers and theorists that could be included in looking at the role of the entrepreneur, but, in a text such as this, only the major contributors from the history of economic theory will be discussed. For a detailed analysis of other theorists and contributors and the development of the theory of the entrepreneur, the student is advised to consult the recommended reading at the end of this chapter (1).

THE ENTREPRENEUR

If we examine conventional economic theory, the term 'entrepreneur' is noticeable only by its absence. In mainstream or neo-classical economic theory, the entrepreneur can be viewed as someone who co-ordinates different factors of production, but the important distinction is that this role is viewed as a non-important one. The entrepreneur becomes merged with the capitalist employer, the owner-manager who has the wealth to enable production to take place, but otherwise does not contain any special attributes. The entrepreneur, if recognized at all, is pure risk taker, the reward being the ability to appropriate profits. It is a remarkable fact that the main body of conventional economic theory has developed without a place for the entrepreneur, yet there is no shortage of writers who have contributed to the development of views on the role and concept of the entrepreneur.

The idea that the entrepreneur has a significant role in economic development has been developed by writers outside the mainstream economic thinking. Their contributions now have an important place, but it is only relatively recently that they have been recognized. As attention has become more focused on the importance of the Small- and Medium-Sized Enterprise (SME) sector for economic development and job creation so greater attention has also been directed at theories of entrepreneurship. We will examine the most important of these theories which are accepted today.

The term 'entrepreneur' is French in origin, a literal meaning might translate as 'one who takes between'. There are some important French writers who contributed views on the role of the entrepreneur, the most important being Cantillon and Say. Cantillon was the first to recognize the crucial role of the entrepreneur in economic development which was founded on individual property rights. Of the three classes in society recognized by Cantillon, entrepreneurs were the important class and were the central economic actors. The other two classes comprised landowners and workers or hirelings. Say also made the entrepreneur the pivot of the economy and a catalyst for economic change and development. The entrepreneur provided a commercial stage in three stages of production. In this way the entrepreneur could be seen as close to the traditional mainstream view of the entrepreneur as someone willing to take the risk of bringing different factors of production together.

Both Cantillon and Say belonged to a French school of thought known as the 'physiocrats', so called because the physical nature of the agrarian economy dominated their thinking. It could be because of this view that developments in the concept of the entrepreneur were not seen as being relevant to the nineteenth century industrial economy. It was much later before more modern concepts of the entrepreneur were developed. Some of these views have been developed within the 'Austrian School' of thought, however, this is such a wide-ranging term that there is not one particular view associated with this school for the entrepreneur. What is different, however, is that the entrepreneur is seen as being crucial to economic development and a catalyst for dynamic change. We turn now to these Austrian school writers who underpin much of the current theories and research into the characteristics of the entrepreneur.

KIRZNER

For Kirzner, the entrepreneur is someone who is *alert* to profitable opportunities for exchange. Recognizing the possibilities for exchange enables the entrepreneur to benefit by acting as a 'middleman' who facilitates the exchange. The Kirznerian entrepreneur is alert to opportunities for trade. He or she is able to identify suppliers and customers and acts as the intermediary. Note that there is no necessity to own resources and and profit arises out of the intermediary function.

These possibilities for profitable exchange exist because of imperfect knowledge. The entrepreneur has some additional knowledge which is not possessed by others and this permits the entrepreneur to take advantage of profitable opportunities. The information is costless, it arises when someone notices an opportunity which may have been available all the time. It can often seem obvious after the service or product has been provided but it still takes someone with additional knowledge to recognize and exploit the opportunity.

The role of information in the market place is important for the Kirznerian entrepreneur. Market exchange itself is an entrepreneurial process, but people can profit from exchange because of information gaps in the market. In this view, the entrepreneur may be seen as little more than a market trader, taking advantage of opportunities to trade; yet for Kirzner the entrepreneur is someone who is still creative. The possession of additional knowledge provides opportunities for creative discoveries. However, in contrast to the Schumpeterian view, below, anyone could potentially possess the additional knowledge and be alert to opportunities for exchange and trade.

SCHUMPETER

By contrast, Schumpeter's entrepreneur is a special person. Although Schumpeter is a writer classified in the 'Austrian School', his views on the entrepreneurial function are quite different from those of Kirzner.

The Schumpeterian entrepreneur is an *innovator*. The entrepreneur brings about change through the introduction of new technological processes or products. For Kirzner, anyone has the potential to be an entrepreneur and they operate within set production constraints. For Schumpeter, only certain extraordinary people have the ability to be entrepreneurs and they bring about extraordinary events. The Schumpeterian entrepreneur changes technological possibilities and convention through innovative activity, and moves production constraints. He or she develops new technology whereas for Kirzner the entrepreneur operates on opportunities that arise out of new technology.

Although the entrepreneur is again an important catalyst for economic change, the entrepreneur is essentially temporary for Schumpeter. Schumpeter predicted the demise of the function of the entrepreneur. Technological advance and change would be carried out by teams of workers and scientists operating in large organizations. This is because, for Schumpeter, large monopolistic firms have distinct advantages over small firms in the technological process.

The idea that large firms are more successful than small firms in new technology-based industries is more correctly attributable to Galbraith. However, this idea has become to be associated with Schumpeter, even though he was more concerned with the advantages of monopolistic market structure than firm size. The basic concept is that the small firm entrepreneur faces considerable disadvantages in Research and Development (R&D); e.g., R&D is expensive; it has long development times; and teams of researchers are able to benefit by feeding off one another's ideas. If the entrepreneur is an innovator, then this argument suggests that he/she will find it difficult to establish new small firms. Technological change is carried out by large firms. The entrepreneur may still exist in large firms—the so-called 'intrapreneur'—an individual who is capable of initiating change in large firms.

The concept that the entrepreneur is someone who is different, someone who is an innovator, is important. Some writers have carried this forward to distinguish entrepreneurs (business owners who wish to develop and expand their businesses) from other small business owners who have no ambition to expand their business or wish to remain merely self-employed. The essential distinguishing feature for such writers is that the entrepreneur is a Schumpeterian innovator, although here the term 'innovator' would be more loosely defined to include a person who wishes to manage change or initiate change in some way. For example, Curran and Stanworth (2) state that:

> Entrepreneurship, rigorously defined, refers to the creation of a new
> economic entity centred on a novel product or service or, at the very

least, one which differs significantly from products or services offered elsewhere in the market (p. 12).

KNIGHT

The commonly held view of the entrepreneur as a calculated risk taker comes close to the view of Knight. For Knight the entrepreneur is an individual who is prepared to undertake risk and the reward—profit—is the return for bearing uncertainty and is an uninsurable risk.

The opportunity for profit arises out of uncertainty surrounding change. If change is perfectly predictable then no opportunity for profit exists. The entrepreneur is someone who is prepared to undertake risk in an uncertain world.

Knight made an important distinction between risk and uncertainty. Risk exists when we have uncertain outcomes but those outcomes can be predicted with a certain degree of probability. For example, the outcome that your car will be stolen or not stolen is uncertain, but the risk that your car will be stolen can be calculated with some degree of probability and this risk can be insured against. True uncertainty arises when the probability of outcomes cannot be calculated. Thus, anyone can set up in business but that person cannot insure against business failure because that particular outcome cannot be predicted with any degree of probability. The entrepreneur is someone who is willing to accept the remaining risk that cannot be transferred through insurance. We have an important distinction established by Knight which has not so far been explored in small firms' research. We include some of the author's own research on risk management and insurance in a later section in this chapter. Issues such as the extent to which the small firm owner assesses, accepts, and transfers risk have not yet been explored in research.

This distinction helps to distinguish a small firm manager from the entrepreneur/owner. One of the characteristics of entrepreneurs (following Knight) could be considered to be the responsibility for one's own actions. If a manager assumes this then he or she is performing some entrepreneurial functions. We can also use this distinction as a criticism of some research into entrepreneurship which concentrates solely on personality traits and ignores management skills.

These distinctions are unfortunately rarely discussed in the small firms' literature. However, an exception is provided by Shailer (3). For example Shailer considers that:

> (The) entrepreneur is now a widely used term, with considerable contemporary diversity in meaning associated with the intended interests of its users. . . . Owner-managers do not necessarily fit any of the current popular definitions of 'entrepreneur' (p. 34).

Shailer prefers to adopt the view of entrepreneurship as a process and refers to a stage of the firm when it is in owner-management. Again we have the important concept of management of the firm, the willingness to accept risks and responsibilities. If the firm grows, it is possible to transfer this entrepreneurial function, but still retain part ownership through the issue of shares. The manager as opposed to the owner now takes on the function of the entrepreneur. The fact that behaviour of the previous owner-entrepreneur is likely to alter has been established (theoretically) by writers such as Jensen and Meckling (4) by applying agency theory. The concept of the importance of small business management skills is also discussed by Ray (5). He considers that the search for the prototype has been ill-conceived and considers that: 'there is no empirical evidence or conceptual base to say much, if anything, about entrepreneurs and risk taking' (p. 347).

Ray considers that we should concentrate on the development of skills and how managers acquire them. These concepts are too frequently ignored and this entrepreneurial and learning process has not yet been adequately researched.

We could say then that the Knightian entrepreneur is anyone who is prepared to undertake the risk of setting up their own business. However, equally it could be any risk taker (and this is a source of criticism). The entrepreneur is someone who has the confidence and is venturesome enough to make judgements about the uncertain future and reward for this is profit.

SHACKLE

Shackle's entrepreneur is someone who is creative and imaginative. Whereas Kirzner's entrepreneur perceives opportunities, Shackle's imagines opportunities. Everyone potentially has this creative ability, which is exercised in making choices.

The role of uncertainty and imperfect information is crucial for the view of the role of the entrepreneur by Shackle. Uncertainty gives rise to opportunities for certain individuals to imagine opportunities for profit. Shackle's entrepreneur is creative and original. The act of imagination is important for identifying the potential of opportunities. This potential is compared to resources available which can lead to the decision to produce, hence the act of entrepreneurship.

CASSON

Casson attempts to synthesize some of these entrepreneurial attributes and concepts that have been discussed with the major writers above. Casson recognizes that the entrepreneur will have different skills from others. These skills enable the entrepreneur to make judgements, to co-ordinate scarce resources. The entrepreneur makes judgemental decisions which involves the reallocation or organization of resources.

Casson emphasizes that entrepreneurs require command over resources if they are to back their judgements and that this is likely to imply that they will have personal wealth. Lack of capital would thus be a barrier to successful entrepreneurship.

Casson's view is closer to that of Knight than other writers. The entrepreneur operates within a set of technological conditions; by making difficult judgemental decisions they are able to enjoy the reward of profit (for bearing uninsurable risk). This enables the entrepreneur to co-ordinate demand and supply under uncertainty.

In Fig. 1.1, the demand curve represents the return to each entrepreneur as their numbers increase and is part of a map of such curves. The supply curve of entrepreneurs depends on access to resources and thus depends on the local economy and environment. Casson's analysis attempts to explain why in some economies entrepreneurs can flourish, yet in other economies, there are low participation rates for people who own their own businesses. For example, the South-East in the UK has higher participation rates of people in small business ownership than the Midlands, which in turn has higher participation rates than

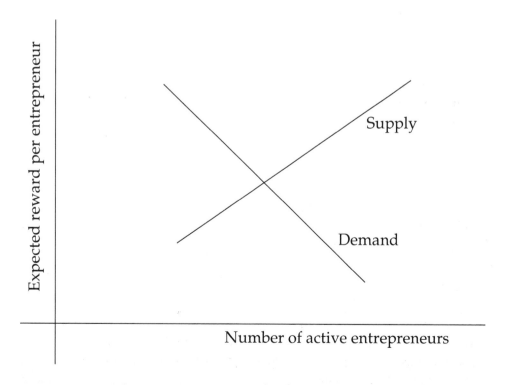

Figure 1.1 Casson's demand and supply of entrepreneurs

Scotland. The low participation rates in Scotland have been attributed, for example, to low home ownership which limits the amount of equity that a potential entrepreneur might have to invest in a start-up firm (6). Thus Casson's point about the access to resources would appear to be an important one. The clear implication when we examine such participation rates is that the environment can be a more powerful influence than any predilection among the local population for entrepreneurship.

Casson's insight is to view change as an accompaniment to entrepreneurship. The pace of change provides opportunities and the entrepreneur chooses which one to back. Entrepreneurs can vie with each other as their numbers increase, the supply of entrepreneurs depending on their access to resources. The supply curve shown in Fig. 1.1 will thus depend on the propensity of any given set of circumstances and the extent to which potential entrepreneurs have access to resources. This will depend on factors such as social mobility, and institutional factors such as the ability to access capital. An equilibrium position will result as shown in Fig. 1.1 from the interaction of these factors.

A number of additional economic writers and theorists have considered the development of the role of the entrepreneur. These include, for example, Thunen who could be seen as a forerunner of Knight. Thunen recognized the function of the entrepreneur as a risk taker, risk which cannot be transferred through insurance, a theme which we will return to later in this chapter. For Thunen, however, the entrepreneur was also concerned with innovation and problem solving.

It would be untrue to say that the neo-classical school of economists added little to the concept of the entrepreneur. For example, Marshall recognized a distinction between the capitalist and the entrepreneur through his 'undertaker' who was alert to opportunities but also innovative in devising new methods of production.

SUMMARY

A consensus has emerged that in conditions of uncertainty and change, the entrepreneur is a key actor in the economy. Two major lines of thinking have developed: the Knightian approach which highlights the risk bearing and uncertainty reducing role of entrepreneurs; and the Schumpeterian approach in which the entrepreneur is an innovator, a forger of new systems and production possibilities. Other perspectives highlight the knowledge and insight of the entrepreneur to possibilities and the role of Kirzner's middleman. This co-ordinating role has been developed and emphasized by Casson, but in addition it is clear that there are other factors which influence participation in entrepreneurship such as access to resources and facilities in the local environment. Finally, it is probably more useful to look at the entrepreneurial function rather than any set of characteristics which are necessary to become an entrepreneur.

We turn now to consider some of the empirical evidence of the factors that influence entrepreneurship. As we have suggested much of research effort has gone into discovering personality traits of the entrepreneur; some of this literature is controversial, since some of it assumes that an entrepreneur must have some special ability that distinguishes him/her from other people. Unfortunately this does not explain why there are low participation rates in entrepreneurship by women and by African-Caribbeans in the UK. As Ram (7) has pointed out the Asian community has high rates of participation in small business ownership/entrepreneurship, yet this has more to do with negative factors of barriers to employment elsewhere than any predisposition for entrepreneurship.

MORE RECENT DEVELOPMENTS

The ideas and concepts surrounding the entrepreneur which have been outlined above are used as a basis by researchers for detecting traits in successful small business people and entrepreneurs. As in any scientific method the theory can be used for developing hypotheses about the behaviour of successful entrepreneurs. These hypotheses are then tested against the observed characteristics of entrepreneurs and small business owners in the real world. However, there are a number of problems with this approach that have been discussed above and in particular:

1. Some regions are more favoured than others at establishing successful small businesses and entrepreneurs and hence their economic development is more successful. The question of whether this is due to characteristics in the population or due to certain aspects of the environment and infrastructure which enable potential entrepreneurs to exploit their skills and opportunities more easily, remains, at this stage, an open one.

   For example, research undertaken for Scottish Enterprise (6), after concern with low participation rates in entrepreneurship, showed that a complex series of factors contributed to low participation rates in Scotland. For example, the historical dependence of the population on a limited number of large employers coupled with inward investment (North Sea oil) had produced a 'dependency culture' , that is, that people were used to depending on large employers for employment. Thus, the thought of going into business on their own account did not come easily to them. Yet other factors were important as well such as lack of finance. This example shows why participation rates might be different in particular regions for varying complex reasons.
2. Concern has been expressed at the existence of latent entrepreneurial talent. For example, why are there so few successful female entrepreneurs? Why is the

participation rate of African-Caribbeans in entrepreneurship low? Again these remain open questions which appear to have no simple solution but rather are caused by a complex combination of social and economic reasons.

Little research has been conducted specifically on these groups in the UK, although a study carried out by the author and Ram (8) with African-Caribbean entrepreneurs suggests that motivations among this minority group in the UK consist of a combination of positive (pull) and negative (push) factors. Positive factors are associated with the attractions of entrepreneurship and negative factors are associated with limited opportunities in the inner-city and deprived urban environments.

3. Attention has focused on the role of networks in successful entrepreneurial development. For example, some research suggests that inter-firm networks contribute to successful entrepreneurship as discussed below.

We know that a high proportion of new firms fail within three years of start-up. For example, in the UK, 30 per cent of new firms cease trading by the third year and 50 per cent by the fifth year (9). In addition, there is only a small proportion that grow to employ 50 workers. One of the factors is the potential loss of control faced by the entrepreneur as the firm grows. New small firms and entrepreneurs that are successful are predominantly located in the South-East in the UK. This suggests that the environment and infrastructure is at least as important as the characteristics of the entrepreneur. It is also likely that the development of inter-firm networks is more advanced in the South-East than in other regions of the UK.

The inter-organizational networks that link firms after they are established have been found to be important to the on-going success of firms (10). Efficient networks that foster good communications between firms contribute to entrepreneurial behaviour and success.

THE ENTREPRENEURIAL PERSONALITY

The second approach to entrepreneurship is to identify certain personality characteristics or 'traits' in individuals that appear to be possessed by successful entrepreneurs. The characteristics literature has been concerned with testing and applying some perceived characteristics in individuals. From this approach, it is possible to argue that the supply of potential entrepreneurs is limited to a finite number of people that have innate abilities, that they have a set of characteristics marking them out as special and have particular insights, not possessed by others. This has led to some controversy and, in terms of policy, it has significant implications. Obviously, if entrepreneurial characteristics are inherent, then there is little to be gained from direct interventions to encourage new start-ups, although indirect interventions into improving the infrastructure or environment may still have an effect. Whether an 'entrepreneurial personality' exists, however, is the subject of controversy and despite attempts to provide prototypical 'lists' of characteristics of the entrepreneurial personality this author, for one, remains sceptical of such approaches.

Some of these personality 'traits' are examined below, although, as will become apparent, the author does not accept the hypothesis that there is a limited supply of potential entrepreneurs. For example, many of the characteristics which are often said to be special to successful entrepreneurs are the same abilities and skills that could be applied to most successful managers and it is therefore difficult to separate out specific characteristics of entrepreneurs.

Some of this research stems from the original work carried out by McClelland (11), who gives the following key competencies of successful entrepreneurs:

- Proactivity: initiative and assertiveness
- Achievement orientation: ability to see and act on opportunities
- Commitment to others.

Much has been made of the need for achievement trait, as though this was the one characteristic that sets potential budding entrepreneurs apart from others, and was, therefore, associated with successful economic development in advanced industrial countries. An implicit assumption with this approach is that the individual bears responsibility for his or her lack of entrepreneurial activity and this proposition could be used by policy makers to divert interventions away from regions that have low rates of participation in small firm ownership.

Considering the work of writers on the entrepreneurial personality and those who might subscribe to the characteristics approach, we can identify certain key characteristics which have been identified in the literature as being important abilities of any entrepreneur:

- McClelland's need for achievement
- Calculated risk taker
- High internal locus of control
- Innovative
- Ambiguity tolerance
- Vision.

Some writers subscribe to the view of McClelland that the key characteristic is achievement motivation, or a high need for achievement, which can be described as a desire to excel, to achieve a goal in relation to a set of standards. High achievers are those that accept responsibility for decisions and for achieving solutions to problems, but standards will be set carefully so that they can be achieved. Satisfaction is gained from the solution to a problem rather than with monetary reward. Yet, partly because such a characteristic is difficult to measure, the evidence has proved to be contradictory.

Another characteristic that has been advocated is the locus of control. Individuals with a high locus of control like to be in control of their environment and of their own destiny. Again, however, as with the need for an achievement trait, it has not been possible to reconcile the conflicting evidence of entrepreneurs with this approach to one or two important personality traits. For a critique of the characteristics literature see Chell *et al.* (12).

As we have said above, researchers have been concerned with whether successful entrepreneurs display psychological traits that separate them out as individuals from others. This approach can be criticized in a number of ways:

1. It is inappropriate to search for a significant single trait.
2. It ignores other environmental factors that may be more important than personality.

A further example is provided by Meredith *et al.* (13) who give five core traits:

- Self-confidence
- Risk taking activity
- Flexibility
- Need for achievement
- Strong desire to be independent.

Again the trait of need for achievement is represented.

In general the following traits have been suggested as important.

- Need for achievement
- Internal locus of control
- High propensity for risk taking
- Need for independence
- Deviants (see below)
- Innovative behaviour.

The deviant personality is associated with the third approach to the entrepreneur, that of the social behavioural school, associated with Kets de Vries. A deviant character is associated with individuals who do not easily fit in with their existing employment, e.g., someone who is out of place in a large firm. However, this would seem to rule out the possibility of the dynamic employee wishing to create change in the large firm, the intrapreneur.

Writers such as Timmons (14) have attempted to summarize the personality characteristics of successful entrepreneurs and to categorize traits that can be acquired and those that are more innate. While Timmons does admit that many of these characteristics can be acquired, that is they can be acquired through learning or from experience, Timmons also considers that there are some attributes which cannot be acquired, that are innate, that perhaps mark out 'born entrepreneurs' from 'made entrepreneurs'.

Timmons considers that both need for achievement and locus of control can be acquired along with other leadership abilities and competencies such as the ability to take responsibility for actions/decisions. Many of these characteristics are management skills. That is, entrepreneurs obviously need to be ambitious but need to be satisfied that they have achieved personal goals and ambitions.

We can assume that profit or monetary reward is not the only driving force behind entrepreneurs. There is also the need to build and achieve personally set goals, implying that entrepreneurs have a high need for achievement in order to establish a growing business or 'entrepreneurial' firm (this is discussed in more detail in Chapter 10). Similarly, the internal locus of control characteristic has been identified as an important characteristic of potential entrepreneurs. A high internal locus of control means that the person needs to be in control of their own environment, to be their own boss. It is perhaps interesting that Timmons considers that these characteristics can be acquired. This approach is one to be welcomed—many of these abilities can be taught or, at the very least, scenarios can be provided which stimulate the acquisition of these skills and abilities.

It is also interesting that Timmons considers that dealing with failure can be an important attribute of entrepreneurs. However, the ability to tolerate failure depends on the culture. In the USA failure is viewed as a learning experience and people can benefit from failure, can learn from their experience and go on to form successful companies as a result. In Britain, our culture is less tolerant of failure and too often highly talented individuals have not been able to recover from failure. The culture and environment is crucial to tolerance of failure. There is little doubt that Britain has lost many potentially successful entrepreneurs, because having failed once, they have not been allowed to recover from that failure, perhaps from an inability to raise capital having been through bankruptcy. Failure is a very valuable learning experience, as many entrepreneurs have admitted. It is a pity in Britain that we too often do not allow potential entrepreneurs a further opportunity so that they can benefit from their experience, apply lessons learned, and build a successful business.

In practice, many of the entrepreneurial characteristics are those associated with any successful manager or indeed with any successful individual. It is thus difficult to justify a separate set of characteristics for a successful career in entrepreneurship.

Timmons also gives additional attributes which are more innate. These are listed as:

■ High energy coupled with emotional stability
■ Creative and innovative ability
■ Conceptual ability
■ Vision combined with a capacity to inspire.

Although it may be claimed that this set of characteristics is more innate in terms of identifying people who are potential entrepreneurs, it is difficult to justify that these abilities mark people out for entrepreneurship. It also does not mean that they cannot be acquired. By the use of planning scenarios and problem-solving it is still possible to demonstrate how opportunities can be exploited, how resources can be acquired, and how creative solutions can be developed.

Some institutions and writers have attempted to develop tests of potential entrepreneurial ability of enterprise. For example, one such approach has been developed by Caird. She has developed a measure of enterprising traits (or entrepreneurial abilities) called the General Enterprise Tendency (GET) (15), used by Durham Business School. It consists of a scale of different questions within the following categories:

12 questions which measure need for achievement
12 which assess internal locus of control
12 to determine creative tendency
12 to gauge calculated risk taking
6 to measure need for autonomy

Entrepreneurial or enterprise tendency tests, however, suffer from the same limitations as the characteristics approach. Not surprisingly, these tests have been found not to be consistent in their application or selection.

Problems arise whenever attempts are made to measure these characteristics. The problems with measurement are that:

1. Characteristics are not stable and change over time.
2. In many cases they are subjective judgements that do not lend themselves to objective measurement. For example, how do we define being innovative? It can simply be the ability to deal with change and cope with new processes and solutions. How do we measure the calculated risk taker? In many respects there are unsatisfactory definitions of these concepts which makes their measurement difficult to justify.
3. Concentrating on personality characteristics means that we are in danger of ignoring environmental and cultural influences which can be just as if not more important than any set of personality traits.
4. Placing too much importance on an inherent set of personality characteristics reduces the role of education and training. Learning can be a very valuable

process that allows potential entrepreneurs to acquire skills to develop methods of business planning. While we would agree that many people are not suited to entrepreneurship, there is still much that can be learned by potential entrepreneurs and this process is far from understood.

There is a danger that these approaches can influence and dominate approaches to small firm ownership and entrepreneurship so that important influences on entrepreneurship such as quality of the infrastructure provided in the environment are ignored. There are a number of problems with these approaches which have been mentioned above. They include ignoring issues such as gender, age, social class, and education, all of which can have a bearing on the propensity of an individual to enter entrepreneurship. Later in this chapter, we turn to one of these issues for special consideration, that of gender, and we examine some of the limited research into female entrepreneurship.

THE ABILITY TO LEARN

Much effort has gone into identifying entrepreneurial characteristics and it has diverted research away from important areas concerning the entrepreneur's ability to learn from problem solving and to gain from their business experience. We do not understand how entrepreneurs learn, yet it is accepted that there is a learning experience from merely establishing a new enterprise. The learning process that is involved in business and enterprise development is poorly understood, yet programmes have been designed and interventions are made in business development. The problem with these interventions (at least in the past) is that they are often task-oriented. They are often built around particular tasks and skills in terms of business planning; for example, they may concentrate on bookkeeping or financial skills, on liquidity or controlling for debt. As such they concentrate on specific tasks of running a business. A failing of such interventions is that they do little to alter the approach of the entrepreneur to solving business problems and learning from dealing with those problems.

Entrepreneurs who become task-oriented are those that are more likely to fail. Entrepreneurship involves a learning process, an ability to cope with problems and to learn from those problems. An ability to recognize why problems occur and to be able to deal with them, and more important understand why they occur, will ensure that the entrepreneur will be able not only to deal with those problems, but to learn from the experience and ensure that processes are put in place within the firm to ensure that either the problem does not occur again or that the firm can deal with the problem. This ability to learn from experiences involves the concept of double-loop learning (16)—a process which involves examining why the problem occurred and to learn from that process. It is a process of learning 'how to learn'. Unfortunately, much of previous research effort has focused on attempting to identify key characteristics of entrepreneurial personalities or key characteristics of growth firms. This approach completely ignores this skill of successful managers and entrepreneurs which is the ability to learn from problems, the ability to acquire and use knowledge from their experience. Entrepreneurship as with any other process is very much a learning process. If we accept that, then rather than attempt to pick successful entrepreneurs or growth firms, we should concentrate on helping entrepreneurs to cope with problems and to learn from their experience. Concentration of much of support intervention is therefore misplaced (although this is beginning to change) because it concentrates on tasks, not on entrepreneurship as a process. Entrepreneurs who are process driven are much more likely to be successful.

The statements made in this section, on the ability to learn, have been unqualified by any citations of research. This reflects the lack of research into the learning process of entrepreneurship and enterprise development and the emphasis of previous research, which has focused on the identification of personality characteristics. There is now a need for re-focusing research away from the emphasis on picking successful entrepreneurs or picking winners, to identifying key issues in the learning and developmental process of entre-preneurship. We can then help business owners to achieve conceptual awareness of this process and help entrepreneurs develop skills in its management, abilities which allow them to learn and act upon their experience.

RISK MANAGEMENT

In this section we return to Knight's concepts of risk and uncertainty and of the entrepreneur as risk taker and manager. It has often been expressed that an entrepreneur is a risk taker but 'not a gambler'. That is, that they will take calculated risks, not gambles (which are seen as uncalculated risks). The author, however, does not find this helpful, since a gambler can just as easily be described as someone who does take calculated risks—a gambler knows the odds against winning, has calculated the chances of beating those odds and hence takes a calculated risk with a financial stake. It is possible to argue that there is little difference between this approach and that of the entrepreneur who has made a calculated risk by putting up a financial stake and has worked out the odds against success. We may describe first attempts to enter business, by definition, as a form of calculated gamble. The entrepreneur can minimize those risks but there is always an element of luck, of right timing. There are always things that can go wrong, after all the entrepreneur is dealing with uncertainty. This is the key insight of Knight, that the entrepreneur is dealing with uncertainty and takes risks that can be calculated just as the gambler takes his or her calculated risks.

It is more helpful to see the entrepreneur as a risk manager as this identifies one of the key concepts to understanding the process of entrepreneurship. In dealing with uncertainty, the entrepreneur has to identify, assess, evaluate, manage and transfer risk. Knight saw risk as a subset of uncertainty. Events that are truly uncertain cannot be predicted with any degree of probability. However, most events are risky; their probability of occurrence can be predicted with a degree of probability. Some events have a greater degree of probability of occurrence attached to them than to others. For example, insurance premiums in the inner city are high because the probability of damage to premises is higher than in other locations. A successful entrepreneur is someone who is able to identify, assess and evaluate the importance of the risk, say, of trading in the inner city. They are able to manage this risk either through preventive measures or through the transfer of risk with insurance, and hence make decisions about trading and market opportunities weighed against the risk of operating in a particular location. A later chapter examines ethnic minority entrepreneurs. In the UK these have been successful entrepreneurs in marginal economic environments. They have successfully managed the risk of operating in that environment by being resourceful, by developing coping strategies, by learning to manage within a limited ethnic market, and developing policies that enable them to break out into mainstream markets. By understanding the process of entrepreneurship in the context of the environment and the degree of risk imposed by that environment, this gives us a greater degree of understanding of what contributes to a successful process of entrepreneurship than attempts to identify sets of personality characteristics or focusing too closely on the role of the entrepreneur as some form of calculated risk-taker.

A successful entrepreneur is someone who can minimize risks either through the limitation of his or her financial stake or by reducing the degree of uncertainty, so that risks can be calculated accurately and decisions can be made with more reliability. He or she will want to know what the potential market is, who the competitors are, and what strategy would be best in the market place. By assessing different risks in terms of the process of production which includes buying materials, supplies, and assessing risks in the market, the entrepreneur engages in uncertainty reducing behaviour that will maximize his or her probability of success.

RISK MANAGEMENT AND THE USE OF INSURANCE

The pre-occupation in applied research with the personality traits of entrepreneurs has meant that little attention has been given to the management skills of entrepreneurs. One set of management skills is concerned with the management of risk. Although Knight identified the importance of risk taking, the entrepreneur needs to be able to assess which risks to accept and which risks to transfer. In this process, the entrepreneur may decide to accept some risk, reduce risk through risk management, or transfer risk through insurance. As indicated before, however, we know little of the extent to which an entrepreneur attempts to perform this function.

The availability of insurance is important because it enables the entrepreneur to transfer risk instead of accepting the full risk liability. For example, if you start in business, you will be faced with a number of risks that can prevent the business operating successfully. These include theft of stocks, fire, damage to vehicles through motor accidents, injury to a member of the public through the actions of your employees or from your products, and injury to visitors on your premises. All of these risks can easily be transferred through insurance policies and in some cases such insurance may be compulsory, e.g., employee liability. Some risks, of course are not transferable. The risk of making losses cannot be transferred through any insurance policy, although it is possible to transfer subsequential losses (from some other risk, e.g. subsequential loss from fire). In addition, the management of risk can reduce the extent of insurance needed, and risk can also be reduced by taking a number of measures that prevent the possibility of accidents. For example, special training for employees in health and safety may reduce the risk of employee accidents and hence reduce the amount of insurance premium required by the insurance company.

Some firms are faced with more risks than others. For example, high technology manufacturing small firms face greater risks than service sector firms. They may have product liability risks and, in addition, if their product is protected by a patent, they face the risk that another firm could copy their product, thus incurring expensive legal action to defend their patent.

The extent to which entrepreneurs undertake both risk management and the transfer of risks through insurance is largely unknown, yet the ability to manage risk (of which insurance is part) is an important subset of management skills for small firm survival. A small survey of high technology small firms undertaken by the author in 1993 does give some indication of the limited use of insurance by this set of firms (17). A postal survey of 300 selected high technology small firms produced a 25 per cent response rate, giving a sample of 76 high technology small firms in the West Midlands. The use of insurance is summarized in Table 1.1. This table shows that there are significant differences in the extent of the use of insurance between the top four risks and other risks that we might expect entrepreneurs to transfer through insurance and specialized risk cover.

Table 1.1 indicates that there are insurance gaps which exist in high technology small firms. For example, we would expect the take-up rate of key man insurance to be higher. The use of more specialized insurance is also low with only 8 per cent of firms taking out cover for the protection of patents and copyright. The low take-up of patent protection may reflect a low application rate of high technology and innovative entrepreneurs to take out patents, which are time-consuming, relatively complicated, and expensive. However, follow-up research

Table 1.1 The use of insurance by a sample of 76 small high technology firms

Risk category	Percentage of firms using risk cover
Motor and vehicles	97
Property and premises	96
Public liability	92
Employer's liability	90
Business interruption/loss of profits	72
Products' liability	57
IT and risk of computer breakdown	32
Goods in transit	12
Health and life insurance	9
Professional indemnity	8
Protection of patents and copyright	8
Key man	5
Personal accident	5
Errors and omissions cover	4
Engineering	4
Travel	4

indicated that up to 30 per cent of the sample were concerned with acquiring patents which would suggest that the low take-up rates of cover are due to difficulties in the insurance environment. The existence of such insurance gaps is a matter of concern and could indicate limited risk management skills and knowledge of insurance by the high technology based entrepreneur. At the time of writing, because of the limited research in this area, we have yet to examine the extent of risk management skills and such knowledge by entrepreneurs. The study went some way to raising the profile of the need for such research and highlighting the importance of the relationship of the small firm with the insurance broker. Ninety-six per cent of high technology small firms in the survey turned to brokers for insurance provision and 87 per cent turned to brokers for advice on insurance, yet interviews with brokers indicated that risk management advice, although available on a fee basis, was rarely used. The relationship with the broker was seen as important by the high technology based entrepreneur, yet apart from our study there has been little investigation of this relationship.

Further discussions with the insurance industry and small firm representatives such as the Federation of Small Businesses (FSB) indicated that risk management and the use of insurance was an important topic that suffered from a low profile in research. A paper by the FSB (18) indicated that insurance was seen as a particular problem by their members (small firm entrepreneurs) especially in the inner city, where the difficulties in obtaining adequate insurance cover were seen as a significant constraint in small firm entrepreneurship start-up and development. For example, insurance premiums in these areas are expensive, yet risk management measures were difficult to impose due to local authority restrictions on the extent of security provisions.

We have discussed the use of insurance in this section because it is part of a subset of management skills of the entrepreneur concerned with risk management. It fits nicely into the Knightian (or Thunen) theory of the entrepreneur as someone who has the ability to assess, evaluate and accept risk. However, it remains, at present, one of the gaps in our knowledge of the management skills of the entrepreneur. In general, we know little about the managerial skills of entrepreneurs and the process involved in how these skills are acquired. Entrepreneurship as a learning process has been ignored in research. Too often research assumes that entrepreneurs have a given set of personality traits and skills. With some research there has been an assumption that entrepreneurs are born and not made, yet this contradicts what we know about the ability of entrepreneurs to overcome difficult environments. There is a learning process during which skills are acquired or developed, although unfortunately, as yet, we know little about this process.

FEMALE ENTREPRENEURSHIP

Although data is hard to come by, it is generally accepted that the activity rates of women in business are much lower than those of men. For example, in the UK, self-employment data suggests that around 5 per cent of women in employment are either self-employed or run their own business. This compares to figures of about 12 per cent for men (Department of Employment (19)). However, during the 1980s, in line with other activity rates for women, the participation rates of women increased at a faster rate than that of men. The national picture is that women are catching up with the activity rates of men as some of the traditional barriers (for entering entrepreneurship) come down but still lag a long way behind those of men.

The sectors where women have higher participation rates are in areas such as personal services. There are some industrial sectors which are largely male preserves and in which women still face barriers. Goffee and Scase (20) have suggested that female entrepreneurship is influenced by two sets of factors:

Table 1.2 Types of female entrepreneur

Entrepreneurial ideals	Conventional gender	Roles
	High	Low
High	Conventional	Innovative
Low	Domestic	Radical

- Attachment to 'entrepreneurial ideals'
- The extent to which they accept conventional gender roles.

Goffee and Scase define entrepreneurial ideals as high motivation for self-advancement, self-reliance, and strong attachment to the 'work ethic'. Conventional gender roles are associated with a subservient role for women to the career aspirations of their partner, a primarily domestic role in supporting their male partner. Based on this distinction they give the taxonomy of female entrepreneurs shown in Table 1.2 and outlined as follows:

1. *Conventional.* Using Goffee and Scase's terminology a conventional female entrepreneur is someone who is highly committed to entrepreneurial ideals and conventional gender roles. The motivation is the need to acquire earnings, but the traditional domestic role is retained. Help received from the partner is very limited.
2. *Domestic.* The domestic female entrepreneur is strongly attached to the traditional gender role, but only moderately committed to entrepreneurial ideals. The motivation for start-up is self-fulfilment. Goffee and Scase argue that in this case the attachment to the traditional female role limits the development of the business because of the priority attached to the partner and family.
3. *Innovative.* The innovative female entrepreneur has rejected the conventional gender role and is highly committed to entrepreneurial success. She is likely to start in areas where she may have encountered obstacles to her career.
4. *Radical.* The radical female entrepreneur regards the business primarily as part of the feminist movement for equality. Thus she has a low attachment to both entrepreneurship and conventional gender roles. In these circumstances the business may be co-owned and operate as a co-operative.

Although the Goffee and Scase approach was useful it is now rather out-dated as a method of classifying 'types' of female entrepreneur. In addition, the concept of 'entrepreneurial ideals' is rather ill-defined. Considerable progress has been made by women in business, but research has yet to catch up with the development of female entrepreneurship. Research (in the UK) into female entrepreneurship has been limited and many studies have often ignored gender issues. Watkins and Watkins (21), with a limited sample of 58 women and 43 male business owners showed that some differences did exist, in particular that women had little prior experience that facilitated their entry into non-traditional areas.

A recent study by Rosa *et al.* (22) promises to go some way to improving our knowledge of female entrepreneurs. As the study points out, however, gender involves men as well as women and that there have been no studies, for example, focusing solely on men. As with entrepreneurship generally, this study shows that factors affecting female entrepreneurship are complex and depend on the environment as well as social factors, and the influence of different factors can vary across different industrial sectors. Among the preliminary findings is that women are less likely to be involved in co-ownership, although there are significant numbers of women in multiple business ownership. The researchers consider that women are fast catching up with male-dominated participation rates in entrepreneurship. For example:

> 'If we speculate that women in business have started from a much lower tradition of achievement, then these figures are remarkable, and may indicate that they are catching up fast' (p. 30).

CONCLUSIONS

We can see that attempts to develop tests on entrepreneurial characteristics owe something to the development of theories of entrepreneurship. Shackle's creator and Schumpeter's innovator are included in the measures of creative tendency. There is Knight's calculated risk taker. The role of co-ordinator of Casson and Kirzner is included by the need to have an internal locus of control and autonomy. These theories have been the guidelines for tests of entrepreneurial ability. Concern with the entrepreneurial personality, however, has diverted attention away from the learning and development process in entrepreneurship and enterprise development, away from the recognition that the individual entrepreneur *acquires* skills and abilities, which are learned from the very process of entrepreneurship, as much as from innate abilities. Much of this learning process is not understood. There is a need to re-focus research away from the investigation of the entrepreneurial personality, which is effectively a *cul de sac*, towards identifying the important factors, of which the environment might only be one, that affect the process of learning and development in entrepreneurship. Support for entrepreneurship can then be better informed to enable individuals to acquire management skills that enable them to learn from their experience and from their solution of problems.

There is little doubt, however, that the environment can be just as important as personal management skills for successful entrepreneurship. This has important implications for policy and the support of SMEs. Some of these issues will re-occur when we examine small business support later in this book. If the environment is not conducive then entrepreneurial talent will lay dormant. The importance of identifying entrepreneurial characteristics lies in encouraging potential entrepreneurs to start their own businesses. Schemes that give blanket coverage run the risk of persuading people to enter business who are not suited to the task of controlling and running their own business (however good the business idea may be) and eventually fail. Indeed the evidence suggests that the majority of small business start-ups will fail. Recent policy developments in England and Wales have been aimed away from blanket coverage to help start-ups and more at helping existing small firms and reducing the high failure rate of start-ups.

Learning outcomes

You should be able to:

1. Understand the main theories and concepts of the entrepreneur.
2. Discuss the application of these theories and concepts to attempts to research the personality of the entrepreneur.
3. Appreciate some of the problems and limitations of research into the personality of the entrepreneur.
4. Appreciate some of the factors that influence the extent of entrepreneurship.
5. Distinguish between the personality of owners and the management skills of small firm owner-managers and the importance of the distinction between ownership and management of a small firm.
6. Understand the importance of risk management and insurance to small firm development and survival.
7. Understand that entrepreneurship is a process of development, not a static state.
8. Understand the need for research into the process of entrepreneurship.

Suggested assignments

1. Students undertake a small research study by interviewing small firm owner-managers about their concepts of management and entrepreneurship. For example, do they consider themselves as entrepreneurs? Small groups of students can each interview one small firm owner and discuss results in class.
2. Students have to debate the skills of entrepreneurs. Students are each given one of two briefs indicating which case they have to argue from:
   - Entrepreneurs are special and have to be born
   - Entrepreneurship skills can be acquired and the environment that fosters entrepreneurship is important.
3. Discussion around a theme such as 'Can entrepreneurship be created?' or 'What difficulties might face inner-city entrepreneurs?'

REFERENCES

1. HÉBERT, R. F. AND LINK, A. N. (1988) *The Entrepreneur: Mainstream Views and Radical Techniques*, 2nd edn, Praeger, New York.

2. CURRAN, J. and STANWORTH, J. (1989) 'Education and Training for Enterprise: Some Problems of Classification, Evaluation, Policy and Research', *International Small Business Journal*, vol. 7, no. 2, pp. 11–22.

3. SHAILER, G. (1994) 'Capitalists and Entrepreneurs in Owner-managed Firms', *International Small Business Journal*, vol. 12, no. 3, pp. 33–41.

4. JENSEN, M. C. and MECKLING, W. H. (1976) 'Theory of the Firm: Managerial Behaviour, Agency Costs and Ownership Structure', *Journal of Financial Economics*, vol. 3, no. 2, pp. 305–60.

5. RAY, D. (1993) 'Understanding the Entrepreneur: entrepreneurial attributes, experience and skills', *Entrepreneurship and Regional Development*, vol. 5, no. 4, pp. 345–57.

6. SCOTTISH ENTERPRISE (1993) *Scotland's Business Birth Rate: A National Enquiry*, Scottish Enterprise, Glasgow.

7. RAM, M. (1993) *Managing to Survive: Working Lives in Small Firms*, Blackwell, Oxford.

8. RAM, M. and DEAKINS, D. (1995) *African-Caribbean Entrepreneurship in Britain*, Small Business Research Centre, University of Central England.

9. BARKHAM, R. (1992) 'Regional Variations in Entrepreneurship: some evidence from the UK', *Entrepreneurship and Regional Development*, vol. 4, no. 3, pp. 225–44.

10. BUTLER, J. E. and HANSEN, G. S. (1991) 'Network Evolution, Entrepreneurial Success and Regional Development', *Entrepreneurship and Regional Development*, vol. 3, no. 1, pp. 1–16.

11. McCLELLAND, D. C. (1961) *The Achieving Society*, Van Nostrand, New Jersey.

12. CHELL, E., HAWORTH, J. AND BREARLEY, S. (1991) *The Entrepreneurial Personality, Concepts, Cases, and Categories*, Routledge, London.

13. MEREDITH, G. G., NELSON, R. E., and NECK, P. A. (1982) *The Practice of Entrepreneurship*, International Labour Office, Geneva.

14. TIMMONS, J. A. (1985) *New Venture Creation: A Guide to Entrepreneurship*, 2nd edn., Irwin, Illinois.

15. CROMIE, S. and O'DONOGHUE, J. (1992) 'Assessing Entrepreneurial Inclinations', *International Small Business Journal*, vol. 10, no. 2, pp. 66–71.

16. PEDLER, M., BURGOYNE, J., and BOYDELL, T. (1991) *The Learning Company: A Strategy for Sustainable Development*, McGraw-Hill, New York.

17. DEAKINS, D. and BENTLEY, P. (1993) *The Small High Technology Firm, Risk Management and Broker Provision of Insurance*, University of Central England, Birmingham.

18. GOODMAN, F. (1994) 'Insurance and Small Firms: A Small Firm Perspective', paper presented to *Insurance and Small Firms Seminar*, University of Central England, Birmingham, April.

19. Department of Employment (1993) '1992 Labour Force Survey', *Employment Gazette*, March.

20. GOFFEE, R. and SCASE, R. (1987) 'Patterns of Business Proprietorship among Women in Britain', *Entrepreneurship in Europe*, Croom Helm, London, pp. 60–82.

21. WATKINS, D. and WATKINS, J. (1984) 'The Female Entrepreneur: Her background and determinants of business choice, some British data', *International Small Business Journal*, vol. 2, no. 4, pp. 21–31.

22. ROSA, P., HAMILTON, D., CARTER, S., and BURNS, H. (1994) 'The Impact of Gender on Small Business Management: Preliminary Findings of a British Study', *International Small Business Journal*, vol. 12, no. 3, pp. 25–32.

RECOMMENDED READING

BARKHAM, R. (1992) 'Regional Variations in Entrepreneurship: some evidence from the UK', *Entrepreneurship and Regional Development*, vol. 4, no. 3, pp. 225–44.

BROWN, B. and BUTLER, J. E. (1993) 'Networks and Entrepreneurial Development in the Shadow of Borders', *Entrepreneurship and Regional Development*, vol. 5, no. 2, pp. 101–16.

BUTLER, J. E. and HANSEN, G. S. (1991) 'Network Evolution, Entrepreneurial Success and Regional Development', *Entrepreneurship and Regional Development*, vol. 3, no. 1, pp. 1–16.

CASSON, M. (1982) *The Entrepreneur: An Economic Theory*, Robertson.

CASSON, M. (1990) *Entrepreneurship*, Edward Elgar, Aldershot.

CHELL, E., HAWORTH, J., and BREARLEY, S. (1991) *The Entrepreneurial Personality, Concepts, Cases, and Categories*, Routledge, London.

CROMIE, S. and O'DONOGHUE, J. (1992) 'Assessing Entrepreneurial Inclinations', *International Small Business Journal*, vol. 10, no. 2, pp. 66–71.

DAVIES, S. P. (1991) 'The Entrepreneurial Capabilities of Rural Furniture Manufacturers in Central Java, Indonesia: a framework and case study', *Entrepreneurship and Regional Development*, vol. 3, no. 3, pp. 253– 7.

HÉBERT, R. F. and LINK, A. N. (1998) *The Entrepreneur: Mainstream Views and Radical Techniques*, (2nd edn), Praeger, New York.

JOHANNISSON, B. and NILSSON, A. (1989) 'Community Entrepreneurs: networking for local development', *Entrepreneurship and Regional Development*, vol. 1, no. 1, pp. 3–20.

RICKETTS, M. (1987) *The Economics of Business Enterprise*, Wheatsheaf, London.

SHAW, B. (1991) 'Developing Technological Innovations with Networks', *Entrepreneurship and Regional Development*, vol. 3, no. 2, pp. 111–28.

SZARKA, J. (1990) 'Networking and Small Firms', *International Small Business Journal*, vol. 8, pp. 16–22.

2 *The Small Firm and the UK Economy*

INTRODUCTION

The role and importance of the Small- and Medium-sized Enterprise (SME) in the UK economy has been the subject of increased attention, particularly in the 1980s and 1990s. One reason for this attention has been the belief that a healthy and vigorous small business sector is important to the performance of the UK economy. Comparisons are often made between UK performance and that of Germany and Japan. Germany has an important medium-sized firm sector, the Mittelstand, but both Germany and Japan have a more important and vigorous SME business sector and both have out-performed the UK economy. A recent report comparing SMEs across Europe (1) commented that in the UK the industrial structure of the economy is still dominated by the large firm sector.

However, the role and importance of the small firm for the health of the economy is not without some controversy (for example, the importance of small firms in job creation). We will be examining some of the arguments later. The small firm sector has recovered importance since the 1971 Bolton Report pointed out a relative decline of the sector in the 1960s. Indeed the UK, at this time, had the smallest small firm sector of any advanced industrial country. First, though, it is necessary to define what we mean by the small business sector. This chapter will begin by examining some definitions of the small business sector, examine the importance of this sector in the economy, and consider some of the issues in the debate concerning the importance of small firms for job creation.

DEFINITIONS

In the previous chapter, we saw that it can be difficult to define both the term entrepreneur and the process of entrepreneurship. Precise definitions of small firms and the small business sector are similarly elusive. Entrepreneurship does not necessarily coincide with small firm ownership, although throughout this book we use the term entrepreneur in connection with small firms. However, the entrepreneurship concept and entrepreneurial skills can be applied to large companies. Unlike entrepreneurship, which is essentially a subjective concept, small firms lend themselves to objective definitions. For example, criteria such as turnover or numbers employed can be applied to distinguish the SME sector. The number of firms which are below certain turnovers or employee size may constitute the SME sector of the economy, although there are difficulties with comparable definitions. We might say that small firms are all those firms that employ less than 50 employees. However, there will be big differences in the size of firms with such a definition across different industrial sectors. For example, a clothing sector firm employing less than 50 will be much smaller than say a chemical firm employing less than 50 and there may well be little comparison between their respective turnovers.

The Bolton Report in 1971 (2) considered that one definition of small firms was inappropriate. Instead they recommended the following alternative definitions:

1. *The employee definition:* Small firms can be classified by some maximum number of employees. However, this will depend on the the nature of capital intensity which varies from one industrial sector to another. Thus, less than 200 employees was considered appropriate for manufacturing, whereas less than 25 was considered appropriate for construction.
2. *The turnover definition:* Bolton gave £50 000 as a turnover definition for small firms in the retail trade—this might be nearer £1m today. This illustrates one of the problems of a turnover definition—inflation can make nonsense of it over time. However, for temporary purposes there are advantages of using turnover definitions, since they are roughly comparable across different sectors.
3. *The characteristics definition:* Bolton gave three essential characteristics of a small firm:

   ■ It has a small share of the market
   ■ It is managed by its owners or part-owners in a personalized way
   ■ It is operated independently.

This third definition is sometimes referred to as an economic definition. The three definitions combined were meant to be used in different circumstances. Turnover might be used in some sectors where there was some consistency in the turnover levels of firms. However, the third definition can be incompatible with some small firms which may have a formal management structure and do not necessarily have a small share of the market.

The multiplicity of criteria of the Bolton Report has been replaced in most circumstances by a European Union (EU) definition of the small- and medium-sized enterprise as an enterprise employing less than 500 employees. As we will see later in the chapter, this definition covers 99 per cent of all the enterprises in the UK. It is now generally accepted that there is a need to identify different sizes of firms within the SME sector. In particular, it has been recognized that very small firms are important to the economy; these are sometimes referred to as micro-enterprises to distinguish them from other small firms.

There are EU definitions that are generally adopted. These use the criterion of number of employees as the distinguishing factor of size according to the following definitions:

Number of employees	*Size of enterprise*
0–< 10	Micro
10–<100	Small
100–<500	Medium

Thus the important Mittelstand sector of Germany would consist of medium-sized enterprises employing between 100 to less than 500 employees. A consensus has emerged that this is an appropriate definition. For example, the 1992 Cambridge Report on *The State of British Enterprise*, (3) adopted the EU definition of less than 500 employees. The result is that this definition is often used, misleadingly, in studies in the small firm sector. We can claim that the definition is misleading because it covers 99 per cent of all firms, as shown in Table 2.1. In fact, even if we reduce the definition to include only those firms that employ 20 or less we would still capture 98 per cent of all the firms in the UK. If we are to use a small firm definition based on number of employees, the evidence in terms of firm size distribution, as shown in Table 2.1, would suggest that we restrict our analysis to firms employing less than 20 employees. Table 2.1 illustrates the importance and growth of the micro-sized firm in the UK. Comparing the UK's SME sector to other European countries, such as that of Germany, seems to show that the SME sector in the UK is dominated by micro-sized firms.

One problem, at least in the UK, as a result of the importance of the micro-enterprise for small firm surveys which include SMEs (<500 employees) is that, statistically, inclusion of the relatively rare medium-sized firm can distort the results of the survey in terms of parameters produced in the survey results.

It is not surprising that some researchers have turned to alternative definitions to operationalize studies with small firms. For example, a 1992 Kingston Small Business Research Centre study (4) of service sector firms operationalized definitions with a 'grounded' definition of size adapted for the different services covered. The researchers considered what the small firm owner and representatives of the sector considered to be small in relation to the economic activities in which they were involved.

Table 2.1   Firm size and share of employment UK 1979–89 (*totals may be different due to rounding)

Firm size	1979 No. (000)	1979 Share of employment (%)	1986 No. (000)	1986 Share of employment (%)	1989 No. (000)	1989 Share of employment (%)
1–10	1597	19.2	2308	27.8	2802	28.6
11–19	109	7.6	84	6.0	92	6.0
20–49	46	6.9	56	8.2	57	7.6
50–99	16	5.3	16	5.8	18	5.8
100–199	15	10.2	9	7.4	9	7.2
200–499	5	8.1	5	9.5	6	10.6
500 +	4	42.8	3	35.1	3	34.2
Totals	1791 *	100 *	2481 *	100 *	2988 *	100 *

Source: *Employment Gazette* (modified) February 1992 and other editions. Crown copyright © Reproduced with the permission of the Controller of HMSO.

It may not be possible to define statistically the small firm or the small firm sector at all. As we will see from the evidence given in the tables, there is no doubt that the small firm has become more important throughout the 1980s and into the 1990s. One of the reasons for the increased importance of the small firm is its ability to respond quickly to change. As the pace of technological change has increased in society, so the ability of the small firm to respond quickly to change has given it an advantage over the large firm. This characteristic of small firms has been called 'flexible specialization' and reflects the ability of the small firm to be both specialized and respond to change. As the demands of society change, it may be that the growth in the importance of the small firm merely reflects those changed demands. In the same way that the UK labour market has changed dramatically with employment no longer based on long term careers with large firms in one occupation and in favour of a more 'flexible' labour force, so the structure of the economy has changed in favour of the small, flexible and specialized firm.

In such circumstances, and in the face of the increasing pace of change, it may be folly to attempt to define the small firm, because what is small, and which small firms are important, are changing anyway. We turn, however, to examine the evidence concerning the importance of small firms in the economy.

THE IMPORTANCE OF THE SMALL FIRM SECTOR IN THE UK

Table 2.1 shows the trends in the numbers and importance of small firms for share of total employment in the 1980s. A striking trend, shown in the table, is the increased numbers and growth in importance of the very small firm or so-called micro-firm that employs 10 or less employees. The numbers of such firms have nearly doubled in the 1980s as has the firms' share of employment. It is also noticeable that the number of firms that employ more than 10 employees has remained virtually static during the same period. Thus most of the growth in the importance of small firms has come from the micro-businesses.

Why there should have been this concentration of growth in micro-firms is less clear. There are reasons associated with the re-structuring of the economy. Large numbers of workers were made redundant in the early 1980s, workers who often had substantial redundancy payments and little prospect of re-training. Faced with lack of opportunity it is not surprising that many people were tempted into starting their own (micro) businesses. However, this factor alone cannot account for the growth in the importance of such businesses in share of employment. Also, because these figures are based on VAT registrations, very small self-employed workers may not register for VAT and may not enter the statistics. The explanation of the growth of these micro-firms is more complex than simple push factors from high unemployment rates and is probably tied to underlying structural changes in the economy, as discussed above—structural changes that had been in place for some time.

Across the EU as well, there has been a significant growth in small firms that employ less than 100. According to a European study (1), between 1988 and 1993 these firms were responsible for creating three million jobs whereas other firm were net losers of jobs, suggesting that there are significant structural changes in all European countries in favour of small firms and entrepreneurs that employ less than 100 employees.

These statistics contrast with the decline in the small firm sector that had been reported by Bolton in 1971. The growth in the small firm sector began soon after Bolton reported and the revival of the small firm sector is a longer process than that reported in Table 2.1. Factors that are put forward include the following:

1. Structural changes in the UK economy, particularly the decline in manufacturing and the growth of the service sector where a smaller size of firm is more 'optimal'.
2. An associated change in the extent of economies of scale, partly associated with technical changes which suit smaller-scale production.
3. The ability of the smaller firm to be more flexible and respond to 'market opportunities', the ability to be both specialized and flexible as discussed above.

4. Changes in government policy and the fostering of the so-called 'enterprise culture'. As discussed in a later chapter, the importance of the impact of policy is debatable.
5. Changes in macro-economic policy in favour of small firms e.g., changes in corporation tax to ensure a fairer treatment of small firms.
6. Private sector initiatives, e.g., enterprise agencies were often established with sponsorship from the private sector.
7. A more important role for the small firm in local authority policy, e.g., some economic development units have launched initiatives to help smaller firms. Contracting out of public sector services has also encouraged the growth of the small firm entrepreneur.
8. High unemployment rates in the 1980s which have forced some workers to start their own enterprise using existing skills and redundancy payments rather than re-training.

The data shown in Table 2.1 is reinforced when we examine turnover levels for small firms. Table 2.2 gives the size distribution of firms based on turnover for 1989 and shows that 97 per cent of all firms had turnover levels of less than £1 million.

Table 2.2   Size distribution of firms based on turnover 1989

Turnover (£000)	Number of firms (000)	Percentage share	Cumulative percentage share
0–14	1046	35	35
15–49	939	31.4	66.4
50–99	345	11.6	78
100–249	339	11.3	89.3
250–499	139	4.6	93.9
500–999	82	2.7	96.6
1000–2499	56	1.9	98.5
2500–4999	20	0.7	99.2
5000–9999	11	0.4	99.6
10,000 +	12	0.4	100
Totals	2989	100	

Source: *Employment Gazette*, February 1992 (modified).
Crown copyright © Reproduced with the permission of the Controller of HMSO.

This gives further weight to the importance of the micro-firm. Remarkably, the table also shows that 35 per cent had turnovers of less than £15000. This makes one wonder at the nature of operation of many small firms. It will become clear that far from being prosperous for many of these micro-firms, much of their time is spent trying to survive from day to day (one reason why there is little forward planning in small firms). As we will see below, being in business for many small firm owners can only be a part-time occupation, generating very small turnover levels.

SMALL FIRM VOLATILITY

It should be clear by now that not only do most small firms struggle to survive on very low turnover levels, many will also cease to exist. Table 2.1 may show a net growth in small firm formation, but the table also hides high volatility due to both high birth rates and high death rates in the 1980s. Births and deaths of firms are illustrated in Table 2.3 for the period 1987–89. This shows that small firm and micro-firm death rates were almost as high as birth rates and this was in a boom period. It is only in the service sector in the micro-firms (less than 10 employees)

Table 2.3   Small firm turbulence 1987–1989

No. of employees	Service sector		Production and manufacturing	
	Births (000)	Deaths (000)	Births (000)	Deaths (000)
1–4	240	166	82	62
5–9	139	133	78	84
10–19	76	101	65	95
20–49	28	45	28	55
50–99	15	28	14	34
100–499	18	42	14	50
500–999	0	2	2	12
1000–4999	3	9	2	21
5000–9999	0	6	0	10
10000+	0	0	0	0
Totals	518	532	284	423

Source: *Employment Gazette*, August 1992.
Crown copyright © Reproduced with the permission of the Controller of HMSO.

that new firm formation exceeds small firm deaths by any significant figure. During a recession period as in the 1990s death rates will have been higher.

These birth and death rates illustrate a side of small firm creation that is too often ignored by the Government and policy makers. The social costs associated with a drive to improve start-up rates are often high. For example, high bankruptcy rates among small firm owners and entrepreneurs, who have often pledged much of their wealth and personal assets into the business, leave many people who have lost more than they put into the business. Due to the bankruptcy laws which require secured creditors to be paid first, small firm creditors are often the last to be paid. During a recession, this situation can lead to a domino effect as one business failure forces other small firms to fail.

The problem of (low) small firm survival rates has been illustrated by Westhead and Birley (5). They show that VAT de-registrations have been highest in the older industrial areas and conurbations leading to high net losses of firms even during the boom period of 1987–90. They comment that:

> This aggregate macro-level analysis reinforces the micro-level evidence that the majority of new firms are doomed to death in their formative years. Deregistration rates were found to be markedly lower in rural environments and significantly higher in urban areas (pp. 56–7).

High business birth rates may look impressive, but they hide the fact that many of the new starts will not survive beyond the first year of operation and most will not survive the first three years of operation. It is a sad fact that policy makers have been too pre-occupied with quantifiable numbers of new firm starts and insufficient concern with the quality of business start-ups that were created during the 1980s. It is only recently that there has been some belated attention given to the quality of new firm start-ups. As we comment below, greater focus on the potential of surviving and growing new firms has led to changes in policy away from blanket coverage and incentives for all new starts, incentives that in the past have encouraged new firm starts that were doomed to fail.

GROWTH FIRMS AND JOB CREATION

The gradual realization that we should be more concerned about the quality of new small firm start-ups has led to greater focus on small firm start-ups that have the potential to grow—the so-called 'fast track' new firms with the potential for job creation. There has been some controversy surrounding the job creation of small firms. Numbers of small firms starts do not give an indication of job creation, nor do we have a picture of whether new firm starts can replace the job losses of larger firms that have continued to rationalize and cut jobs in the 1980s. Some writers have questioned whether small firms can replace the job creating ability of large firms. After all it takes a lot of small firms to create the same number of jobs (ignoring issues of quality and security of jobs created) as one major car plant such as the investment by Toyota in Derbyshire.

The controversy surrounding the role of small firms in creating employment stems from a paper by Birch (6) which claimed that, in the USA between 1969 and 1976, 66 per cent of net new jobs were created by firms employing less than 20 employees. However, the assumptions and conclusions of Birch have been criticized by subsequent writers. In the UK, Fothergill and Gudgin (7) have claimed that firms employing fewer than 25 people only accounted for 0.8 per cent of the growth in total manufacturing output, in the period 1968 to 1975. A more recent study by Daly *et al.* (8) claims that small firms employing less than 20 people were equally important (to large firms) in the UK in job creation between 1987 to 1989.

Daly *et al.* calculate a net fertility index (NFI) by dividing the firm size share of overall employment into the firm size share of net job gain. This fertility index is shown in Table 2.4 and shows that on this measure for the period 1987-9, the major net providers of new jobs were the micro-firms that employed less than 10 employees.

These studies must be treated with caution because of a number of factors:

1. They are usually based on VAT registrations which exclude some of the very small firms (due to the VAT turnover threshold) and do not give a complete picture. (Although adjustments are usually made, it is difficult to allow for non-registrations and de-registrations that are not deaths.)
2. Some small firm creation can lead to job replacement rather than job creation. For example, if an individual starts in business under the Enterprise Allowance Scheme (EAS), they may force another individual out of business (because they are subsidized).
3. Equally some of the job creation may be temporary due to state subsidies or special financing schemes.
4. We have hinted that job creation may be of low quality in small firms. Employees are often non-unionized. The evidence on industrial relations is mixed and Ram and Holiday, for example, show that in small family-run firms relations are not as harmonious as might appear and consist of a form of 'negotiated paternalism' (9).
5. Small firm owners/entrepreneurs work long hours.

It has been suggested that net job generation is only accounted for by a very small proportion of new small firms. For example, only a small minority of firms will grow to employ 50 people. Storey (10) claims that out of every 100 new firm starts only a handful, perhaps three or four, will turn out to be major job creators and high growth potential firms. For example, Storey comments: '. . . out of every 100

Table 2.4   Job creation 1987–9

$$\text{Net fertility index (NFI)} = \frac{\text{Share of net job gain}}{\text{Share of overall employment}}$$

NFI by size of firm

Firm size (no. of employees)	Service sector	Production
1–4	2.7	6.3
5–9	1.0	2.1
10–19	0.4	1.0
20–49	0.8	0.8
50–99	0.9	1.1
100–499	0.9	0.8
500–999	1.1	1.6
1000–4999	0.8	0.2
5000–9999	0.3	0.3
10000+	0.7	0.4

Source: *Employment Gazette*, August 1992.
Crown copyright © Reproduced with the permission of the Controller of HMSO.

small firms, the fastest growing four firms will create half the jobs in the group over a decade' (p. 113).

Using data from manufacturing firms in the north of England for the period 1965-78, Storey shows that out of 774 firms surviving to 1978, only 5 per cent had more than 50 employees and only 1 per cent had more than 100 employees. It is not surprising that only a minority of firms will grow to any size given that national data such as that shown in Table 2.1 indicates that 97 per cent of all firms employ less than 20 people. More important, however, is the contention that a very small number of firms will create the major proportion of new jobs. For example Storey calculates '. . . over a decade, 4 per cent of those businesses which start would be expected to create 50 per cent of employment generated' (p. 115).

A study by Gallagher and Miller (11) supports the contention that a majority of jobs will be created by a small minority of firms. From a study of 2000 new firms in Scotland and 20 000 in the South-East, they found that in Scotland, 11 per cent of firms created 68 per cent of the jobs and in the South-East 18 per cent of firms created 92 per cent of jobs. However, Daly *et al.* (8) with national data shown in Table 2.4 for the period 1987–9, claim that the growth of employment is more dispersed and slower than the evidence given above might suggest. They claim that over 50 per cent of net job generation is accounted for by firms moving from less than five employees to less than 10 employees. That is, the existence of fast-track new firms or 'high flyers' is less important than has been claimed for job generation. However, the contention that only a few fast-track firms will create the majority of jobs has influenced policy. As will be seen later in Chapter 7, emphasis in policy has shifted from blanket coverage to the concept of identifying winners and helping fast-track or growth firms to achieve their potential. While this concept is sound in theory and is supported by the balance of evidence (since the Daly *et al.* data may be seen as an exception that only covers a two year period) there has yet to emerge any consistent criteria or policy for identifying these fast-track growth firms.

REGIONAL VARIATIONS

Using VAT data, Keeble and Walker (12) show that there are very significant regional variations in the growth of new and small businesses. The data reveals a north–south divide in new firm formation during the 1980s. Table 2.5 shows that the South-East, South-West and East Midlands have much higher enterprise formation rates than the North, Scotland and Northern Ireland. These regional differences in new firm formation rates add weight to our argument in Chapter 1 that the environment is a powerful factor in entrepreneurship. Keeble and Walker model a series of factors that affect firm formation, growth and death. Significant factors for both formation and growth are local population growth, capital availability, and professional and managerial expertise. They also find that support from enterprise agencies does help to reduce the death rates.

Scottish Enterprise as mentioned in Chapter 1, following their own research into new firm formation in Scotland, have launched their own strategy for improving the business birth rate in Scotland (13). However, the analysis of Keeble and Walker would suggest that the low population growth in Scotland and lack of home ownership will continue to limit new firm formation in Scotland. Recent research by the author (1995) (14), with high technology small firms in the West Midlands and Scotland, illustrated that the gap between the two regions (which the strategy of Scottish Enterprise is trying to close) in new firm formation rates for new high technology small firms is quite daunting with a very much smaller proportion of high technology small firms in Scotland formed in the last five years, than in the West Midlands.

The significance of home ownership as a means of providing collateral and equity is a theme that will be considered in Chapter 4. Home ownership can reduce the liquidity constraints that face entrepreneurs (15,16) and influence the

Table 2.5 Regional variation in new firm formation rates 1980–90

Region	Number of new firms (000)	Formation rate[1]
South-East	850	100.3
South-West	190	99.7
East Anglia	79	95.8
East Midlands	140	79.3
Wales	93	77.5
West Midlands	180	72.1
Yorks and Humberside	158	70.3
North-West	207	68.7
Northern Ireland	39	61.1
Scotland	134	55.4
North	77	55.3
UK	2,147	81.4

Note 1: Per 1000 civilian labour force, 1981.
Source: Keeble and Walker (12).

propensity to enter entrepreneurship. It is a constraint that has been identified as significant by Scottish Enterprise in its enterprise strategy.

CONCLUSIONS

We have concentrated on the importance of small firms in the UK economy. Historically, the UK's small firm sector, however defined, has been less important than other developed nations which have enjoyed better economic performance and growth, notably Germany and Japan. Greater attention in the 1980s and through the early 1990s has been paid to the small business sector for its potential in generating jobs and providing the engine for new economic growth. The result is that it is now received government policy that the small firm sector will provide the main vehicle for recovery from the recession and will be the main provider of jobs during the rest of the 1990s.

Close examination of small firm statistics, however, in the UK reveal that the vast majority of small firms are not major job creators and 98 per cent will probably never employ more than 20 people. Much of the balance of evidence suggests that high growth small firms are very rare, perhaps only three or four for every 100 new firm starts. While the number of small firms has increased, especially in micro-firms employing less than 10 people, this pattern is very uneven throughout the UK with large regional (and sectoral) variations.

The decade of the 1980s may in the future be called a decade of small firm growth in the UK. This is in both absolute and relative (as a proportion of employment) terms. However, it is often forgotten that it has also been a decade of high volatility in the small firm sector: high business birth rates are accompanied by high business death rates. Many people have been encouraged to start their own business who do not have the management skills to survive, and so some new firms are doomed to failure in the first year of trading. The social costs are high, due to the personal tragedies that lie behind the bland statistics. In the 1970s, losing your job did not mean losing your home; now a more frequent story can be the loss of everything when the business fails, often putting intolerable strains on the small firm entrepreneur's family. In addition, the quality of many of the jobs created have been questionable, often low paid, part time, and insecure. Secondary labour markets have expanded in line with the growth of small firms in the 1980s.

Although the Government will claim that it has fostered the successful growth of the small firms sector during this decade, there are a number of factors that suggest that the growth would have occurred to some extent anyway, since small firms are better equipped to meet the rapidly changing demands of the 1990s.

There are signs that we have learned some lessons from the 1980s decade of small firm growth. The emphasis in policy is beginning to switch to quality rather than quantity. Germany has a more important SME sector, but new firm starts are likely to be of higher quality than new firm starts in the UK. Policy is now focusing on quality, although we will see later, that as yet, few criteria have been developed to target fast growth firms.

Learning outcomes

Students should be able to:

1. Analyse the major trends in small firm creation in the UK.
2. Discuss the factors that account for these trends.
3. Evaluate the importance of new small firms for job creation.
4. Discuss different definitions of the small firm and SME sector.
5. Construct visual presentations of the resurgence in the importance of the SME sector.
6. Appreciate the volatility associated with the growth in the small firm sector.
7. Identify the social costs associated with small firm failures.

Suggested assignments

1. Students analyse and present data on new firm formation and the small business sector working in small groups.
2. Students discuss reasons for differences in small firm formation rates in different regions in the UK as shown in Table 2.5. Why should the South perform better than the North?
3. Class or group discussion of the factors that affect business start-up, a topic which we will return to after examining a case study of clients of a local enterprise agency and a case study start-up in the next chapter.

REFERENCES

1. THE EUROPEAN OBSERVATORY FOR SMES (1994) *Second Annual Report*, EIM Small Business Research and Consultancy, Netherlands.

2. HM GOVERNMENT (1971) *Report of The Committee of Inquiry on Small Firms (Bolton Report)*, HMSO, London.

3. CAMBRIDGE UNIVERSITY SMALL BUSINESS RESEARCH CENTRE (1992) *The State of British Enterprise*, Cambridge University, Cambridge.

4. CURRAN, J., BLACKBURN, R. A., AND WOODS, A. (1992) 'Profiles of the Small Enterprise in the Service Sector', paper presented to the 14th National Small Firms Policy and Research Conference, Blackpool, November.

5. WESTHEAD, P. AND BIRLEY, S. (1994) 'Environments for Business De-registrations in the UK, 1987–90', *Entrepreneurship and Regional Development*, vol. 6, no. 1, pp. 29–62.

6. BIRCH, D. L 'The job generation process' *MIT study on neighbourhood and regional change*, MIT.

7. FOTHERGILL, S. AND GUDGIN, G. (1979) *The job generation process in Britain*, Centre for Environmental Studies.

8. DALY, M., CAMPBELL, M., ROBSON, G., AND GALLAGHER, C. (1991) 'Job-creation 1987–89: the contributions of small and large firms', *Employment Gazette*, November, pp. 589–94.

9. RAM, M. AND HOLIDAY, R. (1993) 'Keeping it in the Family: Small Firms and Familial Culture', in Chittenden, F., Robertson, M., and Watkins, D., *Small Firms: Recession and Recovery*, Paul Chapman, London.

10. STOREY, D. J. (1994) *Understanding the Small Business Sector*, Routledge, London.

11. GALLAGHER, C. AND MILLER, P. (1991) 'New Fast Growing Companies Create Jobs', *Longe Range Planning*, vol. 24, no. 1, pp. 96–101.

12. KEEBLE, D. AND WALKER, S. (1993) 'New Firms, Small Firms and Dead Firms: Spatial Patterns and Determinants in the UK', *Regional Studies*, vol. 28, no. 4, pp. 411–27.

13. SCOTTISH ENTERPRISE (1993) *Improving the Business Birth Rate: A Strategy for Scotland*, Scottish Enterprise, Glasgow.

14. DEAKINS, D. AND PADDISON, A. (1995) *Risk Management and the Use of Insurance by High Technology-Based Entrepreneurs*, Paisley Enterprise Research Centre, University of Paisley.

15. EVANS, D. AND JOVANIVIC, B. (1989) 'An estimated model of Entrepreneurial Choice under Liquidity Constraints', *Journal of Political Economy*, vol. 97, no. 4, pp. 808–27.

16. BATSTONE, S. AND MANSFIELD, E. (1992) 'Births, Deaths and Turbulence in England and Wales', in Robertson, M., Chell, E., and Mason, C. (eds), *Towards the Twenty-first Century: the Challenge for Small Business*, Nadamal Books, Macclesfield, pp. 179–208.

RECOMMENDED READING

BANNOCK, G. AND DALY, M. (1990) 'Size distribution of UK firms', *Employment Gazette*, May, pp. 255–8.

CURRAN, J. (1986) *Bolton 15 Years On: a review and analysis of small business research in Britain 1971–86*, SBRT, Milton Keynes.

DALY, M., CAMPBELL, M. ROBSON, G., AND GALLAGHER, C. (1991) 'Job-creation 1987–89: the contributions of small and large firms', *Employment Gazette*, November, pp. 589–94.

DALY, M. AND McCANN, A. (1992) 'How Many Small Firms?', *Employment Gazette*, February, pp. 47–51.

HM GOVERNMENT (1971) *Report of The Committee of Inquiry on Small Firms*, (Bolton Report), HMSO, London.

3 *Issues in Business Start-up*

INTRODUCTION

This chapter provides a case study example of a start-up business, Greenwed Ltd as well as the results of an evaluation study carried out for a West Midlands local enterprise agency with the agency's clients. It will give you an opportunity to compare evidence from the survey and the case study with the concepts that have been discussed in the previous two chapters. We will see that the study of the enterprise agency's clients confirms the view that for many small businesses, incomes are very low and that most are concerned with day to day survival. We use the survey, however, to examine the importance of different constraints that face start-up businesses such as the availability of finance, premises, and motivation. We also consider some observations on the clients who did not start and the potential importance of constraints that prevented non-start.

The Greenwed Ltd case study provides our first opportunity to analyse a business as a case study. It is typical of many start-up businesses that formed the bulk of new small firms that were set up in the 1980s. The motivation came from an experienced and qualified individual who left employment with a large firm to set up his own business because he recognized market opportunities that the large firm could not exploit. As is the case with many entrepreneurs we cannot pigeon-hole him into a particular category since he demonstrates abilities of several different concepts of the entrepreneur including Kirzner's alertness and Schumpeter's innovator, yet by sinking personal wealth and assets into the business, he could also be categorized as a Knightian risk taker.

The material presented provides the basis for a number of suggested assignments at the end of the chapter. Alternatively, the material may be used as a basis for class or small group discussion. Greenwed Ltd provides the first of our case studies used in this book. The location of the case studies is not meant to be restrictive to issues discussed in the chapter as there are elements that could be developed and discussed under other topics. Thus, Greenwed Ltd may be referred to under sources of finance or under innovation. However, it has been included here because it illustrates a number of important issues in start-up, including access to markets, resources, and relationships with large firms.

The survey of enterprise agency clients, in contrast, provides an opportunity to review the personal and business characteristics of small firm founders. For example, who is the typical small business founder? We discuss these personal characteristics in terms of age, gender, and family, and the business characteristics such as turnover and sources of finance used. Until now, we have looked at the national data of small firms, their importance, and the numbers of new firms, small firms, and death rates. We have yet to examine any evidence of detailed characteristics of the typical small firm and the typical small firm owner. The case study and the survey discussed in this chapter provide an opportunity to put some depth of information upon the bare bones of national data.

Note: Questions for class discussion are included under different sections of the survey report.

THE RESULTS OF AN EVALUATION STUDY WITH A LOCAL ENTERPRISE AGENCY

The following results are extracted from a research report and evaluation study carried out for a local enterprise agency in the West Midlands. The study involved start-up businesses that had been established for less than three years and attempted to include clients of the agency that had not started or had started and subsequently ceased trading. The study was designed to investigate issues in start-up support, but a considerable amount of data was collected from the respondents that took part in the survey. This data forms an unusually rich source of information specifically concerned with issues in start-up e.g., on the motivations and aspirations of founders, on the constraints that they face and on why they subsequently cease trading. We do not attempt to look at issues in small business support here, since this will be an important topic considered later. Data have been extracted from the survey to form the basis of a discussion on the characteristics, motives, constraints, and aspirations of new small business founders.

The survey, conducted on behalf of the enterprise agency, involved a detailed postal questionnaire that was mailed to 700 clients. A response rate of 17 per cent of usable replies was obtained giving a total sample size of 118 clients. Of these 63 (53 per cent) clients were still trading at the time of the survey, 42 (36 per cent) had decided not to start, and 13 (11 per cent) had started but subsequently ceased to trade. A number of initial points need to be made:

1. The low response rate is quite typical of postal questionnaires and is statistically acceptable, i.e., the sample is large enough to be confident about the findings, that they are accurate and representative.
2. The questionnaire was very detailed and represented a compromise between the need to obtain data and the likelihood of obtaining a response. In the light of the 'heavy' questionnaire and the target population from which the sample is drawn, the response rate was acceptable.
3. Obtaining replies and data from small firms that have subsequently failed is notoriously difficult due to the lack of motivation of such clients. This accounts for the small sample from this group, and obviously, any conclusions on the reasons for the cessation of trading need to be treated with caution.
4. The sample will inevitably be biased since the population from which it is drawn comprises exclusively the clients of one enterprise agency. It is likely that some, potentially successful, founders will not bother to approach an enterprise agency for advice. These may well have some characteristics that will be different from the sample involved in this study. However, these characteristics are more likely to involve issues surrounding personal motivation. We can be confident that other data discussed, such as the findings concerning the business characteristics, is likely to be representative of start-ups in general.
5. The study is also likely to be biased because of the geographical location of the enterprise agency. More about this below.
6. Finally, the study was carried out in 1990 when the national and local economies were still in a relatively buoyant state; economic growth was positive and the economic climate was generally favourable for small business start-up.
7. As mentioned before, discussion questions are included under different sections of the report.

All these factors need to be borne in mind when discussing the results.

THE MAIN FINDINGS
The results can be categorized into four main sections:

1. Personal characteristics of the small business founder, such as age, sex, marital status, etc.

2. Business characteristics of the small business such as turnover and sources of finance.
3. Issues and constraints in subsequent business development, including the personal goals of the small business founder.
4. Reasons for non-start and for the cessation of trading.

1. PERSONAL CHARACTERISTICS OF THE FOUNDER

The personal characteristics included age, sex, marital status, number of dependants, and previous employment status. No ethnic entrepreneurs responded because of the location of the enterprise agency in a predominantly white, middle class, suburban geographical area of the West Midlands. There were undoubtedly ethnic entrepreneurs represented in the agency's clients, but it is likely that the motivation to respond in the survey would be particularly low in this client base. Some of the personal characteristics of the founders are given in Table 3.1:

Table 3.1   Some personal characteristics of the agency's clients (whole sample)

Characteristic

Gender	60% male	40% female	
Marital status	64% married	36% not married	
Spouse working	68% working of those married	32% not working	
Dependants	46% of sample had dependants		
Mean no. of dependants	1.4		
Employment status before start-up	37% employed	49% unemployed (registered)	14% unemployed (not registered)
Age	See below		

The age distribution of clients of the agency shows the 'age-launch' window which is typical of the start-up characteristics of business founders. This distribution is given in Table 3.2 and is drawn as a bar chart in Fig. 3.1.

Table 3.2 The age distribution of the agency's clients

Age	No. of respondents
Under 25	16
25–29	20
30–34	29
35–39	10
40–44	15
45–49	10
50–54	7
55–59	7
60 and over	4
Total	118

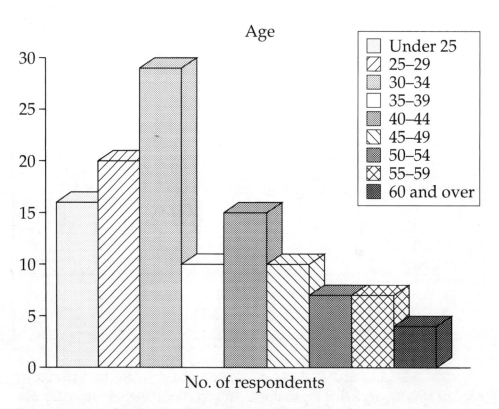

Figure 3.1   Age distribution of the agency's clients

———————— *Questions for discussion* ————————

There are a number of issues that could be discussed, including:

1. Why is the age of 30–45 considered to be an age-launch 'window'?

2. What particular difficulties might older or younger entrepreneurs face?

3. Would you expect the age of the founder to be correlated with any other business characteristic, e.g. capital at start? business sector? motivation?

4. What difficulties will a potential entrepreneur face who is within the age launch window age range?

5. Why might family support and the number of dependants be significant in business start-up?

6. What difficulties do female entrepreneurs face that would account for the distinct gender bias demonstrated by this survey's results?

7. What support could or should be given to increase the percentage of female entrepreneurs?

8. Why might previous employment be significant in business start-up?

9. Can marital status affect start-up? Married, single, or divorced?

ISSUES ASSOCIATED WITH GENDER

Rather belatedly, there has been increased attention given to the low start-rate of female entrepreneurs. A number of enterprise agencies in the UK now run Women into Business seminars. There are examples of enterprise agencies that have been specifically set up to encourage female entrepreneurship. Women into Business seminars attempt to tackle some of the perceived problems that women face such as 'lack of confidence'.

The survey did find that women clients saw confidence as being a more important issue than did male clients and women also felt that a lack of self confidence to be more of a reason for not starting a business than did men. However, this view, that women lack confidence, may be seen as patronizing. It also may obscure more significant constraints that face female entrepreneurs such as a lack of equal treatment by finance providers (intentional or otherwise) when assessing new business propositions.

There may be additional factors, associated with personal characteristics, which can explain why clients or potential business founders with a good proposition may not enter business. For example the study found that there were significant differences in the fear of failure between married men, single men, and single women. It was single women that feared failure the most and this may be a significant factor that prevents start-up.

2. BUSINESS CHARACTERISTICS

Business characteristics are those associated with the performance of the business after start-up. For the purposes of the study this limits the sample to those that were still trading (63) and those that had started trading but since ceased (13). These business characteristics included trading status, family support, industrial sector, number of employees, turnover, use of the Enterprise Allowance Scheme (EAS), and sources of finance.

2.1 Trading status

The legal form of the business is often not given a lot of attention by the founder. It is obviously easier to set up as a sole trader than as a company and this is reflected in the study's results on trading status shown in Table 3.3.

Table 3.3 Trading status of start-up clients

Legal form	Percentage of respondents
	(n = 74)
Sole trader	81
Partnerships	10
Limited company	8
Co-operative	1

Questions for discussion

One or two questions arise on the significance of legal form for business start-up. For example:

1. Should different support provision be given to co-operatives? If so, does it matter whether they are worker co-operatives or producer co-operatives.

2. Why does being a sole trader remain so popular as a legal form for business start-up despite the known disadvantages of this legal form?

3. What disadvantages might accrue in the economy from a high proportion of start-ups in the form of sole traders?

2.2 Family support

Of the agency's clients that started in business, 22 per cent employed members of their family in the business. The significance of family support has been commented on by other writers (1). It is known that family support can be a significant factor in successful business start-up.

——————— *Question for discussion* ———————

Apart from employment in what ways will family support be significant?

2.3 Industrial sector

It is known that the majority of start-ups are in the services sector and that this sector has been the most significant for the creation of new jobs in the 1980s (2). It is not surprising then, that the study found that 62 per cent of the agency's clients had started in services and only 38 per cent in manufacturing and construction. In fact the proportion in manufacturing was higher than might be expected from national figures and probably reflects the importance of manufacturing in the West Midlands.

——————— *Questions for discussion* ———————

Again there are a number of questions which we can discuss about the bias towards start-ups in services:

1. Does creation of service sector based small firms have consequences for the sustained recovery of the UK economy?

2. Should support be geared at the encouragement of more manufacturing and the removal of perceived constraints?

2.4 Employment

When examining employment creation we must remember that the majority of start-ups had been trading for less than one year, and that some firms had ceased trading. However, the number of employees at different stages is given in Table 3.4.

Table 3.4 Number of employees

Period	Full time employees	Part time employees	No. of firms
At start	32	11	74
At 6 months	19	18	60
At 1 year	9	7	38
At 2 years	9	4	17

Questions for discussion

1. What changes are shown in the table and what factors might account for these changes?

2. What implications might exist for support agencies in their delivery of training and advice to new business founders?

2.5 Turnover

Turnover figures are given in Table 3.5. They show a high proportion of firms with very low turnover levels. There could be a number of reasons for this such as part time start while the founder retains part time employment, the reliance on the Enterprise Allowance Scheme, and the high proportion of firms that were in their first year of trading.

This confirms the view, discussed in a previous chapter, that of any sample of new small firms, only a very small minority will be high growth performers. However, it is difficult to tell with this sample since there may well be high growth firms within the sample that are yet to emerge. However, it is

Table 3.5 Turnover

Turnover level	Proportion of firms (n = 69) %
Less than £5000	40
£5000 to less than £10 000	17
£10 000 to less than £15 000	13
£15 000 to less than £20 000	10
£20 000 to less than £50 000	13
£50 000 and over	7

known that only a very small percentage of new small firms are high performing firms. One of the implications lies in small firm support. If high growth firms can be identified there is an argument that support would be better targeted at them, rather than giving advice to all potential founders as occurs at present.

2.6 The Enterprise Allowance Scheme (EAS)

The EAS will be discussed at different times in the book, since it is a topic that occurs in sources of finance and in the discussion of attempts to create an Enterprise Culture. However, it is obviously an important issue in start-up since it is a scheme which is specifically designed to encourage small firm start-up. The original blanket coverage of the scheme has been reduced since control has passed to the Training and Enterprise Councils (TECs) and Local Enterprise Companies (LECs), although qualifications to enter the scheme remain fairly minimal. At the time the survey was undertaken there was a minimal period of unemployment to qualify for the scheme. Nevertheless, 62 per cent of clients had applied for the EAS, and of these 82 per cent had qualified.

—————— Questions for discussion ——————

1. Why does the EAS cause a possible displacement effect?

2. What advantages might exist for keeping the EAS?

2.7 Sources of finance

Sources of finance are discussed in more detail later but the results of this study are given in Table 3.6.

Table 3.6   Importance of sources of finance

Source	Mean score
Personal savings	3.0
Family and friends	1.43
Bank overdraft	1.31
Personal assets	0.75
Bank loan (secured)	0.62
Bank loan (unsecured)	0.49
Other loan	0.43
Re-mortgage	0.31
Insurance policy	0.25
Local authority	0.13
PYBT	0.11

Note: Mean score is based on a scale of 0 to 5 (from 0 = no importance to 5 = very substantial importance).

The clear importance of personal savings is shown at start-up.

Question for discussion

In what ways does Table 3.6 illustrate the financial problems of start-up for small firms?

3. ISSUES IN BUSINESS DEVELOPMENT

The importance of finance is also reflected in business development. The study found that, primarily, small firm owners were limited from expanding by financial resources; then competition from other businesses; human resources; physical resources; and then administrative resources.

We found that only a small proportion of businesses used IT. Only 26 per cent of starters had introduced any form of computer based technology, although of those trading it was found that 41 per cent did have plans or were likely to introduce some form of IT.

3.1 Motives

The importance of motives for new small business owners are given in Table 3.7. This table indicates that satisfaction and independence are the most important motives for the establishment of a new small business.

Table 3.7 Motivation of founders

Importance of motive	Mean score
Satisfaction	4.4
Independence	4.1
Financial	3.6
Picking people you work with	3.4
Building an enterprise that can survive	3.0
Status	2.5
Leading others	2.1

Note: Mean score is based on a scale of 0 to 5 as in Table 3.6

It may be interesting to note that leading others is given a low priority, yet it will automatically follow from business success. It may mean that new small firm owners do not plan for such personal development.

——————— *Question for discussion* ———————

What other issues will emerge as the small firm grows and increases the number of employees?

The skills and characteristics of successful entrepreneurs will be discussed in a later chapter, but the study showed that the founders perceived their most important skills to be planning and controlling, followed by negotiating skills, and those associated with acting as a figurehead.

4. REASONS FOR NON-START AND THE CESSATION OF TRADING

We have to be tentative about any conclusions in this section because of the smaller sample sizes involved. However, our findings are worth consideration as possible barriers and constraints that:

- ■ prevent start-up
- ■ possibly contribute to the cessation of trading.

4.1 Factors that prevent start-up

In rank order the problems that clients anticipated and stopped them starting up were:

- Insufficient start-up finance
- Anticipated cashflow problems
- Change in home circumstances
- Cost of business premises
- Unacceptable risk
- Inappropriate location of business premises
- Competing demands from family/domestic sources
- Lack of knowledge of accounting/financial techniques
- Anticipated problems of outlets
- Inappropriate sizes of outlets.

Personal problems were rated as a different category and the most important personal problems that prevented start-up in rank order were:

- Financial commitments
- Family commitments
- Fear of failure
- Lack of general self-confidence
- Adequate current job satisfaction
- Inadequate encouragement from spouse/partner
- Not having mastery of the tasks or jobs they would encounter.

It seems that there were four key issues:

- Availability and access to sufficient finance
- Confidence
- Associated (lack of) knowledge
- Support.

4.2 Factors in business failure

Finally, there are some very tentative findings on why businesses subsequently cease to trade. The rank order again of the important factors were:

- Lack of knowledge of marketing
- Competing task demands from family/domestic sources
- Problems of outlets
- Lack of market awareness of their product/service
- The costs of business premises
- Inappropriate business premises
- Insufficient mark up
- Unacceptable risk
- Change in home circumstances
- Inappropriate size of premises.

Other factors such as too much debt or capital tied up in stock do not seem to be a problem, but the sample is too small to come to any definite conclusions on this matter.

SUMMARY

This survey can be compared to other larger surveys, e.g., the Cambridge Survey (3), but these surveys are often of existing, well-established small firms. This survey covers typical new starts. It is a (biased) picture of business start-up.

The main characteristics to emerge from this survey of new small firms are that:

1. A strong gender bias exists towards male founders.
2. There is a distinct age-launch window of business start-ups.
3. The majority of new firm starts have very low turnovers.
4. Only a very small proportion will be fast growing small firms.
5. Family support is a significant factor.
6. The majority of new firm starts were in the service sector.
7. The majority were reliant on personal equity for start-up finance. The main source of external finance was the bank overdraft.

GREENWED LTD

The following case study is designed to illustrate some of the constraints that a small business may face that has been in business for a short time and wishes to expand. The case study is based on the experiences of a real entrepreneur who had recognized market opportunities and needed specific resources (both financial and others) to be able to exploit them. The name of the business and the owner have been changed to protect confidentiality, but all other material is based upon the real experiences of the entrepreneur concerned (as is the case for all businesses in this book which are used as case studies). The case study will also serve as a preliminary exercise before attempting a more detailed case study assignment also based on a real business.

AIMS

1. To provide examples of real world experiences and problems of small business management.
2. To prepare students for a more detailed case study assignment.
3. To enable the discussion of problems in small business management.
4. To illustrate the problems of skill shortages in local labour markets.

Greenwed Ltd

The information in this document is strictly confidential. The author is grateful for permission by the entrepreneur to use the material that follows.

BACKGROUND

Greenwed Ltd is an individually owned limited company that was formed two years ago by Malcolm Preece. Malcolm had worked for 21 years as a skilled joiner and later a project manager for medium-sized organizations and companies in the building and shopfitting trade. For the previous eight years Malcolm had been in middle management. Malcolm had recognized an opportunity to offer quality-built shopfittings and other work on a general basis with emphasis on quality and a belief that a small firm has advantages of flexibility and innovation in design for the particular market with which he was familiar. Malcolm was also able to use his extensive contacts to generate work as a consultant on new projects, e.g., shop fronts and design.

With a belief that the company could be launched with very little capital and with the basis of a firm order and a paid deposit, Malcolm decided to launch Greenwed Ltd with himself and his wife as nominal shareholders (i.e., the minimum number of shareholders and nominal capital of £1 shares).

Malcolm was able to acquire an old Transit van with the help of a loan from family. To begin with he secured work using his skills as a joiner and later to establish his name for quality. At this time, Malcolm did not have any premises and could work from home.

The launch became successful very quickly and Malcolm was able to take on staff and sub-contract work, sub-contracting being common practice in the shopfitting and construction industry. After six months he was employing six people directly and had up to 19 people on sub-contract work.

The need for suitable premises where he could store materials was beginning to become a constraint, with the office being located in the garage at home and his wife as accountant. To begin with, he was able to negotiate a sub-lease of a small yard for storage of timber and other materials used for the shopfitting trade. During this initial early stage of the first six to nine months of the business, Malcolm was able to cope with the standard work coming in, which was for small contracts of less than £100 000. Any additional work that could not be handled could be contracted out. Obviously, Malcolm could not do all the quality fitting himself and finding suitable people, who were qualified joiners and could be relied upon to do a first class job to Malcolm's specifications, was becoming a problem.

Personally, Malcolm was highly skilled with good contacts and experience of what was required for major contracts in the shopfitting trade. However, he had no enterprise or financial training and was 'learning by doing' as the business expanded. This may work for a time, particularly where someone has the flexibility and ability to learn quickly and adjust. However, the business was so successful and expanding at such a rate that it became impossible for Malcolm to handle everything.

The company's project management work had begun to develop and it needed additional office staff for management and bookkeeping purposes.

THE NATURE OF DEMAND

Shopfitting was still the prime business of Greenwed Ltd, but the demand for this is subject to seasonal factors. It is essentially demand derived from retailers who may have peak sales at Christmas. However, in order for shops to be ready to meet this demand they place their orders during the summer. Thus peak demand for Greenwed Ltd is from July to September. The distinct seasonal nature of demand meant that this created some bottlenecks during the busy periods, as well as inevitable slack periods during the winter. This is less of a problem if work can be sub-contracted but with project management additional staff were being employed who had to be paid in the quiet periods.

EQUIPMENT NEEDS

Second-hand Transit vans were used at first which could be picked up cheaply but required high maintenance. After two years of operation Greenwed Ltd needed to modernize its vehicles and some of its equipment.

POTENTIAL

After two years of operation Greenwed Ltd had established a reputation for high quality shopfitting and innovative design of shop interiors, some design work being sub-contracted to Greenwed Ltd's specifications. Malcolm felt that considerable potential for growth in the company had yet to be realized:

1. Project management was beginning to be established and the employ-ment of a contracts manager full time would enable this potential market to be cultivated and developed.
2. Malcolm needed to focus his activity on the management of the growth of the company, using other skilled labour where possible so that he could focus on management.
3. Alternative markets needed to be explored and researched. Spin-offs may

exist in retailing materials and timber products that are used or connected with the shopfitting business.

4. More general domestic and property conversions or extensions offer considerable scope for expansion based on existing skilled resources and labour or on a sub-contract basis. Contacts with designers and architects would enable a design service to be offered as well as construction.

5. The flexibility of remaining as a small business has permitted a competitive pricing policy due to low overheads. However, there was a pressing need for suitable office and storage space. Greenwed Ltd would still hope to break into new markets by being able to offer the same strengths of flexibility and competitiveness.

6. Greenwed Ltd has successfully developed market-nicheing to offer the independent retailer a competitive service but with the experience and knowledge that has been gained from operating with larger concerns. Customer care services can consequently be much higher for the smaller company. There remains much potential to be exploited from this market nicheing.

TRENDS IN RETAILING

Huge investments by multiple stores have increased the square footage of the typical supermarket into the modern 'superstore' sometimes in out-of-town developments. Alternatively, smaller retailers have aimed at niche markets with multiples of smaller stores, e.g., Lloyds the Chemist, Threshers, and Body Shop.

To service this category of retailer with competitive systems and the essential corporate image nationwide, the shopfitting industry has been forced to change and develop large-scale operations. However, the pronounced seasonal nature of the market, pointed out before, is a problem which is compounded in a large firm. For example, they have to recruit middle management to cope with demand at peak periods only for these skills to be redundant in the slack periods. Consequently, these larger concerns have high overheads.

Greenwed Ltd has exploited this situation by offering the smaller retailer a flexible but high quality service at competitive rates. The service is provided as required on demand. There is no direct competition to Greenwed Ltd. The larger companies are unable to respond effectively to the demands of the smaller retailer and have their own efficiency problems from carrying senior management on high salaries during slack periods. Greenwed Ltd has shown its strength in this area throughout the recession. In the future Greenwed Ltd is well placed to expand its market share of the small independent retailer that many larger shopfitting companies are unable or unwilling to serve.

ENVIRONMENTAL FACTORS

Shopfitting has become an extremely wasteful industry by fitting disposable materials that are 'thrown away' after a short life period. This is becoming increasingly important as waste disposal sites are becoming scarce, and the public are becoming more aware of 'green' issues. It is likely that major retailers will be put under pressure to use more environmentally favourable products not just on their shelves but in their shelves. They will also be forced to look at alternatives as the cost of disposal of existing systems increases.

The DIY market also is dominated by waste and disposal problems. Materials are often supplied in bulk and tend to be of poor quality. Greenwed Ltd believes that there is demand for high quality fittings in DIY and also demand for recyclable products.

There was also an opportunity to create a 'timber scrapyard', where good quality components would be available either as off-cuts or recycled from other projects which would be available on a self-select basis. Greenwed Ltd handled, daily, a wide variety of surplus and recycled products from the shopfitting industry. Instead of these materials going for waste or disposal as previously, they could be exploited to provide high quality products direct to the general public as DIY materials.

Greenwed Ltd intended to offer an environmentally friendly service to the general public, individual tradesman, and the small shopkeeper. In order to do this, however, new premises were needed and an expansion of employment to draw in management and office/sales skills.

GREENWED LTD

MANAGEMENT ACCOUNTS FOR THE PERIOD FROM
1 NOVEMBER 1991 TO 31 AUGUST 1992

PROFIT AND LOSS ACCOUNT FROM THE PERIOD
1 NOVEMBER 1991 TO 31 AUGUST 1992

	£	£
SALES AND CONTRACT INCOME		212 284
COST OF SALES		
Purchases	32 148	
Sub-contracting	126 101	
Delivery charges	531	
Plant and equipment hire	709	
Waste disposal	366	
Closing stock	(1 398)	158 457
GROSS PROFIT		53 827
OTHER INCOME		
Interest		14
		———
		53 841
EXPENSES		
Directors	14 888	
Secretarial services	426	
Rent and rates	1 176	
Light and heat	240	
Motor expenses	5 105	
Vehicle hire	2 149	
Leasing	1 877	
Travel	1 180	
Mobile phones	1 732	
Telephone	1 151	
Insurances	325	
Repairs and maintenance	262	
Printing and stationery	1 946	
Cleaning	379	
Legal fees	1 365	
Accountancy	1 350	
HP interest	257	

Bank interest	973	
Bank charges	603	
Loss on sale of vehicles	345	
Depreciation	2 240	
		42 457
NET PROFIT		11 384

BALANCE SHEET AS AT 31 AUGUST 1992

	£	£
FIXED ASSETS		
Motor vehicles	5 830	
Plant and equipment	1 104	
Fixtures and fittings	2 427	
	9 361	
Property improvements	1 462	
		10 823
CURRENT ASSETS		
Stock	1 398	
Debtors	39 969	
Pre-payments	306	
Bank	25 014	
Cash	400	
	67 087	
CURRENT LIABILITIES		
Creditors	11 628	
Accruals	2 313	
Hire purchase	5 440	
PAYE	10 696	
VAT	15 520	
Overdraft	20 927	
	66 524	
NET CURRENT ASSETS		563
		11 386

CAPITAL AND RESERVES
Called up share capital   2
Profit and loss account   11 384
                                              ————
                                               11 386
                                              ————

PLANS FOR EXPANSION

The need for new premises and extra staff is becoming acute for Greenwed Ltd. From estimates of future contracts and sales, Greenwed Ltd forecasts that it can generate £300 000 as income in the next financial year. This forecast depends on having premises and storage space for its timber products. The company plans to expand its vehicles by leasing additional cars and vans. The company estimates that it needs an additional £50 000 to meet additional expenses if it is to finance expansion as follows:

Additional staff costs	£30 000
Premises (rental)	£10 000
Vehicles	£10 000

Additional expenditure on plant and equipment can be met by the company's reserves.

Questions on Greenwed Ltd

1. To what extent does Malcolm Preece fit the typical characteristics of small firm owners.
2. Identify the resources that Malcolm Preece needed to start the business.
3. What constraints and problems did Malcolm face in the first year of operation?
4. What are the characteristics of demand for shopfitting and what problems does this give for a new entrant to shopfitting?
5. What potential marketing opportunities are open to Greenwed Ltd and how can it best exploit these?
6. Analyse the profit and loss account and balance sheet of Greenwed Ltd at the end of the first year's trading in terms of (i) profitability and (ii) liquidity.
7. What are the main strengths and weaknesses of Greenwed Ltd?
8. Assume the role of bank manger. Would you lend £50 000 to Greenwed Ltd? Justify your decision.

Learning outcomes

At the end of this chapter, students should be able to:

1. Describe the typical important personal and business characteristics of new start-up firms and entrepreneurs.
2. Discuss the reasons for some of these characteristics.

3. Identify and discuss the importance of constraints in early growth business development.
4. Discuss the potential advantages and disadvantages of financial support for new firm formation in the form of 'blanket' schemes such as the Enterprise Allowance Scheme.
5. Analyse the features of a market opportunity such as that demonstrated by Greenwed.
6. Identify and discuss resources required for a new-start firm.
7. Describe the important sources of finance for new-start entrepreneurs and firms and the strategies that might be adopted to overcome (financial) constraints.

Suggested assignments

1. You work as a management consultant to small firm owners/entrepreneurs. You have been assigned by Greenwed Ltd to identify their potential and recommend possible courses of action. You have been given the following tasks:
   (a) Identify the financial strengths and weaknesses of Greenwed Ltd from the balance sheet and profit and loss account.
   (b) Identify the main constraints that you consider Greenwed Ltd to be facing at the present time.
   (c) Identify the options open to the company in terms of raising the required finance.
   (d) Present your recommendations for a course of action as though presenting them to the managing director.
   These tasks should be researched carefully by considering all potential sources of finance. Any materials that you can provide to improve your presentation will be given credit.
2. Students participate in small group discussions and consider the questions/issues on Greenwed Ltd. Students present their findings on these questions to the group.

REFERENCES

1. CURRAN, J. (1986) *Bolton 15 Years On: A Review and Analysis of Small Business Research in Britain 1971-1986*, Small Business Research Trust, London.

2. DALY, M. and MCCANN, A. (1992) 'How Many Small Firms', *Employment Gazette*, April, pp. 47–51.

3. CAMBRIDGE REPORT (1992) *The State of Enterprise in Britain*, Cambridge Small Business Research Centre, Cambridge University, Cambridge.

4 *Sources of Finance*

INTRODUCTION

This chapter will be predominantly concerned with sources of finance for entrepreneurs and small and medium-sized enterprises (SMEs), taking definitions of SMEs as given in Chapter 2. Thus, for many small firms, certain sources of finance are not available due to entry barriers. For example, many entrepreneurs and SMEs are automatically excluded from certain financial sources, such as the Stock Exchange, and face difficulties raising certain types of finance such as long term loans because of the automatically higher risk associated with firms who have little equity in the form of share capital. In the majority of cases the only equity is going to be that of the proprietors. This chapter will give an overview of the sources of finance and some time will be spent examining theoretical issues that provide the foundation for an examination of this important area. This chapter is linked to a case study, Peters and Co., which gives a practical example of a start-up proposition that is seeking finance. There are a number of possible assignments that can be set based upon the case study.

It is worth making a distinction between the theoretical basis of entrepreneurs' and SMEs' finance and what we know about the sources of finance that they actually use. For example, it is easy to hypothesize from what has been said above, about the difficulties facing entrepreneurs and small firms; that such entrepreneurs and small firms are likely to rely heavily on personal savings and equity for long term finance, and perhaps trade credit for short term finance. However, these hypotheses need to be balanced about what actually happens, i.e., the empirical evidence. Unfortunately, a lot of the empirical evidence is rather *ad hoc*, i.e., drawn from small surveys or anecdotal evidence. We will consider each in turn.

There are a variety of sources of finance available to the entrepreneur and small- and medium-sized firm. These can be classified as internal and external. Internal sources of finance include the personal equity of the entrepreneur, usually in the form of savings re-mortgages, or perhaps money raised from family and friends. After the initial start-up of the firm, retained profits and earnings provide internal capital. Usually within an SME it is normal for internal sources to provide the major proportion of the firm's capital and financial structure. External finance can be drawn from a number of sources. The principal sources for the SME and entrepreneur are going to be advances from banks, equity from venture capitalists and informal investors, and short term trade credit. Other external sources may include leasing, hire purchase, and factoring. In addition to these sources, in the UK, the small firm entrepreneur may qualify for grants or 'soft loans' from government bodies such as the DTI (e.g., Regional Selective Assistance—RSA); or qualify for other schemes such as the Small Firms' Loan Guarantee Scheme (SFLGS); or for start-ups, the Enterprise Allowance Scheme (EAS). Local government may also provide loans and grants, and there a number of agencies that have attempted to set up their own financing schemes for small firms. These may include venture capital and loans from enterprise agencies, Training and Enterprise Councils (TECs), or in Scotland the Local Enterprise Companies (LECs), development agencies, enterprise boards, and Inner City Task Force Funding.

Whether SMEs and entrepreneurs do face real difficulties in raising external finance can be disputed; but the concern with this area by policy makers has given rise to a barrage of assistance that is now available to small firms and entrepreneurs. Whether these schemes are effective is another issue, which we touch upon later, but they have arisen at least in part because of theoretical concerns which suggest that small firm entrepreneurs will be at a disadvantage in raising finance compared to large firms. In particular concern has centred on whether SMEs and entrepreneurs face finance gaps, because the supply of relatively small amounts of finance that small firms require, less than £200 000, can be uneconomic to provide and subsequently monitor by financial institutions especially when considering sources of equity capital. We turn to consider these issues in more detail.

ISSUES IN SOURCES OF FINANCE FOR SMEs AND ENTREPRENEURS

1. FINANCE GAPS

If gaps arise they do so because of mis-matches between supply and demand. The existence of a finance gap will arise because demand from small firms is greater than the willingness of financial institutions to supply the finance at current market conditions. For finance such as bank loans these gaps may be termed credit rationing. A gap may exist such as that illustrated by Fig. 4.1, where demand exceeds the available supply at current market rates of interest.

In Fig. 4.1 total advances that small firms would like to take up are given by ob. However, the amount that banks are willing to supply is given by oa. Hence the existence of a debt gap given by the distance ab. Governments can attempt to close this gap by shifting the supply curve of (debt) finance to the right by the

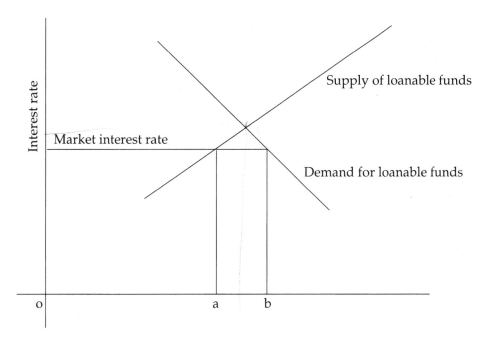

Figure 4.1 Demand and supply for bank credit. Notes: (i) The market interest rate is likely to be established below the equilibrium level due to state and Bank of England regulation. (ii) The demand for loanable funds is assumed to consist of homogeneous and 'good' propositions seeking bank finance implying a 'gap' that could be met by rationing

introduction of schemes such as the Small Firms' Loan Guarantee Scheme (SFLGS).

The discussion, so far, however, is an over-simplification of the market for small firm entrepreneurs' finance. For example, we are assuming that all propositions from small firms that banks receive are homogeneous. This will, patently, not be the case and we would expect some propositions to be more favourably treated than others. An equally important point arises about whether the 'good' propositions receive finance and whether the 'poor' propositions do not. This is the problem of adverse selection which is discussed in more detail below.

Finance gaps, however, have been recognized for over 60 years. They were first highlighted by the Macmillan Report of 1931 (1), and subsequently termed the 'Macmillan gap'. Macmillan found, at the time, that small businesses and entrepreneurs would find it difficult to raise amounts of less than £200 000, equivalent to £4m today. The Stock Exchange required a minimum figure of this amount to allow the trading of equity capital in a firm. There is little doubt that this gap has been substantially narrowed with the development of the venture capital industry in the UK. However, various official reports and other researchers have pointed to the continued existence of an equity gap in the UK. For example, it has been mentioned by the Bolton Report in 1971 (2), the Wilson Report in 1979 (3), and for a recent study see Mason, Harrison, and Chaloner (4). There is general consensus that there is still a gap for raising equity of amounts below £250 000. This equity gap for SMEs and entrepreneurs still exists because of the following reasons:

1. It is not economic to issue shares for relatively small amounts of equity on the Stock Exchange (e.g., commission costs are high for small issues of less than £1m).
2. Difficulties can exist in getting a listing on the Stock Exchange. This did become easier with the development of the Unlisted Securities Market (USM) and the Third and Over the Counter (OTC) markets, but the need for a trading record of at least three years is a barrier to many small firms. The recent announcement of the demise of the USM (1993) is testimony both to the problems of entrepreneurs and small firms in the raising of equity and to the problems of providers in the administration of markets for relatively small amounts of equity capital. At the time of writing, attempts are being made to re-start these alternative stock markets for smaller firms, through the launch of an Alternative Investment Market (AIM) and attempts to start regional stock markets. It remains to be seen, however, whether they will be any more successful than previous alternative stock exchanges.
3. It is not economic for venture capitalists to provide relatively small amounts of equity capital. The reasons for this are that venture capital companies will want to monitor the performance of the company closely, because they supply equity not debt capital and are consequently not guaranteed a return. Furthermore, the costs of arranging the finance and the appraisal of propositions are generally fixed costs (5).
4. Following on from point 3, venture capitalists require high rates of return because they are assuming higher risks than the banks. Only certain high performing entrepreneurs and firms, the high growth firms, will be able to achieve the high rates of return required by venture capitalists who have in turn to satisfy the requirements of the shareholders in the venture capital fund. As a consequence of this, venture capitalists tend to concentrate on certain sectors of the economy only, or on certain types of finance such as Management Buy-Outs (MBOs). For consideration of these issues see Dixon (6). Recent figures on the formal venture capital industry show that the majority of the sector's funds are invested in MBOs and Management Buy-Ins (MBIs) (7), so that the importance of this sector for the finance of SMEs and entrepreneurs is limited. For example, in 1988 62 per cent of all venture capital in the UK went into MBOs and MBIs (8).
5. Venture capitalists will apply a 'due diligence' procedure to any proposition that

is being considered for investment. This will take a considerable period of time and only a small proportion of applications for formal venture capital eventually receive funding after the due diligence procedure. Less than 5 per cent of applications for such formal venture capital will receive funding from this sector.

6. Venture capitalists will also require an exit route for the sale of their shareholding after a period of time with their investment in the entrepreneurial concern. The normal method of seeking an exit route for such a holding will be to seek an Initial Public Offering (IPO) on the Stock Exchange. Thus, venture capitalists will seek high growth entrepreneurial concerns that can be turned within a short period (say five years) into public companies and provide an IPO as an exit route for their holding and their funds.

7. Venture capitalists will also seek to take an active part in the management of the company to safeguard their investment. They will seek to add value to their investment through an active role in the management and use their networking capabilities to open up additional opportunities for the growth of the entrepreneurial concern. The extent to which venture capitalists can add value has been one of the concerns in the venture capital sector.

The equity gap and informal venture capital

Various alternative sources have been suggested as ways of reducing the equity gap. The Business Expansion Scheme (BES), discussed in more detail below, was a government response to the problem. Informal risk capital, provided by informal investors or 'business angels' has attracted attention recently as a means of providing small amounts of equity capital to small firms to close the equity gap. The major work in this area in the UK has been completed by Mason and Harrison (9, 10), who argue that the informal venture capital sector has enormous potential for closing the equity gap which is, as yet, largely untapped. They estimate that the total venture capital that may be available if properly tapped would be in the order of £4 billion to £5 billion, which places it potentially on a par with the formal venture capital sector. However, the significance for small firms is far greater because, according to Mason and Harrison, business angels would be more patient than the formal sector, less likely to want to be directly involved in the firm and be willing to invest small amounts of capital in line with the needs of entrepreneurs and the owners of small firms.

The major problems that exist in this sector concern the search costs for investors and firms who have to match each others' requirements, since business angels will have their own preferences for different types of firm and investment. In order to overcome these problems Mason and Harrison have suggested that non-profit making agencies (e.g., TECs and LECs) should set up matching services. Their work has been influential in persuading the Government to establish a pilot scheme with a limited number of TECs to provide a matching service for business angels and entrepreneurs.

Mason and Harrison (10) have shown that the informal venture capital sector (business angels) is well developed in the USA and claim the following advantages of business angels:

1. Business angels are willing to invest small sums of perhaps less than £50 000 that will meet the needs of start-up entrepreneurs and existing small firms.
2. The time spent in analysing propositions is much shorter than the formal venture capital sector where the due diligence procedure can take many months.
3. Business angels are less likely to seek quick exit routes and will be more patient than the formal venture capital sector.
4. Business angels will be satisfied with lower returns since there is no need to satisfy shareholders of a venture capital company. They may invest because they have an interest in the industry or business sector and they can bring their own expertise (however, they will not have the same network of contacts as venture capitalists).
5. Business angels may be more suited to high technology based entrepreneurs and small firms that have special seed capital requirements in order to finance the research and development process. It can be argued that business angels have the patience and the expertise necessary in order to invest in high technology based entrepreneurs.

While it is unquestionable that the informal venture capital sector does have a lot of potential for closing the SME and entrepreneurial equity gap, there remain, nevertheless, some disadvantages with business angels associated with the administration of any scheme to link angels with entrepreneurs that need finance. These disadvantages include:

1. There is no formal matching procedure established. Not only are business angels difficult to find, they have to be matched to suitable entrepreneurs that they are interested in funding. Such search costs are difficult to finance and administer adequately.
2. There may be limited expertise that the business angel can give to the entrepreneur. Hence value-added may be problematical and business angels will not be able to tap into extensive networks of contacts that are well established by venture capitalists (to help the growth potential of entrepreneurs). These matching problems include search costs for both suitable entrepreneurs with suitable propositions for investments and suitable business angels that can match funding and preferences to the proposition.
3. It has been claimed that many entrepreneurs and small firm owners do not want external equity holders since the loss of control and dilution of equity takes away some of their independence and decision-making ability, an independence that may have been a prime motivating factor in start-up.

Overall, however, there is little doubt that there is much potential that could be developed from a proper harnessing of business angels to small firm entrepreneurs that are actively seeking small amounts of equity.

Recent research has also highlighted the under-utilized potential of corporate venturing for developing sources of equity and venture capital for entrepreneurs and small firms. According to McNally (11) there is under-utilized scope for corporate venturing particularly for high technology concerns where corporations can contribute to specialized venture capital funds and contribute expertise to improve the available networking skills from venture capitalists.

Given the existing constraints, it is not surprising that entrepreneurs and small firms will rely on debt finance as the principal source of external finance. As a consequence the banks are the principal institutions approached by entrepreneurs and small firms, although there are difficulties, theoretically, here as well. These difficulties can produce debt gaps, such as that illustrated in Fig. 4.1, where small firms may wish to borrow finance externally but for a number of reasons the banks are unwilling (or occasionally, due to a Bank of England directive, unable) to supply this finance. We shall now consider these issues associated with bank finance in more detail.

2. FINANCE AND THE BANKS

The problems that exist theoretically can be analysed using theory from the economics of information. When conditions of uncertainty combine with asymmetric information (where providers and borrowers have different sets of information), we get two problems for the banks:

- Adverse selection,
- Moral hazard.

Adverse selection occurs when either the bank provides finance for a venture that subsequently fails or refuses finance for a venture that would have been successful. It may occur because the bank does not have all the available information or that the information is imperfect. The difficulty here is that the information required by the bank to assess perfectly the risk of the proposition is not costless to obtain. However, it can be argued that banks should reduce the mistakes they make, since they should have the skills and resources necessary to increase the frequency of correct decisions.

Moral hazard is more difficult to control for the bank. Once an entrepreneur has raised the bank loan, there is no guarantee that they will act in the best interests of the bank. In theoretical terms this is an example of a principal–agent situation, with the bank as principal, who engages the borrower as agent to undertake the proposition, resulting in a profit for both sides. Therefore, moral hazard is a monitoring problem and for relatively small amounts of finance it is not economic for banks to monitor performance closely. For this reason, banks will usually require security, yet this contributes to the problems facing entrepreneurs. Those entrepreneurs without substantial equity and insufficient security will fall into the debt gap.

We have argued that bank assessments of small firm applications for loan finance are examples of decision making under uncertainty incorporating asymmetric information for the provider and the client. The foundations of analysis of possible mismatches between supply and demand that can occur under these conditions have been laid down by Akerlof's seminal 1970 paper (12). Writers have developed the significance of these conditions for finance theory using a principal–agent framework (13, 14, 15). However, the relevance of these insights is limited when considering the finance of entrepreneurs and small firms that have restricted access to financial markets. Concepts of moral hazard and adverse selection, however, are still important and have been further refined by later writers (16, 17, 18).

Stiglitz and Weiss have shown that the problems of moral hazard and adverse selection are likely to produce credit rationing, insufficient credit available for all sound propositions (19). It is possible to argue that these problems can lead to a credit glut (20) and a report by Aston University suggested that growing firms who wished to expand and were sound propositions were able to raise finance when they needed to (21). However, comprehensive surveys by Binks *et al.* in the UK have revealed the expected mismatches between providers (the commercial banks) and clients suggested by the theoretical papers 1988 and 1993 (22, 23).

Research by the author and Hussain (24, 25) and the author and Philpott (26) has revealed that adverse selection certainly occurs in the UK and that risk assessment practices of UK bank managers are considerably different from their counterparts in Germany and Holland. The argument is that criteria used in Germany and Holland for risk assessment are different and less likely to lead to adverse selection. Deakins and Hussain took on the role of entrepreneurs seeking a funding proposition from 30 bank officers in the UK for a new venture. They hypothesized that banks would require financial and managerial information in risk assessment of propositions from new entrepreneurs. They expected bank officers to place more importance on the abilities and experience of the entrepreneur, since financial information which might appear as financial projections of income and costs in the cashflow forecast will be subject to uncertainty and treated with caution. Of course, with new propositions there is no financial track record of profitability and other criteria which may be used to assess existing propositions such as liquidity, sales growth, debtors, and other measures of financial performance. If the new entrepreneur involves an application of new technology, we have the added factor of technological uncertainty. For these propositions, they expected the banks to develop networking methods with outside institutions that can provide information on the assessment of the technology and the technical abilities of the entrepreneur that would help to reduce the more acute problem of asymmetric information.

We found that, of the 30 bank officers, 50 per cent would have backed the proposition yet 50 per cent would not, but that there was also considerable variation in the approach of different officers. They also noticed that there was a bias in approach to financial criteria whereas important management criteria were discounted. Table 4.1 illustrates the importance of different information for their proposition. We can see from this table that only 10 per cent of managers considered small business experience and enterprise ability to be important. Further research by the author and Philpott (26) with German bank officers revealed much greater importance in Germany placed on managerial information.

Table 4.1 Criteria used or sought on the proposition

Information	Percentage of managers
Gearing	83
Entrepreneurs' personal financial position	73
Forecasted balance sheet and P&L account	66
Entrepreneurs' drawings	63
Entrepreneurs' contacts in industry	60
Timing of income payments	60
Contingency plans	57
Entrepreneurs' personal collateral	50
Market research	50
Entrepreneurs qualifications and careers	43
Cashflow assumptions	40
Entrepreneurs starting separately	37
Role of IT consultant	33
IT development costs	27
Business/managerial strategy	13
Enterprise and small business experience	10

Notes:
(i) n = 30.
(ii) These are selective criteria.

Source: Deakins and Hussain (24).

This research has been extended recently by Fletcher (27) with 38 Scottish bank managers. Taking the same proposition as used in the Deakins and Hussain study, but with modifications to allow for slightly different economic conditions and the Scottish environment, Fletcher found a number of significant differences between the Scottish bank managers and the findings of the author's study. A greater proportion of Scottish bank managers (68 per cent) were prepared to back the proposition and some Scottish bank officers were prepared to back the proposition without security, despite the relatively high gearing of the proposition. Some of the differences are illustrated in Table 4.2. Fletcher attempts to account for the differences by reference to the different banking structure and relationships in Scotland. The three Scottish banks, The Royal Bank of Scotland, The Bank of Scotland, and the Clydesdale Bank operate with closer relationships to their business customers than the main English clearing banks. This, coupled with the different environment (e.g., there is less owner-occupied housing in Scotland), might account for some of the differences found in practice between English and Scottish bank managers, with Scottish bank managers closer to the German approach where greater emphasis is placed on the entrepreneurs' abilities and managerial experience.

Table 4.2   English v. Scottish bank managers' decisions

Score out of 10	Number of officers English	Scottish
0	1	1
1	4	3
2	4	1
3	3	2
4	3	5
5	1	1
6	3	4
7	10	13
8	1	7
9	0	1
10	0	0
Total	30	38

Source: Deakins and Hussain (24) and Fletcher (27).

3. THE ROLE OF SECURITY

We can also hypothesize that bank officers will stipulate requirements on the small business owner which may involve frequent monitoring information, to reduce moral hazard. However, a cost minimization approach will also include using methods that ensure commitment on the part of the entrepreneur. We would expect collateral to have an important role because it can ensure commitment and also provides a fail-safe method for the bank to recover losses in the case of the form of adverse selection that involves selecting a business failure. In conditions of uncertainty, signalling is obviously important and following Spence (28), a number of writers have developed theoretical implications of this (29, 30, 31). The importance of signalling commitment has also been recognized (32). Thus, liquidity constraints and uncertainty combine to encourage the provider of finance to require security when this is available. Also Chan and Kannatas have pointed out that the type of security maintained by the entrepreneur can supply information for the provider (33).

Collateral, however, is not without costs and its own problems, e.g., there are valuation problems, there might be depreciation to consider; and it might be necessary to revalue collateral at intervals. The taking of collateral, then, needs to be balanced against the costs of management for the bank. Also, the taking of collateral does nothing to reduce adverse selection. It merely provides a method for the bank to recover (some) potential losses where it considers risks to be high. However, if we assume that bank mangers are risk averse, we can expect that collateral will be required where risks are perceived to be high, e.g., with new technology entrepreneurs or with propositions that have high gearing.

Table 4.3. shows the importance of general criteria from the study with English bank managers. While security requirements do not appear to be of high importance, in practice they will often be critical requirements where risk is perceived to be high, such as with our proposition that was discussed with 30 bank managers. For example, of those that would have backed the proposition all required security. The importance generally of gearing (the ratio of debt to equity) as a criterion is reflected in Table 4.3, which reinforces the view that financial information such as the gearing level are critical factors for bank managers in the UK.

Theoretically, adverse selection should not occur if the bank has perfect information and can rely with certainty on cashflow predictions. Following Altman (34), we have argued that it is necessary to define two different categories of adverse selection. Firstly, the bank officer could approve a proposition that turns out to be a business failure. Secondly, the bank could refuse to accept a proposition that turns out to be a business success. We define these categories as Type II and Type I errors respectively. (The reader should note that this reverses the Altman classification.) We consider that bank officers are overly concerned with avoiding Type II errors (partly because Type I errors will not be discovered) and that this contributes to excessive adverse selection.

Table 4.3   Importance of criteria used to assess lending propositions

Criteria	Rank order	Mean score	STD deviation
Trading experience	1	4.43	0.5
Projected income	2	4.37	0.85
Existing profitability	3	4.3	0.6
Equity stake	4	4.18	0.69
Repayment of previous loans	5	4.12	0.76
Gearing	6	3.82	0.9
Client an existing customer	7	3.78	0.76
Net profit to sales	8	3.75	0.89
Previous loans	=9	3.73	0.69
Personal guarantees	=9	3.73	0.69
CVs of clients	11	3.7	0.76
Trade debtors	12	3.65	0.71
Liquidity ratios	=13	3.62	0.85
Gross profit to sales	=13	3.62	0.85
Trade creditors	15	3.57	0.85
Charge on personal assets	16	3.55	0.65
Fixed charge on business assets	17	3.52	0.91
Floating charge	18	3.00	1.07

Note: 6 point scale used from 0 to 5.

Systems that control for Type II errors may minimize risk, but they also miss profitable opportunities associated with business propositions that might contain higher risk but provide profitable opportunities for growth in the business of the bank. These hypotheses provide theoretical explanations of why bank officers may turn away small firm propositions that have high potential for growth and profitability.

4. SOME EMPIRICAL EVIDENCE

In terms of empirical research, it is known from various sources that entrepreneurs and small firms are highly dependent on internal sources of finance, as might be expected from our discussion above. Research by Cambridge University's Small

Table 4.4 External sources of finance from a sample of 1185 small firms

	Percentage of respondents receiving additional finance from:
Banks	83.7
Venture capital	6.5
Hire purchase/leasing	44.6
Factoring	6.0
Trade credit	8.5
Partners/working shareholders	19.5
Other private individuals	5.6
Other sources	9.7

Source: Cambridge Small Business Research Centre (35).

Business Research Centre in 1992 (35) indicated that bank finance was by far the most important source of finance for entrepreneurs and SMEs. Table 4.4 gives their figures. The Cambridge study found that 65 per cent of their sample of 2000 SMEs and entrepreneurs had attempted to raise finance from external sources in the previous three years. This figure represents a considerable improvement on the 26 per cent found by the Bolton Report (1971) but it still may represent some degree of introspection by small firms and entrepreneurs in seeking finance. It may also, however, represent the existence of barriers to obtaining finance. This may have two identifiable consequences:

1. It will affect the speed and growth of their development and confirms that few firms are high growth performers.
2. It raises the question of whether sufficient entrepreneurs and small firms are available that are actively seeking equity finance to make matching schemes for business angels and entrepreneurs worth while.

It is likely that internal sources and the entrepreneur's equity will be very important for start-up finance. Using our study of start-up small firms and entrepreneurs (Sparrow and Deakins (36)), discussed in Chapter 3, we report the results in Table 4.5. Although, it shows that a high proportion of start-ups do use bank finance, a more significant feature is the comparative importance of personal savings which are rated significantly higher than bank finance in importance as a source of finance.

Table 4.5 Start-up finance for a sample of firms in the West Midlands

Source	Percentage of respondents	Importance (mean score)
Personal savings	75	3.0
Bank overdraft	37	1.31
Family and friends	37.5	1.4
Unsecured bank loan	15	0.49
Secured bank loan	17	0.62
Enterprise Allowance Scheme (EAS) ·	62(i)	n.a.

Note: (i) The importance of the EAS is accounted for by the large majority of respondents which were trading for less than one year.

Source: Deakins and Sparrow (48).

Question for discussion

Do female entrepreneurs face disadvantages when raising finance compared to male entrepreneurs?

It has been suggested that if entrepreneurs and small firms face problems in raising finance and are faced by finance gaps, then female entrepreneurs and small business owners face more acute problems since their propositions may not be taken (as) seriously by funders or they may face disadvantages through lack of equity, security, and possibly support from their spouse. It is only very recently that systematic and careful research has been carried out on this important topic. Two studies have adopted careful research methodology which overcomes some of the limitations of previous (more *ad hoc*) attempts to research this issue.

Firstly, Read (37) has examined the question of whether bank managers have any preference for lending to men rather than women. She examined matched samples of 40 pairs of male and female entrepreneurs and found 'more similarities than differences' in their relationships with the bank and their use of overdrafts and loans. However, she did find some evidence of patronizing treatment of a minority of the female entrepreneurs by the bank and some differences in the relationship suggesting that women adopt a different strategy when dealing with the bank manager.

Secondly, Rosa *et al.* (38) have also made a careful study of the differences between male and female entrepreneurs. They find that differences in terms of capitalization and economic performance between male and female entrepreneurs are complex, but women significantly are likely to have lower levels of capitalization and hence levels of external finance. However, as they comment, given that female entrepreneurs have started from a much lower base, they conclude that the performance of female owned businesses has been quite remarkable and that they are 'catching up fast' with male owned businesses.

ETHNIC MINORITY ENTREPRENEURS AND FINANCE

The take-up of sources of finance may be different when we examine the use of finance by ethnic minority entrepreneurs. It is possible to claim that the finance of ethnic minority entrepreneurs is a special case and there has been considerable attention (and research) on the use of finance by them. This issue is also dealt with in a separate chapter on ethnic minority entrepreneurs and the reader should also refer to Chapter 6.

Rather than suffering from any disadvantage in restricted access to financial markets, it has been claimed by Ward and Jenkins (39) that ethnic minority entrepreneurs have a competitive advantage due to the access to informal sources of finance in the extended network of family contacts that exist, for example, in the Asian community. This theme, that Asian entrepreneurs have advantages in seeking finance, has been continued by Jones *et al.* (40) who argue that bank managers are more likely to treat propositions from Asian entrepreneurs more favourably (than other ethnic minority entrepreneurs) due to the success of the Asian community in promoting and fostering entrepreneurship. A study by Curran and Blackburn (41) has also shown that African-Caribbean entrepreneurs have less use of bank finance than Bangladeshi or Greek-Cypriot entrepreneurs.

Further research by the author *et al.* (42) in a study of 34 ethnic minority entrepreneurs in the West Midlands has demonstrated, however, that the importance of the reliance upon informal contacts, particularly in the Asian community, for finance is declining. When examining the change in the importance of different sources of finance as firms develop, we found that bank overdrafts and trade credit became the most important sources of external finance, whereas the reliance on family and kin contacts declined. Even for start-ups, we found that there has been a decline in this traditional reliance on family and kin contacts for sources of finance. Table 4.6 shows the change in importance from start-up to current use in our sample.

We claim that this increased reliance upon bank finance may put ethnic

Table 4.6 Change in order of importance of the sources of finance for a sample of 34 ethnic minority entrepreneurs

Source	Rank order	Mean score (change)
Bank overdrafts	1	+1.9
Trade credit	2	+1.0
Bank loans	3	+1.0
Building societies	4	+0.2
Other sources	5	+0.2
Personal assets	6	+0.1
Insurance policies	7	+0.1
Venture capital	8	−0.2
Family/kin contacts	9	−0.5
Internal sources	10	−1.1

Source: Deakins *et al.* (42).

entrepreneurs at a disadvantage, since they are located in inner city areas and may face disadvantages of securing finance through the limited value of the property in these areas. A follow-up study carried out again by the author *et al.* (43), which examined the relationship between the entrepreneur and the bank manager through combined demand and supply-side interviews, found that there was evidence of good practice by bank managers (such as involvement in the local community) but that this practice was extremely variable and that there is still considerable untapped potential through better practice by the banks. For example, more specific provision by the banks through the provision of ethnic minority units and positive deployment of staff would go some way to improve relationships and overcome some of the inhibitions on the part of potential ethnic minority entrepreneurs.

It is better to deal with the finance of ethnic minority entrepreneurs in the context of the special issues that they face. For example, they face particular business development issues associated with breaking out into new markets outside their ethnic communities and finance is only a small part of this developmental problem. We also found that African-Caribbean entrepreneurs face particular disadvantages when seeking finance and this has led to a special study (43). These issues are dealt with in more detail in Chapter 6 which deals specifically with issues faced by ethnic minority entrepreneurs.

RELATIONSHIPS BETWEEN ENTREPRENEURS AND SMALL FIRMS AND THE BANKS

Work on the relationship between the entrepreneur/small business owner and their bank has been carried out in the comprehensive surveys by Binks *et al.* (23, 44), carried out for the Forum of Private Business. Bank charges, although frequently cited in the press, may not be the most important concern to small business owners and entrepreneurs; but Binks *et al.* did find that only 26 per cent of respondents thought that bank charges were good value for money. There have been improvements by the banks, particularly in staff training and developing specific posts such as 'Enterprise Managers', but entrepreneurs do have genuine grievances if charges are not itemized and the bank operates a hands off policy. This is something that the banks have tried to correct with their Small Business Charters. However. Binks considers that: 'Bank charges, interest rates and the banks' demand for collateral remain important constraints on small firms' (45).

GOVERNMENT SCHEMES

The recognition that the availability of finance is a major constraint for the start-up and growth of entrepreneurs and small firms, coupled with the need to have a strong SME sector in the economy, has led to the introduction of a number of state schemes designed to relieve some of the aspects of these constraints and the difficulties that face small firms. These are outlined briefly below.

1. ENTERPRISE ALLOWANCE SCHEME (EAS)

This scheme was originally designed to encourage unemployed people to start up their own business. It provides a grant designed to tide over the new business during the first year of operation. The actual level of grant varies slightly depending on the region since the scheme is now operated by the Training and Enterprise Councils (TECs) and Local Enterprise Companies (LECs), under different names such as Business Start-Up, but is approximately £2,000 or £40 per week in the first year of trading. Under the TECs and LECs the qualifications for the scheme can vary, e.g. you do not have to be unemployed, but normally have to demonstrate that you have a viable business plan. In some TECs and LECs some capital input is required from the entrant to the scheme.

The use of the EAS is declining as the TECs and LECs question the effectiveness of such a blanket coverage scheme, with the result that the EAS or Business Start-Up is only available in some areas where TECs or LECs still consider that it is viable to operate the scheme. The EAS has been criticized as a less than optimal use of state resources, since:

- It creates businesses that are not viable.
- It subsidizes inefficient businesses.
- It may create unemployment when other businesses are forced to stop trading by 'unfair competition', since EAS businesses are subsidized.

Despite these criticisms, one evaluation study has claimed remarkably high survival rates of 75 per cent or more after the first year of trading (46).

2. SMALL FIRMS' LOAN GUARANTEE SCHEME (SFLGS)

Designed as a scheme of last resort lending for entrepreneurs who have limited security. A major problem with the scheme is that financing propositions have to be put forward to the DTI by the banks to qualify for support and the banks have not been enthusiastic supporters. Sometimes, the banks have pushed forward marginal and high risk ventures onto the scheme. These factors have contributed to a low take-up of the scheme.

The present Government has attempted to make the scheme more attractive, increasing the proportion of the state guarantee (from 70 per cent to 85 per cent) and reducing the premium interest rate which the scheme employs. These changes were introduced in the budget of 1993 and now the Government agrees to underwrite 85 per cent of the loan, with the banks holding the other 15 per cent of the liability. The government part of the scheme is expensive, since the interest rate is subject to a premium above the usual rate charged to small firms by banks. This premium is charged to make the scheme self-financing and to cover the losses incurred where there are defaulters. The premium charged also depends on the nature of the loan. At present, a loan with a fixed rate of interest is subject to a 0.5 per cent premium, and the variable rate loans are subject to 1.5 per cent. The problem with the premium is that it does reduce the retained earnings of the firm, which may affect its business development. Again this is a possible reason for the low take-up rates of the scheme. The amount borrowed under the scheme can be up to a maximum of £250 000 over a period of 7 years.

3. BUSINESS EXPANSION SCHEME (BES)

The 1992 Finance Act announced the abolition of this scheme owing to the fact that it was failing to meet the needs of entrepreneurs. The scheme operated by giving tax breaks to investors prepared to take an equity stake in a business. It was intended to fill the equity gap. Unfortunately, although the scheme started with good intentions, the rules were changed and much of the investment capital raised went into property companies in the South-East. The scheme, therefore, became a housing policy instrument and part of the tax avoidance industry. There became little point in continuing with the scheme and hence it was withdrawn by the end of 1993.

It has been replaced by the Enterprise Investment Scheme (EIS); dubbed by some as 'son of BES' it remains to be seen whether this scheme will be any better at directing investment (through tax breaks) to small manufacturing firms and entrepreneurs.

4. OTHER SCHEMES

There are a variety of state schemes available to help the entrepreneur and small firm. These are often in the form of grants or awards. The main grants available come under Regional Selective Assistance, which is intended to assist entrepreneurs and small firms in designated areas of the UK that have been targeted and are often given for the purchaser of manufacturing premises. The enterprise initiative was also in the form of a grant and enabled the SME owner and entrepreneur to purchase the time of a management consultant to improve the operation of the firm.

Awards are available to high technology entrepreneurs and firms under the Small Firms Merit Award for Research and Technology (SMART) and Small Firms Award for Projects Under Research (SPUR). Both schemes are part of the DTI's assistance to high technology based firms that may have difficulty in raising funding for innovative products. Although these schemes may give high technology small firms and entrepreneurs much needed assistance, their effectiveness can be questioned since, by their nature, they reward the successful entrepreneurs that have already undertaken some development of their product. The SMART scheme is a competition that rewards winners who are likely to be high technology entrepreneurs that may have already been successful in raising finance, although the scheme is also meant to help small firm entrepreneurs that are having difficulty attracting finance to develop products. There has been little published research on the effectiveness of these schemes for helping high technology based entrepreneurs to raise additional finance that leads to the commercial development of their new product. Caird (47) has carried out some research with Scottish winners of the SMART award. Of the 24 entrepreneurs interviewed, the largest number were in health care and medical products, followed in importance by high technology products and computer software. Since the research was examining perceptions of the innovation process with the entrepreneurs, Caird does not offer any clues as to the effectiveness of the scheme for the entrepreneurs involved.

MUTUAL GUARANTEE SCHEMES

Considerable attention has focused recently on the potential of Mutual Guarantee Schemes (MGSs) for reducing funding gaps, especially for existing firms that are seeking finance to expand. It remains the case that MGSs have been successfully established in European countries such as Spain, France, and Germany, yet at the time of writing there is not one pilot MGS established in the UK, despite the fact that the European Commission has made funds available for this purpose.

We postpone the discussion of MGSs in more detail until Chapter 8. Although they represent an alternative funding scheme, they are not the direct result of government attempts to set up alternative funding. Rather, in principle, they result from voluntary associations of firms which then bargain as one body with a major bank or financial institution. This does not, of course, preclude authorities from assisting firms in some ways (perhaps through providing administration costs), but we leave a more detailed discussion until later because, for this author, the high potential of MGSs is better discussed in relation to entrepreneurs and small firms concerned with innovation, which can be seen to have special funding requirements and constraints compared to other entrepreneurs and small firms. Therefore, more detailed discussion has been left until Chapter 8.

CONCLUSIONS

In this chapter, we have taken an overview of the important issues in the finance of SMEs and entrepreneurs. Much of this discussion has centred on finance gaps and their implications for entrepreneurs and small firms. We have tried to show, theoretically, why these gaps might emerge given problems of uncertainty and asymmetric information.

We have shown that entrepreneurs and SMEs continue to be dependent on banks for external finance despite schemes that attempt to improve the availability of equity capital. We have shown that entrepreneurs also face problems in raising bank finance and that UK bank practices of risk assessment can be variable and that adverse selection (where potentially viable projects are not receiving finance) is higher than it needs to be.

By now you should be able to discuss the importance of alternative sources of finance for entrepreneurs and SMEs and the advantages and disadvantages of the most important of these sources. You should also have an understanding of why small firms and entrepreneurs are at a disadvantage compared to larger firms in financial markets and also have an appreciation of the problems that face providers of finance.

Learning outcomes

At the end of this chapter students should be able to:

1. Discuss the importance of alternative sources of finance for entrepreneurs and small- and medium-sized enterprises.
2. Describe why entrepreneurs and SMEs are at a disadvantage compared with large firms in financial markets.
3. Appreciate some of the problems that face the providers of finance to the SME sector.
4. Compare survey results and known national characteristics on the importance of sources of finance for start-up entrepreneurs and existing ventures.
5. Describe research findings comparing risk assessment practices of English and Scottish bank managers and be able to indicate the main differences in these practices.

Suggested assignment

We have not included a suggested assignment at the end of this chapter, since it is followed by a full case study in the following chapter. Instead it is suggested that students complete assignments associated with the case study.

REFERENCES

1. HM GOVERNMENT (1931) *Report of The Committee on Finance and Industry (Macmillan Report)*, CMND 3897, HMSO.

2. HM GOVERNMENT (1971) *Report of The Committee of Inquiry on Small Firms (Bolton Report)*, CMND 4811, HMSO.

3. HM GOVERNMENT (1979) *Interim Report on The Financing of Small Firms (Wilson Report)*, CMND 7503, HMSO.

4. MASON, C. HARRISON, R., and CHALONER, J. (1991) *Informal Risk Capital in the UK*, Venture Finance Research Project, Working Paper no. 2, University of Southampton.

5. HARRISON, R. T. and MASON, C. (1991) 'Informal Investment Networks: A Case Study from the UK', *Entrepreneurship and Regional Development*, vol. 3, no. 2, pp. 269–79.

6. DIXON, R. (1991) 'Venture Capitalists and the Appraisal of Investments'. *OMEGA*, vol. 19, no. 5.

7 MURRAY, G. and ROBBIE, K. (1992) 'Venture Capital in the UK', *International Journal of Bank Marketing*, vol. 10, no. 5, pp. 32–40.

8. PRATT, G. (1990) 'Venture Capital in the UK', *Bank of England Quarterly Review*, vol. 30, pp. 78–83.

9. MASON, C. M. and HARRISON, R. T. (1991) 'A Strategy for Closing the Small Firms' Finance Gap', paper presented to the 14th National Small Firms Policy and Research Conference, Blackpool, November.

10. MASON, C. M. and HARRISON, R. T. (1992) *Promoting Informal Venture Capital: Some operational considerations for business introduction services*, Venture Finance Research Project, Paper no. 5, University of Southampton.

11. McNALLY, K. N. (1994) 'Sources of Finance for UK Venture Capital Funds: The Role of Corporate Investors', *Entrepreneurship and Regional Development*, vol. 6, no. 3, pp. 275–97.

12. AKERLOF, G. (1970) 'The Market for Lemons: qualitative uncertainty and the market mechanism', *Quarterly Journal of Economics*, vol. 89, pp. 488–500.

13. MIRRLEES, J. A. (1974) 'Notes on Welfare Economics, Information and Uncertainty' in Balch, M., McFadden, D. and Wu, S. (eds), *Essays in Economic Behaviour Under Uncertainty*, North Holland.

14. MIRRLEES, J. A. (1975) *The Theory of Moral Hazard and Unobservable Behaviour*, Nuffield College, Oxford.

15. JENSEN, M. C. and MECKLING, W. H. (1976) 'Theory of the Firm: Managerial Behaviour, Agency Costs and Ownership Structure', *Journal of Financial Economics*, vol. 3, pp. 305–60.

16. HARRIS, M. and TOWNSEND, R. M. (1981) 'Resource allocation under asymmetric information', *Econometrica*, vol. 49, pp. 33–64.

17. HELLWIG, M. (1987) 'Some recent developments in the theory of competition in markets with adverse selection', *European Economic Review*, 31, pp. 319–25.

18. MAGILL, M. AND SHAFER, W. (1991) 'Incomplete markets' in Hildenbrand, W. and Sonneschein, H. (eds) *The Handbook of Mathematical Economics*, vol. IV, North Holland.

19. STIGLITZ, J. and WEISS, A. (1981) 'Credit Rationing in markets with imperfect information', *American Economic Review*, vol. 71, pp. 393–410.

20. DE MEZA, D. and WEBB, D. (1987) 'Too much investment: a problem of asymmetric information', *Quarterly Journal of Economics*, vol. 102, pp. 281–92.

21. ASTON BUSINESS SCHOOL (1991) *Constraints on the Growth of Small Firms*, DTI, HMSO.

22. BINKS, M., ENNEW, C., and REED, G. (1988) 'The Survey by the Forum of Private Business on Banks and Small Firms' in Bannock, G. and Morgan, V. (eds), *Banks and Small Businesses: A Two Nation Perspective*, Forum of Private Business, Knutsford, Cheshire.

23. FORUM OF PRIVATE BUSINESS SURVEY (1993) *Small Businesses and Their Banks*, Forum of Private Business, Knutsford, Cheshire.

24. DEAKINS, D. and HUSSAIN, G. (1991) *Risk Assessment By Bank Managers*, Birmingham Polytechnic Business School, Birmingham.

25. DEAKINS, D. and HUSSAIN, G. (1992) 'Overcoming the Adverse Selection Problem', paper presented to the 15th National Small Firms Policy and Research Conference, Southampton, November.

26. DEAKINS, D. and PHILPOTT, T. (1993) *Comparative European Practices in the Finance of Small Firms: UK, Germany and Holland*, University of Central England Business School, Birmingham.

27. FLETCHER, M. (1994) 'Bank Lending to Small Firms by Scottish Bank Managers', paper presented to the 17th National Small Firms Policy and Research Conference, Sheffield, November, and in *International Journal of Entrepreneurship Behaviour and Research* (1995), vol. 1, no. 2.

28. SPENCE, A. M. (1974) *Market Signalling*, Harvard University Press.

29. CRAWFORD, V. and SOBELL, J. (1982) 'Strategic information transmission', *Econometrica*, vol. 50, pp. 1431–51.

30. QUINZII, M. and ROCHET, J. C. (1985) 'Multidimensional signalling', *Journal of Mathematical Economics*, vol. 14, pp. 261–84.

31. CHO I-K. and KREPS, D. (1987) 'Signalling games and stable equilibria', *Quarterly Journal of Economics*, vol. 102, pp. 179–221.

32. MILGROM, P. and ROBERTS, J. (1982) 'Limit pricing and entry under incomplete information: an equilibrium analysis', *Econometrica*, vol. 50, pp. 443–59.

33. CHAN, Y. and KANNATAS, G. (1985) 'Asymmetric Valuations and the role of collateral in loan agreements', *Journal of Money, Credit and Banking*, vol. 17, no. 1, pp. 84–95.

34. ALTMAN, E.I. (1971) *Corporate Bankruptcy in America*, Heath Lexington.

35. CAMBRIDGE SMALL BUSINESS RESEARCH CENTRE, (1992) *The State of British Enterprise*, Department of Applied Economics, Cambridge University, Cambridge.

36. SPARROW, J. and DEAKINS, D. (1991) 'The Delivery of Small Business Support: an analysis of areas for strategic intervention by business support services', paper presented to British Academy of Management seminar, Manchester Business School, Manchester, April.

37. READ, L. (1994) *Raising Bank Finance: A comparative study of the experiences of male and female business owners*, Venture Finance Working Paper no. 11, University of Southampton, Southampton.

38. ROSA, P., CARTER, S., and HAMILTON, D. (1994) 'Gender and Determinants of Small Business Performance: Preliminary insights from a British study', paper presented to the 17th National Small Firms Policy and Research Conference, Sheffield, November.

39. WARD, R. and JENKINS, R. (1984) *Ethnic Communities in Business: Strategies for Economic Survival*, CUP.

40. JONES, T., McEVOY, D., and BARRETT, J. (1990) 'Raising Capital for the Ethnic Minority Small Business', paper presented for the ESRC Small Business Research Initiative, University of Warwick, Coventry, September.

41. CURRAN, J. and BLACKBURN, R. (1993) *Ethnic Enterprise and the High Street Bank*, Small Business Research Centre, Kingston Business School, Kingston.

42. DEAKINS, D., HUSSAIN, G., and RAM, M. (1992) *The Finance of Ethnic Minority Small Businesses*, University of Central England Business School, Birmingham.

43. DEAKINS, D., HUSSAIN, G., and RAM, M. (1994) *Ethnic Entrepreneurs and Commercial Banks: Untapped Potential*, University of Central England Business School, Birmingham.

44. FORUM OF PRIVATE BUSINESS (1991) *Small Businesses and their Banks*, Forum of Private Businesses, Knutsford.

45. BINKS, M. (1993) *Financial Times*, 19 January.

46. MANPOWER SERVICES COMMISSION (1988) *Enterprise Allowance Scheme Evaluation, Final Report*, MSC, Sheffield.

47. CAIRD, S. (1994) 'Sources of Technological Innovative Ideas and Their Significance for Commercial Outcomes in Small Companies' in Oakey, R.P. (ed.), *New Technology-Based Firms in the 1990s*, Paul Chapman, pp. 57–67.

48. DEAKINS, D. and SPARROW, J. (1990) Evaluation of Local Enterprise Agency Report, Birmingham Polytechnic Business School, Brimingham.

RECOMMENDED READING

ACOST (1990) *The Enterprise Challenge: overcoming barriers to growth in small firms*, HMSO.

BANNOCK, G. (1991) *Venture Capital and The Equity Gap*, National Westminster Bank, London.

DEAKINS, D. and HUSSAIN, G. (1991) Risk Assessment By Bank Managers, Birmingham Polytechnic Business School, Birmingham.

STANWORTH, J. and GRAY, C. (eds) (1991) *Bolton 20 Years On*, Paul Chapman, London (Chapters 4 and 6).

WALKER, D. (1989) 'Financing The Small Firm', Small Business Economics, **1**, pp. 285–96.

5 Sources of Finance: Case Study and Suggested Assignments Peters and Co.

INTRODUCTION AND BACKGROUND

The following information is based on a real business. The names of the three entrepreneurs concerned have been changed but otherwise all information is based on their actual business, including financial costings and research. The information provided is for a start-up venture which is seeking to raise finance from banking or other institutions. You are provided with the following sets of information:

1. Summary of the proposition.
2. Business plan for the following three years for Peters and Co.
3. Information on the three entrepreneurs who are to be equal directors in the concern.

A number of suggested assignments are given at the end of the case study. It can be used, for example, to provide a scenario for a role play, or more generally as the basis for a discussion.

The case study is meant to focus on the importance of different sources of finance for a start-up and infant business.

Research and tutor's note: It should become obvious to the reader that this case study was used, in a different form, in the research that was conducted with bank managers, reported in Chapter 4. Some of the information has been changed and up-dated and the cashflow has been modified, but the essential base of information is still the same.

The author has found that asking students to role play the role of three entrepreneurs has been a valuable way for them to prepare for eventual start-up interviews with real bank managers. Having knowledge of what bank managers are likely to ask has been particularly valuable in this exercise.

The case itself is not intended to be a typical start-up and there are a number of questions that could be posed regarding the secure career of the three directors concerned and the opportunity costs (and hence the risks) of such a start-up. The case is not intended to highlight issues of risk taking but could well be used to highlight these issues and the role and function of the three entrepreneurs compared to the theory and role of entrepreneurs discussed in Chapter 1.

Suggested assignments are given at the end of the case study.

SUMMARY OF THE PROPOSITION

THE THREE PROPRIETORS

The three proprietors are all qualified as chartered quantity surveyors (QS). Two of them are working for a major UK QS partnership which has offices throughout the UK. Noel Peters, who is to be the managing director for Peters and Co, has nine years' experience with local authorities and seven years' experience with the UK QS practice; his qualifications include a BSc in QS. He has been rapidly promoted and is a senior partner. He has worked on schemes up to £100 million in value. Graham Davis is a colleague of Noel Peters with 20 years' experience in the QS industry. He heads up the cost planning unit at the UK practice. Tony Franks has been a chief QS with a local authority and cost centre manager before leaving to be the managing director of a company in private practice. Tony has 30 years' experience in QS and the construction industry. More details are provided on the individual proprietors later.

THE SERVICE

The business would offer traditional cost and auditing control of QS through, for example billing of quantities, which is the traditional costing service of QS. In addition, the business would use its experience to offer project and facility management. Experience in project management means that the business can draw on the skills and expertise of the proprietors to offer this service. The business also hopes to offer an integrated IT construction service. This marks a difference from the standard traditional QS costing and auditing service. The business will offer a bespoke service by applying CAD/CAM techniques to the design, construction, and costing of projects. This use of information technology offers exciting opportunities to break the mould of traditional QS. A project could be designed, costed, and controlled using information technology applications that allow the customer to vary specifications and produce different costings as part of the service.

To develop this service the business will employ an 'automization director'. This person, Joe Wilcot, has worked with Noel Peters before on developing CAD/CAM techniques in the QS industry and the present employers of Peters and Davis, Gleeds. A section of the business plan is devoted to a 'strategy for growth' which concentrates on the role of IT and new technology in the construction industry. If the business is successful it is likely that Joe Wilcot will be brought in as a full director. The directors are excited about the development of a revolutionary housing product developed by Joe. If this takes off then they have been promised a good percentage of the QS work involved.

In the first six months that the business is in operation, the proprietors have identified a further service that could offer potential for the growth of a separate service particularly for local authority housing departments and housing associations—the provision and targeting of an energy auditing service.

THE MARKET

Potential clients are to be drawn from the both the private and public sectors. Obviously the fragile nature of the recovery means that the business will have to market for clients actively. However, there are still some areas that have major growth potential as construction projects, e.g., in hotels and leisure. The development of housing associations also offers major potential. The proprietors believe that the advantages of the flexibility of a small firm could be used to their advantage in the recovery. This ability of a small firm to control costs, react quickly to opportunities, and to be flexible is likely to be an important factor in the success of this proposition.

THE ROLE OF THE DUTCH COMPANY

A section of the business plan is devoted to the association with a company in the Netherlands that has developed the application of IT and new technological developments to the construction industry on the continent. A number of options are under discussion at the present time. The proprietors have had a number of meetings with representatives of this company and have secured agreement for some investment by it but the deal has yet to be ratified. The options at present include cash injection in return for an equity stake, a fee arrangement, or a more loose association with the business using software and technology developed by the Dutch company.

THE BUSINESS RATIONALE

Both Noel and Graham have been frustrated for some time working for Gleeds at their inflexibility and slow progress in adopting new integrated CAD/CAM techniques and new technology. They both feel that they have achieved as much as they can within their present environment and feel that the time is right, despite the fragile nature of the recovery in construction, to launch their own business. They are bringing Tony in because he has contacts in the construction industry and also has experience of running a small company himself. They are hopeful that they will be able to take some customers with them when they leave to start up the business. In addition, the role of the automization director will be significant as new technology is adopted in the construction industry. Joe Wilcot has developed a revolutionary housing product which is currently being patented and has generated a lot of interest. Peters and Co. will receive a great deal of work as a result if this new technology and product is adopted in the construction industry. The potential could be huge since the product is ideally suited to the needs of housing associations for low cost housing. Housing associations now have the majority of state funding that is devoted to housing construction.

BUSINESS PLAN: Peters and Co.

Strictly confidential

No contact to be made with present employers under any circumstances

SUMMARY OF PROPOSALS

Peters and Co. is being established to provide cost control and management services to the construction industry. The company will focus on four principal areas of service:

- Cost control
- Project management
- Facility management
- Construction information technology.

These areas will form the basis for the growth and expansion of the business where our expertise in cost control and project management will be the main activity in the initial stages. From this base, growth will develop into the other areas which will then provide a comprehensive construction and property service to clients.

Although the directors are chartered quantity surveyors (QS) by training, they all acquired specialized skills during their careers to respond to the changing demands and needs of their clients. Peters and Co. bring

---

these people together to form a partnership that will be unfettered by QS tradition.

A strong association with a Dutch company, the Brink Groep, will widen business opportunities for both parties and will also provide advantages for technical development and joint initiatives in other markets.

THE DIRECTORS

The directors are chartered quantity surveyors as follows:

Noel Peters BSc FRICS

Currently a partner with a national QS practice. He will be managing director with principal responsibility for policy and future business direction.

Graham Davis ARICS

Currently an associate with a national QS practice. He will be the technical director with specific responsibilities for cost control and the integration and expansion of the business in IT areas for both the partnership and the clients.

Tony Franks

Currently employed as managing director of a specialist construction company. He will be responsible for financial matters within the firm and provide expert contractual advice to clients.

All three directors have excellent experience and knowledge of the UK construction and QS industry and have gained a wide range of business contacts.

BUSINESS PHILOSOPHY

The company will offer an exceptional personal service based upon the knowledge, expertise, and involvement of the directors. Experience has proved that a commitment to use and develop the most up-to-date computer technology, including the integration of CAD systems with cost control techniques, will provide the firm with a major advantage over its competitors.

To maintain this philosophy we aim to provide:

1. An expertise that encompasses costing, planning, and management, ranging over all aspects of property and construction related activities.
2. The establishment of a working environment that can provide security for all members of the organization and that will manifest itself into the service we reflect towards our clients.

The firm is envisaged as presenting an image that combines quality of service and personal attention with particular emphasis on standards of presentation. To enhance this image we intend to establish a permanent presence in Bath with easy access to all road and rail links. We are currently negotiating a lease for an office with a prestigious city centre location.

STRATEGY FOR GROWTH

The problem with traditional QS service
The standard QS appointment provides for a cost monitoring role. This is reactive and not acceptable as it will not be good enough to cope with the demands of clients who want security and certainty of price in their dealings with the construction industry. Clients' concerns are reflected primarily in the growth of the 'Design and Build' sector of the market where over 20 per cent of commercial work is executed in this way. In this area the traditional QS service has a limited role to play.

We also believe that the presence in the UK of European clients and investors from other countries seeking a marketing foothold in Europe has already affected the attitude and approach of the UK construction industry; the Single European Market will accelerate this change.

Cost control
We will concentrate on cost control by restructuring the fee arrangement to allow us to maximize the service in areas of value management, project planning, and risk avoidance.

Our clients will see budgetary control that will seek to reduce the risk of major cost/time overruns which are the hallmarks of the UK construction process.

Project management
Because project management is difficult to achieve, the current trend is to appoint a project manager with no direct responsibilities. We believe good project management should be cost linked so that the timeframe is viewed at every turn in regard to the cost effects. This requires us to be involved in the auditing of the design process, including the programming•of the design input, as well as the more traditional aspects of project management.

Facility management
There is much evidence that many consultant firms are seeking to diversify as the market changes and workload declines. Our growth and expansion into facility management is calculated to maximize our market share and provide a wider base from which to operate and so stabilize our fee income.

This work will provide an extension to our role to form a more general property management service. Facility management provides the opportunity to be appointed for work where major new build schemes are envisaged—this being a natural progression from the facility management role.

IT in the construction industry

Peters and Co. believes that there is dearth of data with which to make key decisions that affect the building process. Thus, the key procedure in all the above areas is to capture, analyse, and store all pertinent information on computer databases. This will be structured in a way that will allow the data to be transferred throughout the cost control and construction process. It is intended to offer this service to clients by expanding into a support role for bespoke applications.

The growth of the firm will see an automization director, previously identified (Joe Wilcot), who will take a consultancy role in the interim while the market is established. The link with the Brink Groep will also help to support this strategy.

Summary

This range of operations will see a mixture of professional disciplines employed within the firm. The strategy seeks to provide an embracing cost control service to guide clients at any point in their dealings with construction and property.

The potential market is extensive, being in the order of £1500 million to £2000 million of fee income in the UK. We believe that we can establish a share of this market that will see us as a 30-strong practice within eight years with a turnover of at least £2.5 million.

THE POTENTIAL MARKET

We are confident that our contacts will provide suitable commissions in the following areas:

1.   Private sector:
     - Commercial (offices and retail)
     - Industrial
     - Hotels
     - Leisure

2.   Public sector:
     - Housing associations
     - State schools

■ Local authorities
■ Central government agencies.

We fully recognize the difficulty in launching a new firm and to help us in the launch period we have negotiated agreements with two contacts who will actively market on our behalf. One of these contacts has a detailed involvement with educational establishments where he has extensive contacts both at local and national levels. The other contact already provides general marketing for other organizations and has a proven track record. These people will act on the basis of commission.

ASSUMPTIONS ON CASHFLOW

Due to the continued severe downturn in the UK construction market we expect to receive minimal fee income in the initial seven months of trading. We hope to secure one medium sized contract and several smaller contracts in the first six months.

As we become more established and recovery takes place, we anticipate an increase in our market share in line with that recovery. At the peak of the fourth year of trading we anticipate an income per month of £45 000 and to have secured approximately £22 million worth of work (five or six medium sized jobs). The cashflow shows a consequent increase in staffing levels for this growth.

It should be noted that we expect all directors to achieve an earnings capacity of £75 000 per head, per annum.

The figures take no account of re-investment to fund other areas of growth such as facility management and the expected increase in automization.

PROPOSED START DATE

The provisional start date is set for 1 January 19XX. This would mean the funding would need to be in place by 1 December 199XX.

One or more of the directors intends to start earlier than this date in order to concentrate on matters in connection with a business start-up and to establish some of the basic procedures needed to allow the firm to run efficiently from the launch date.

PROPOSALS FOR AN ASSOCIATION WITH THE BRINK GROEP, HOLLAND

There are several alternatives that we consider might be of interest to the parties and we outline them as follows:

1. A venture stake in the firm where the Brink Groep becomes a shareholder. We believe that we have much to offer the Brink Groep in new areas of research such as value engineering and risk management. With this closer relationship we would be able to mould a professional service for a European operation using the Brink Groep marketing identity. This would assist the Brink Groep to establish a network of European offices.

   This degree of involvement would heavily encourage the Brink Groep to market Dutch clients who may wish to work in the UK and would create a stronger drive to establish an automization arm earlier than would otherwise be possible.

   Under this scenario the suggested cash involvement of the Brink Groep would be £40 000 in return for a 20 per cent shareholding.
2. The Brink Groep to secure fee earning work for Peters and Co. A pre-agreed commission rate for this work would be paid by Peters and Co. in the form of a shareholding up to an agreed maximum with cash arrangements thereafter.
3. The Brink Groep to become a minority shareholder of Peters and Co. with, say, a 5 per cent share of the equity for a direct capital injection of £10 000.
4. A more loose association with Peters and Co. promoting the software of the Brink Groep with us providing general or bespoke databases to be used in conjunction with such software.

GENERALLY

We are currently arranging our finance for the venture through major banks or venture capital companies.

The proprietors are also injecting £30 000 into the business and accepting the risk of leaving well paid jobs to set up this venture.

THE THREE DIRECTORS

Noel Peters
Experience

1968–69	Trainee, Worcester County Council
1969–73	Four-year sandwich course, BSc in QS
1973–77	Assistant QS with QS partnership
1977–81	QS and cost planner, Gloucester County Council
1981–85	Cost planning group leader at Hackney Borough Council
1985 to date	Partner with Gleeds, one of UK's major QS partnerships

In the last five years Noel has been rapidly promoted at Gleeds. He has been prepared to take on and develop IT applications in the QS field. He has enjoyed direct managerial responsibility for the securing and execution of major commercial work, working on schemes ranging in value from £1 million to £100 million. He deals with the main clients at both local and national level.

His personal details are that he is married with two teenage sons and owns his own property, currently valued at £150 000 with a mortgage of £50 000.

He is well paid at Gleeds with an annual salary in excess of £40 000 excluding expenses and perks. Thus he is giving up well paid, secure employment to take the risk of launching this company. He believes that the only way to make further progress in the application of IT is to develop applications with his own business.

Graham Davis
Experience
1969–79   QS with three firms in private professional practice
1979–85   Senior QS
1985 to date Associate partner at Gleeds

Graham currently heads up the cost planning unit at Gleeds and has concentrated in recent years on developing fast track contractual procedures in the commercial sector, together with developing computerized systems to reflect the changing climate of the industry and to assist in the preparation of cost control and tender documentation. Graham has good contact with both local and national clients and has generated a high fee income in recent years.

His current salary is in excess of £30 000 excluding perks.

Graham has worked closely with Noel on a number of projects to develop IT applications and both have been involved in a number of demonstrations to important major clients.

Graham is married with two teenage daughters and owns his own property valued at £120 000 with a mortgage of £30 000.

Tony Franks
Experience
1959–67   Junior partner in family building company
1967–73   Commercial manager with masonry sub-contractor
1973–76   Senior QS with QS partnership
1976–90   Chief QS, Dorset County Council
1990 to date MD of private construction company

Tony is a regular lecturer in law to the industry and also lectures at Bath University. He has extensive practical site management experience and has a wide circle of public sector contacts. He was for many years responsible for strategic and project cost planning advice. As chief QS and cost centre manager he assumed responsibility for the whole range of QS functions as well as fee accountability for the department. He was responsible for selection and vetting of contractors and consultants.

Tony has close links, professionally, with Noel and Graham and has worked on a number of contracts with them. He has some very good administrative and small business experience and understands company and commercial law.

Tony built the bungalow that he presently lives in some 20 years ago and has paid off any outstanding debts. The bungalow has been valued at £120 000.

PETERS AND CO.

CASHFLOW PROJECTIONS

(Note: base rates at the time were 12% pa; interest charges were based on +3% over base rate.)

PETERS AND CO - CASHFLOW YEAR 1

19XX	JAN	FEB	MAR	APRIL	MAY	JUNE	JULY	AUGUST	SEPT	OCT	NOV	DEC	TOTALS
INCOME	0	0	1000	2000	3000	3000	3000	8000	8000	8000	12000	12000	60000
CAPITAL	30000	0	0	0	0	0	0	0	0	0	0	0	30000
TOTAL INCOME	30000	0	1000	2000	3000	3000	3000	8000	8000	8000	12000	12000	90000
EXPENSES													
DRAWINGS	6000	6000	6000	6000	6000	6000	6000	6000	6000	6000	6000	6000	72000
HEALTH INSURANCE	90	90	90	90	90	90	90	90	90	90	90	90	1080
NHI PAYMENTS	677	677	677	677	677	677	677	677	677	677	677	677	8124
STAFF COSTS	0	0	0	0	0	0	0	0	0	0	0	0	0
OVERHEADS	1142	1142	1142	1142	1142	1142	1142	1142	1142	1142	1142	1142	13704
RENTAL ITEMS	3963	0	0	3963	0	0	3963	0	0	3963	0	0	15852
FURNITURE	2000	0	0	0	0	0	0	0	0	0	0	0	2000
CARS	1000	1000	1000	1000	1000	1000	1000	1000	1000	1000	1000	1000	12000
TRAVEL	333	333	333	333	333	333	333	333	333	333	333	333	3996
HARDWARE	270	270	270	270	270	270	270	270	270	270	270	270	3240
SOFTWARE	608	608	608	608	608	608	608	608	608	608	608	608	7296
PI COVER	4500	0	0	0	0	0	0	0	0	0	0	0	4500
MARKETING	333	333	333	333	333	333	333	333	333	333	333	333	3996
BROCHURE	1500	0	0	0	0	0	0	0	0	0	0	0	1500
VAT (REBATE)	0	0	0	-4029	0	0	-2629	0	0	-2629	0	0	-9287
INTEREST/CHARGES	0	-303	0	0	467	0	0	1449	0	0	2055	0	3668
TOTAL PAYMENTS	22416	10150	10453	10387	10920	10453	11787	11902	10453	11787	12508	10453	143669
NET CASH FLOW	7584	-10150	-9453	-8387	-7920	-7453	-8787	-3902	-2453	-3787	-508	1547	
OPENING BALANCE	0	7584	-2566	-12019	-20406	-28326	-35779	-44566	-48468	-50921	-54708	-55216	
CLOSING BALANCE	7584	-2566	-12019	-20406	-28326	-35779	-44566	-48468	-50921	-54708	-55216	-53669	

PETERS AND CO - CASHFLOW YEAR 2

19XX	JAN	FEB	MAR	APRIL	MAY	JUNE	JULY	AUGUST	SEPT	OCT	NOV	DEC	TOTALS
INCOME	13000	13000	15000	17000	17000	17000	21000	21000	21000	18000	16000	16000	205000
CAPITAL	0	0	0	0	0	0	0	0	0	0	0	0	0
TOTAL INCOME	13000	13000	15000	17000	17000	17000	21000	21000	21000	18000	16000	16000	205000
EXPENSES													
DRAWINGS	6000	6000	6000	6000	6000	6000	6000	6000	6000	6000	6000	6000	72000
HEALTH INSURANCE	90	90	90	90	90	90	90	90	90	90	90	90	1080
NHI PAYMENTS	677	677	677	677	677	677	677	677	677	677	677	677	8124
STAFF COSTS	0	0	0	2318	2318	2318	2318	2318	2318	2318	2318	2318	20862
OVERHEADS	558	558	558	558	558	558	558	558	558	558	558	558	6696
RENTAL ITEMS	4988	0	0	4988	0	0	4988	0	0	4988	0	0	19952
FURNITURE	0	0	0	0	0	0	0	0	0	0	0	0	0
CARS	1250	1250	1250	1250	1250	1250	1250	1250	1250	1250	1250	1250	15000
TRAVEL	500	500	500	500	500	500	500	500	500	500	500	500	6000
HARDWARE	513	513	513	513	513	513	513	513	513	513	513	513	6156
SOFTWARE	454	454	454	454	454	454	454	454	454	454	454	454	5448
PI COVER	4500	0	0	0	0	0	0	0	0	0	0	0	4500
MARKETING	417	417	417	417	417	417	417	417	417	417	417	417	5004
BROCHURE	0	0	0	0	0	0	0	0	0	0	0	0	0
VAT (REBATE)	-2629	0	0	-3599	0	0	-2811	0	0	-2811	0	0	-11850
INTEREST/CHARGES	0	2225	0	0	2148	0	0	1736	0	0	999	0	7108
TOTAL PAYMENTS	17318	12684	10459	14166	14925	12777	14954	14513	12777	14954	13776	12777	166080
NET CASH FLOW	-4318	316	4541	2834	2075	4223	6046	6487	8223	3046	2224	3223	
OPENING BALANCE	-53669	-57987	-57671	-53130	-50296	-48221	-43998	-37952	-31465	-23242	-20196	-17972	
CLOSING BALANCE	-57987	-57671	-53130	-50296	-48221	-43998	-37952	-31465	-23242	-20196	-17972	-14749	

PETERS AND CO - CASHFLOW YEAR 3

19XX	JAN	FEB	MAR	APRIL	MAY	JUNE	JULY	AUGUST	SEPT	OCT	NOV	DEC	TOTALS
INCOME	26000	26000	26000	30000	30000	30000	38000	38000	38000	38000	40000	40000	400000
CAPITAL	0	0	0	0	0	0	0	0	0	0	0	0	0
TOTAL INCOME	26000	26000	26000	30000	30000	30000	38000	38000	38000	38000	40000	40000	400000
EXPENSES													
DRAWINGS	6000	6000	6000	6000	6000	6000	6000	6000	6000	6000	6000	6000	72000
HEALTH INSURANCE	90	90	90	90	90	90	90	90	90	90	90	90	1080
NHI PAYMENTS	677	677	677	677	677	677	677	677	677	677	677	677	8124
STAFF COSTS	6956	6956	6956	6956	6956	6956	6956	6956	6956	6956	6956	6956	83472
OVERHEADS	729	729	729	729	729	729	729	729	729	729	729	729	8748
RENTAL ITEMS	6050	0	0	6050	0	0	6050	0	0	6050	0	0	24200
FURNITURE	2000	0	0	0	0	0	0	0	0	0	0	0	2000
CARS	1250	1250	1250	1250	1250	1250	1250	1250	1250	1250	1250	1250	15000
TRAVEL	500	500	500	500	500	500	500	500	500	500	500	500	6000
HARDWARE	697	697	697	697	697	697	697	697	697	697	697	697	8364
SOFTWARE	575	575	575	575	575	575	575	575	575	575	575	575	6900
PI COVER	5000	0	0	0	0	0	0	0	0	0	0	0	5000
MARKETING	500	500	500	500	500	500	500	500	500	500	500	500	6000
BROCHURE	0	0	0	0	0	0	0	0	0	0	0	0	0
VAT (REBATE)	-2811	0	0	-4472	0	0	-3247	0	0	-3247	-3655	0	-13777
INTEREST/CHARGES	0	662	0	0	21	0	0	-1405	0	0	0	0	-4377
TOTAL PAYMENTS	28213	18636	17974	19552	17995	17974	20777	16569	17974	20777	14319	17974	228734
NET CASH FLOW	-2213	7364	8026	10448	12005	12026	17223	21431	20026	17223	25681	22026	
OPENING BALANCE	-14749	-16962	-9598	-1572	8876	20881	32907	50130	71561	91587	108810	134491	
CLOSING BALANCE	-16962	-9598	-1572	8876	20881	32907	50130	71561	91587	108810	134491	156517	

Suggested assignments

1. ROLE PLAY ASSIGNMENT

Student requirements
You are required to:

1. Familiarize yourself with information on the venture.
2. Prepare for a role play exercise by taking the role of one of the entrepreneurs who will be allocated to you by agreement.
3. Research additional information on sources of finance and risk assessment by financial institutions; see references from material on sources of finance.
4. Carry out the role play exercise by arranging an interview with the bank manager (member of staff).
5. Complete an individual project report on 'Issues in Start-up of SMEs and Finance for Start-up Entrepreneurs'

This project will indicate the role of the main institutions including banks, venture finance companies, and government schemes. Your report must be wordprocessed and be a minimum of 3000 words. In your report you should attempt to relate your material to start-up entrepreneurs such as those involved with Peters and Co. It is important that you bring concepts such as finance and entrepreneurship.

ASSESSMENT CRITERIA

1. Knowledge of material and additional research.
2. Confident and persuasive presentation.
3. Appreciation of the strengths and weaknesses of the business.
4. Evidence of preparation for specific questions on financial information such as knowledge of gearing, profit, and forecasted financial information.
5. Students work in groups of three but will be expected to answer questions individually and will be assessed individually. This will account for 30 per cent of the assessment.
6. Completion of individual report on issues in start-up and sources of finance for new entrepreneurs using role play information and additional literature references. This will account for the remaining 70 per cent of the assessment.

SUGGESTED ASSESSMENT WEIGHTING

Role play interview: 30 per cent (note: students can be allocated individual

marks although they will prepare for the interview in groups).
Written report: 70 per cent

2. CASE STUDY ANALYSIS AND REPORT
Students analyse the case study as bank manager.

Requirements
Your role is that of a bank manager. You are required to analyse the start-up proposition of Peters and Co. and give a funding decision on whether you would provide the required finance or not.

Students are required to justify their decision by bringing in concepts concerning start-up finance and issues in the start-up of firms.

Produce a written report giving your decision. Students are required to include financial analysis of the projections in the business plan. Students may qualify their answer, for example, that they do or do not require security to fund the proposition.

3. ROLE PLAY
Students divide the role of the bank manager and proprietors between them, working in groups of four where possible.

Additional reports are required from the students on sources of finance for small firms with particular emphasis on the sources of finance for start-up entrepreneurs.

Assessment criteria as above.

Learning outcomes

At the end of this case study and the associated assignments you should be able to:

1. Discuss how this case differs from the majority of small firms and typical start-ups as shown by Chapters 2 and 3.
2. Describe the roles and main functions of the three entrepreneurs and discuss how these match the concepts of entrepreneurs discussed in Chapter 1.
4. Understand some of the financial constraints involved in a non-standard start-up.
5. Appreciate and account for the importance of bank finance as a source of external finance for entrepreneurs and small firm owners.

6. Be prepared to answer questions from bank managers on any start-up proposition for a new firm, including that of your own business.
7. Describe the advantages of a 'team start' as opposed to a sole individual start-up.

6 Ethnic Minority Entrepreneurship

PREVIEW

We have mentioned in the Introduction to this book that much of the material has been drawn from the research programme carried out by a small group of colleagues during a relatively short period of time at the University of Central England. One of those research projects concerned ethnic minority entrepreneurs. During this period we carried out a number of research projects, involving a series of interviews with ethnic minority entrepreneurs in the Midlands. This chapter draws a lot of its material from this research. There were a number of different stages of the research and these included:

1. A first stage study involving interviews with 34 ethnic minority entrepreneurs on their business development problems, focusing on finance.
2. A second stage study involving re-interviews with a sub-sample from the first stage and interviews with bank managers in the West Midlands.
3. A separate study with African-Caribbean entrepreneurs involving interviews with 41 entrepreneurs in four different inner city locations in the UK, which was made possible by funding from the Leverhulme Trust.

This work was carried out with the author's colleagues Monder Ram and Guhlum Hussain and the author would like to acknowledge their contribution to much of the material. In addition, material has been used that was presented at two seminars held at the university during this time and the author would also like to acknowledge the contribution of the main speakers at those seminars and the comments of the participants. The presentations and comments of participants have also helped to enrich the material.

It is admitted that much of the focus of these research studies was on finance and financing relationships. Rather than include this material in the chapter on finance, Chapter 4, material has been separated and an attempt made to place it in the context of other issues concerned with ethnic minority entrepreneurs. This chapter will inevitably concentrate on finance and while claiming that it is a central issue in ethnic minority enterprise development, the author would be the first to admit that there are many other issues concerning motivation, development, management, and strategies for ethnic minority entrepreneurs. To do justice to these would require a fairly substantial book on its own. At the same time the author believes that a separate chapter is warranted on ethnic minority entrepreneurs, placing the finance issue in the general context of the development of ethnic minority entrepreneurship in Britain.

INTRODUCTION

The predominance of ethnic minority entrepreneurship in some areas of Britain has led to attempts to explain this phenomenon. For example, writers have sought to explain the motivations of such entrepreneurs, and the issues they face, particularly the inherent characteristics of ethnic minority small firms and entrepreneurs who are often 'stereotyped' as concentrated in particular industrial sectors. The most notable stereotyping has been applied to Asian entrepreneurs who are often typecast as 'corner shop' retailers and seen as concentrated in the retailing, catering, and clothing sectors. As we will see, this stereotypical and stylized view of the Asian entrepreneur is out-dated. Ethnic minority entrepreneurs cannot be grouped into convenient categories based on industrial sector. In addition, the term Asian entrepreneur covers a wide range of distinct ethnic groups with their own characteristics such as Sikh, Muslim, and Hindu. Further, although Asian entrepreneurs are the most often described and discussed, there are many other ethnic minority groups in the UK with their own entrepreneurial characteristics. Those that have been studied include African-Caribbeans, Bangladeshis, and Greek-Cypriots.

In Britain's economic history, ethnic immigrants have traditionally been of crucial importance to economic development. This is a tradition that goes back to groups such as the Huguenots. These ethnic groups have often been willing to accept new practices or bring new skills that facilitate significant economic developments. That tradition can be seen to be of continual significance in the modern economy where Asian entrepreneurs were the first to open retail outlets on Sundays, pre-dating a modern movement towards Sunday opening in most retail sectors. Ethnic entrepreneurs have also been willing to develop economic capabilities in areas which are shunned by 'mainstream' or white entrepreneurs. These may be economically marginal areas such as inner city areas which have been long deserted by white entrepreneurs. The location of these inner city areas has significant implications for ethnic minority entrepreneurs. Not only does the location often limit the available market to the ethnic enclave, it also makes the acquisition and availability of resources, especially finance and insurance, very difficult or (in the case of insurance) expensive.

Literature concerned with the development of ethnic minority entrepreneurs has mushroomed in response to the increased attention paid to this sector during the last decade. Attempts to explain the importance of ethnic minority entrepreneurs concentrate on the relative primacy of 'negative' or 'positive' factors in the motivations and development of ethnic minority small firm owners, e.g., Ward and Jenkins (1) or Waldinger *et al.* (2). The debate surrounds whether or not the discriminatory factors faced by ethnic minorities in the labour market are the predominant motivating factors in business ownership and entrepreneurship or whether positive entrepreneurial factors such as a group's background experience of business ownership are more important in the motivation decision. Although Curran and Blackburn (3) have indicated that motivational factors such as 'independence' were significant in entry to entrepreneurship, there is little doubt that a history of disadvantage and discrimination has led to the concentration of ethnic minority firms and entrepreneurs in marginal areas of economic activity.

Although there are a number of issues that still remain unresolved in motivation, such as the low participation rate of African-Caribbeans in small business ownership, attention has shifted from start-up to enterprise development issues. For example, ethnic minority entrepreneurs are perceived to be located in ethnic niche markets, such as Asian clothing firms supplying the needs of the Asian community or African-Caribbean hairdressers supplying a service that meets the needs of the African-Caribbean community. The issue of 'break-out' from this reliance upon ethnic niche markets has come to the fore and has been recognized as a policy issue for ethnic minority entrepreneurs. For example, the Ethnic Minority Business Development Initiative (EMBI) of 1991 (4) pointed to the need for ethnic minority entrepreneurs to become accepted into the 'mainstream'. This issue has been examined recently through case study material by Ram and Hillin (5) and is discussed in more detail below. To begin with, however, following the work of Blackburn (6) we review the state of ethnic enterprise in Britain.

The importance of the extended family and its role as a supplier of resources, such as finance and family labour, have been highlighted by much of the early literature (1). This factor may have been of significance in the early part of the last decade for Asian entrepreneurs, yet there is some evidence that the availability of sources of external finance, such as bank finance, has always been an important factor, both for start-up and enterprise development of ethnic minority owned small businesses.

A number of recent studies have confirmed that, certainly for business development, ethnic minority small firms are dependent on bank finance. For example, Curran and Blackburn's study of African-Caribbean, Bangladeshis, and Greek-Cypriot entrepreneurs found that 61 per cent were using institutional sources of finance (3, 6). As we will examine later, it is the relationship with the bank manager that can be crucial to the development of the ethnic minority small firm and a critical factor in the ability of these firms to break out of traditional ethnic community markets. At the time of writing, research that we are carrying out with African-Caribbean entrepreneurs shows that (in contrast to say Asian entrepreneurs) such entrepreneurs are particularly reliant upon internal sources and, in contrast, make little use of bank finance (8). Much of African-Caribbean entrepreneurship is new and recent, but they do not have the extended contacts within their community that might provide informal sources of equity finance. They are perhaps at the same stage of development as Asian entrepreneurs were a decade ago. We claim as a consequence that the potential future enterprise development of this group is in danger of stalling because of the inability to use bank finance. Asian entrepreneurs over the past decade have been able to reduce dependence on their own community for finance enabling continued successful entrepreneurship and enterprise development.

The work of Curran and Blackburn (3) with Bangladeshis and African-Caribbeans (A/Cs) illustrated some differences in their relationships with commercial banks (for example, that A/Cs were less satisfied with their bank). Ram and Sparrow (9) have shown that Asian entrepreneurs may engage in a wide range of commercial activities. These studies illustrate the need to treat ethnic minority firms as heterogeneous. Stereotypical or stylized views of ethnic minority firms as concentrated in a narrow range of industrial sectors are now out-dated. Despite this, the issue of 'break-out' remains important. Even in new industrial sectors, an ethnic minority entrepreneur's customers may be predominantly from their own community. It still remains the case, as we will see later, that for an ethnic minority entrepreneur, it is more difficult to become established and undertake significant enterprise development than for an equivalent white entrepreneur.

The loss of potential business development and hence wealth creation, due to this problem of the ethnic market niche, is difficult to gauge but as we have pointed out, there remains considerable untapped potential in the development of ethnic minority entrepreneurship and small businesses (7). The potential of ethnic minorities in economic development has been highlighted by recent statistical analysis of census data by Ballard and Kalra (10) who show that one of the demographic features of ethnic minorities is their considerably younger age profile. For example, 33 per cent of the ethnic population is under 16 years of age compared with 19.3 per cent of the white population. This would seem crucial to the future economic development of Britain and especially marginal, inner city areas which are still the predominant location for ethnic minority entrepreneurs.

THE PATTERN OF ETHNIC MINORITY ENTERPRISE IN BRITAIN

As Blackburn (6) points out, entry into self-employment is very uneven between ethnic minority groups. As Table 6.1 shows, self-employment rates are among the highest in Pakistani and Bangladeshi groups and lowest in Black (West Indian and African) groups, with participation rates of 22.7 per cent compared to 6.7 per cent respectively. Also as Blackburn says: 'What is striking about the data is the relatively low proportion of the self-employed who are classified as Black who employ others' (p. 2). This indicates that not only are participation rates low among African-Caribbeans, but the size of African-Caribbean firms are likely to be much smaller than firms owned by other ethnic groups. These observations are confirmed in our recent study (11). From an in-depth study of 41 African-Caribbean entrepreneurs, we found that such businesses are typically small (average employment created was only three full time employees and average turnover was only £125 000) and young (the average age of the business being only four years). It must be remembered, however, that given the young age of such African-Caribbean entrepreneurs and the location of the majority in the inner city, such entrepreneurs have made significant progress and are probably catching up

Table 6.1 Key data on ethnic minorities in Great Britain (000)

	All	White	Ethnic Minorities				
			All	Black	Indian	Paki-stani/ Bangla-deshi	Mixed/ other
Total population	54 860	51 843.9	3 006.5	885.4	840.8	636.1	644.3
Total of working age	33 589.5	31 701.9	1 887.6	582.1	547.1	344.9	413.6
Proportion self-employed	12.9	12.8	15.1	6.7	20.0	22.7	16.2
Proportion self-employed with employees as % of all self-employed	33.9	33.5	42.0	24.2	43.3	44.8	48.4

Source: Blackburn (6).

with other ethnic minority entrepreneurs in terms of enterprise development and the establishment of a significant presence in the inner city. African-Caribbean entrepreneurs are currently at a critical stage in their development and we call for special measures, such as specialized units, to ensure that African-Caribbean entrepreneurs can achieve further business development.

The potential contribution of ethnic minority entrepreneurs to the regeneration of inner city areas is confirmed by national data which illustrates the concentration of ethnic minorities in the traditional conurbations. Blackburn (6) illustrates the dependency of ethnic minority businesses on their ethnic communities. The limited economic wealth and high unemployment of such communities often limits ethnic minority entrepreneurs in terms of enterprise development.

Curran and Blackburn (3) have surveyed 76 ethnic minority entrepreneurs from three groups in three different localities. The three groups were African-Caribbeans, Bangladeshis, and Greek-Cypriots and were selected from London, Sheffield, and Leeds.

On motivation, perhaps surprisingly, they found that positive factors associated with the desire to be independent were higher than expected and they claim that this was on similar levels to white owned businesses. To some extent, the strong motivational factors are confirmed by our own research with 41 African-Caribbean entrepreneurs (11). For example over 80 per cent agreed with positive statements concerning ambition and control of their environment. Yet our research also showed that, for a significant minority, negative factors associated with the lack of opportunity elsewhere were also important. For example, over 40 per cent agreed that they had faced discrimination in previous employment. In such circumstances, discrimination and the lack of opportunities in the labour market are significant 'push' factors. Such entrepreneurs are often more highly qualified than equivalent white entrepreneurs[1]. Both Curran and Blackburn and our study confirm that ethnic minority small firm owners are relatively well qualified.

Among the inter-minority group differences found by Curran and Blackburn were that Greek-Cypriots had the longest established and largest businesses, and that African-Caribbean entrepreneurs had the smallest businesses, both in terms of turnover and number of employees.

As discussed in Chapter 4, one of the crucial resources affecting ethnic

---

1. Initial analysis on motivation factors with African-Caribbean entrepreneurs shows that a 'mix' of positive and negative factors were important in start-up and motivation. Negative factors as motivators include the lack of employment opportunities (although this may also be a significant factor for white entrepreneurs) and the lack of career opportunities when in employment. It may be that African-Caribbean entrepreneurs have the characteristics that we would expect for white entrepreneurs. However, evidence of discrimination and frustrated career ambitions was found to be a factor with some of the African-Caribbean entrepreneurs.

minority entrepreneurial development is the availability of finance. It is obviously a crucial resource if break-out of ethnic niche markets is to be obtained and hence vital to the future development of ethnic minority entrepreneurship as well as to the future health and well-being of the UK economy. Hence, much of the the rest of this chapter focuses on the role of finance and relationships with financial providers.

ETHNIC MINORITY ENTREPRENEURSHIP AND FINANCE

Curran and Blackburn confirm much of the author's previous research carried out with ethnic minority entrepreneurs (7, 12). This shows that small firms owned by ethnic minority entrepreneurs are no different from white owned small firms in being heavily dependent on the banks for external finance. However, Curran and Blackburn find that reliance on the bank finance was much less significant for African-Caribbeans; our research confirms that African-Caribbean entrepreneurs are much less dependent on bank finance than both white entrepreneurs and Asian entrepreneurs.

As Curran and Blackburn suggest, this could be due either to reluctance to approach bank institutions through perceived discrimination, or it could be due to differences in approach by the banks to different minority groups. Curran and Blackburn suggest that the differences between the groups in the use of bank finance can be accounted for by differences in business problems (rather than different treatment by the financial institutions). For example, Blackburn (6) states:

> However, although the results show a relative disadvantage in securing finance by the Afro-Caribbeans, it is not as bleak as suggested by others. . . . Many of the problems expressed by the business owners were business problems rather than race-related. . . . (p. 29).

This contention, that the problems encountered by certain minority groups such as African-Caribbeans in raising bank finance are due to business problems such as the quality of their business plans, is one that we would contend with (7). We have shown that the bank managers can have pre-conceived views of different ethnic groups and that the quality of information from African-Caribbeans is often at least as good as from other minority groups. For example, we found that bank managers were often of the opinion that the poorest prepared business proposals came from Muslim groups and in such circumstances would rely on recommendation and introductions.

We found that one of the problems that African-Caribbeans faced was that bank managers often did not have a lot of experience of dealing with such groups (because of their relatively low representation in the business population), whereas they were often experienced in dealing with business proposals from Asian entrepreneurs. We also found that the practice and experience of bank officers varied considerably. We found evidence of good practice, but often bank policies of moving on staff militated against building up good relationships with ethnic minority groups. As we comment later, there is still much that the banks could do to improve the potential of ethnic minority groups through developing best practice, such as involvement in the local ethnic community. It is not surprising that the experience of African-Caribbeans is considerably different from that of other minority groups. We are continuing to find that African-Caribbean entrepreneurs face particular difficulties due to limited markets and low profiles in our current research.

AFRICAN-CARIBBEAN ENTREPRENEURS AND FINANCE

The research reported in this chapter represents part of the results from a much larger research project with African-Caribbean entrepreneurs[2]. The data reported in this section represents preliminary analysis of quantitative data. The full research project involved semi-structured interviews with 41 African-Caribbean entrepreneurs covering a comprehensive survey of business development issues with the identified entrepreneur. At the time of writing the analysis of the research is still continuing. These issues included motivation, the importance of family influence and tradition, the extent to which the entrepreneurs were dependent on ethnic markets and the problems identified in obtaining resources. One of these crucial factors was finance. The interviews were all face-to-face, recorded and carried out at four locations in the UK: Birmingham, Liverpool, London, and Manchester.

Finance had been identified as a crucial limiting factor in business development in our previous research with ethnic minority entrepreneurs in the West Midlands, reported in Chapter 4(7), and especially the availability of bank finance. The findings from this study indicated that raising bank finance was a particular problem for African-Caribbean entrepreneurs compared to other ethnic minority entrepreneurs.

Table 6.2 shows the importance of sources of finance at the start of trading for African-Caribbean entrepreneurs. As expected African-Caribbean entrepreneurs are reliant upon personal savings and trade credit. It is noticeable that bank overdrafts rather than loans are more important at this stage of African-Caribbean enterprise development.

---

2. The contribution of the Leverhulme Trust is acknowledged which provided the funding to carry out the research with African-Caribbean entrepreneurs, from which some of the material for this chapter is drawn.

Table 6.2 Sources of finance at start-up for African-Caribbean entrepreneurs

Source	Rank order	Mean score	Std dev
Personal savings	1	3.4	1.9
Family	2	1.6	2.2
Trade credit	3	1.0	1.7
Bank overdraft	4	1.0	1.8
Personal assets	5	0.8	1.7
Other	6	0.8	2.2
Bank loan	7	0.5	1.4
Venture capital	8	0.4	1.0
Insurance policy	9	0.1	0.7
Building society	10	0.02	0.16

Notes: (i) 6 point scale used from 0 to 5
        (ii) n = 41
Source: Ram and Deakins (11).

As noted earlier at start-up, generally, bank finance is not important. A relatively small number of African-Caribbean entrepreneurs from the sample were actually using any form of bank finance. For example, only 30 per cent were using bank overdrafts at the start and only a handful, 12 per cent, were able to obtain bank loans. These are much lower figures than we might expect from a sample of white entrepreneurs. For example, compare these figures to those of start-up firms reported by our study of white start-up entrepreneurs in Chapter 3—they were roughly comparable to the African-Caribbean firms, being young and small yet they had a higher use of bank finance. If we compare these results to large surveys of white owned businesses such as the Cambridge Small Business Centre's Report (13), we find that African-Caribbean entrepreneurs hardly register in terms of the use of bank finance. The Cambridge report found that over 60 per cent of small and medium sized firms used some form of external bank finance.

It is possible to argue that African-Caribbean entrepreneurs did not seek such finance at the start. It is always possible that the expectation of discrimination will deter such entrepreneurs from making an approach to the bank. However, there were some comments of perceived bias against them by our respondents from the transcripts of the interviews. This confirms the view that African-Caribbean entrepreneurs suffer from inadequate access to bank finance at start-up.

Table 6.3 illustrates the importance of sources of finance for current use (at

Table 6.3 Current sources of finance for African-Caribbean entrepreneurs

Source	Rank order	Mean score	Std dev
Personal savings	1	2.4	2.1
Trade credit	2	1.9	2.0
Bank overdraft	3	0.9	1.6
Bank loan	4	0.9	1.7
Personal assets	5	0.8	1.7
Family	6	0.7	1.6
Other	7	0.6	0.6
Insurance policy	8	0.3	1.5
Building society	9	0.3	1.0
Venture capital	10	0.1	0.9

Notes: (i) 5 point scale used from 0 to 5
         (ii) n = 41.
Source: Ram and Deakins (11).

the time of the interview) by the African-Caribbean entrepreneur. Comparing Table 6.3 to Table 6.2 shows that African-Caribbean entrepreneurs are still very reliant upon internal sources as their business develops. It is possible to hypothesize that such entrepreneurs should make more use of bank finance as their business develops (50 per cent had experienced some growth in sales). The majority of the entrepreneurs were concerned with business development and expansion, yet there was very little change in the use of bank finance and a continued dependence on internal sources. The basic conclusion has to be that they do not make much use of banks for start-up or development finance. This could be due to suspicion, distrust, or introspection on the part of the African-Caribbean entrepreneur. However, we have little evidence that these problems stem from inherent business problems or poorly prepared business plans that might contain insufficient information. In some cases, qualitative evidence would support the contention that they face problems with raising external and bank finance.

There is a small increase, as we would expect, in the number of entrepreneurs that are using bank finance as the business develops. For example, 31 per cent use some form of bank overdraft, but only 12 per cent rate it as important for the finance of their business. Similarly, with bank loans, 29 per cent make some use of bank loans, yet only 12 per cent rate them as important sources

Table 6.4 Change in importance of sources of finance from start-up to current use for African-Caribbean entrepreneurs

Source	Rank order	Mean score	Std dev
Trade credit	1	+ 0.9	1.5
Bank loan	2	+ 0.5	1.6
Building society	3	+ 0.2	0.8
Insurance policy	4	+ 0.1	1.6
Personal assets	5	+ 0.0	1.7
Bank overdraft	6	− 0.1	2.0
Venture capital	7	− 0.3	1.0
Other	8	− 0.3	1.6
Family	9	− 0.9	1.7
Personal savings	10	− 1.0	2.0

Notes: (i) Calculated separately from Tables 7.2 and 7.3
(ii) n = 41
Source: Ram and Deakins (11).

of finance for their businesses. Given that our previous research has found that bank managers have experience of dealing with Asian entrepreneurs but not black entrepreneurs it is not surprising that African-Caribbean entrepreneurs are discouraged from even applying for bank finance.

There is tremendous potential in the future development of African-Caribbean entrepreneurs since they are under-represented in UK small business ownership (14). At the present time we have to conclude that this potential talent is not being harnessed and encouraged by the support infrastructure in the UK.

Table 6.4 shows the change in importance of sources of finance. Bank loans do increase in importance, but it must be remembered that these only account for a minority of the entrepreneurs. If you compare Table (6.4) to Table 4.6 (p. 88), you will notice that there is less significant change compared to the majority of Asian entrepreneurs that were represented in Table 4.6. Although, Table 6.4 does indicate a decline in the importance of personal savings and the family it is noticeable that all the changes are relatively small. There is some increase in the importance of bank loans, but the overall message is that there has been little change in the importance of different sources of finance since start-up for African-Caribbean entrepreneurs. Bank finance remains of minor importance.

FINANCE AS A CONSTRAINT

Table 6.5 shows the most important problems that African-Caribbean entrepreneurs felt they faced in rank order. Respondents were supplied with a list of potential problems and asked to rank the most important five in order of importance. It is significant that ability to raise both long term and short term finance are seen as the most important constraints by the entrepreneurs. Although finance comes at the top, the ability to break into new markets is also rated highly and illustrates the current importance of the 'break-out' issue for minority and African-Caribbean entrepreneurs.

ALTERNATIVE SOURCES OF FINANCE

(a) Loan Guarantee Scheme (LGS)

Although 39 per cent of African-Caribbean entrepreneurs were aware of the Loan Guarantee Scheme (LGS), only a small handful had applied for finance under this scheme. In total this amounted to less than 7 per cent. This illustrates that government attempts to raise the profile of the LGS are likely to fail. Our previous research with bank managers had also shown that at best the improvements to the LGS were perceived as 'cosmetic'.

(b) Business angels

Considerable attention has been paid to the potential of business angels for

Table 6.5 Most important business problems for African-Caribbean entrepreneurs

Business problem	Rank order
Ability to raise long term finance	1
Ability to raise short term finance	2
Obtaining suitable skilled staff	3
Breaking into new markets	4
Obtaining suitable premises	5
Relationships with buyers	6
Relationships with suppliers	7
Dependence on a few buyers/sellers	8
Delegation	9

Source: Ram and Deakins (11).

mainstream businesses. We have argued before that attempts to provide 'match-making' services for ethnic businesses and especially for African-Caribbean entrepreneurs are unlikely to work due to the invisibility problem of business angels. Having said this, however, we did find that well over half of the African-Caribbean entrepreneurs were aware of the concept and not surprisingly would consider an investment from a business angel, given the problems faced by such entrepreneurs in obtaining long term finance.

(c) Task-force and inner-city funding

There was some evidence of awareness of this form of funding, with 56 per cent of respondents aware of it. At the time of writing, we have not analysed the full transcripts of the interviews to comment on respondents' experiences.

RELATIONSHIPS BETWEEN ETHNIC MINORITY SMALL FIRMS AND THEIR BANK MANAGER

We have examined the relationship between the ethnic minority entrepreneur and the bank manager in some detail in our previous research (7). In particular, we have reported the results of a combined demand and supply study with ethnic minority entrepreneurs and commercial bank managers in the Birmingham area. We concluded that there remains considerable unfilled potential from the further development of ethnic minority entrepreneurs and businesses. For such entrepreneurs, which were mainly Asian, we confirmed that they were dependent on banks for external finance, as discussed above and by previous writers (3, 15).

As shown in Chapter 4 (especially Table 4.6) the results from our study have shown that as ethnic minority businesses develop, they become more reliant upon bank finance after start-up. In many cases, ethnic minority businesses were reliant upon short term finance for their long term development. The study also highlighted the importance of security which we see as a key issue for the continued development of ethnic minority businesses. Although, banks' requirements for security have been highlighted for small firms in general, we argue that it becomes a key issue in the case of ethnic minority entrepreneurs and small firms because of their location in marginal environments and in inner city areas, where properties have limited equity values.

The research employed both qualitative and quantitative techniques with 42 interviews with ethnic minority entrepreneurs and seven interviews with bank managers at different levels of management in commercial banks. Although we asked to interview experienced bank managers, we found that their experience varied considerably. We also found that there was considerable difference in bank manager practices.

Relationships are critically affected by the extent of trust, by bank manager attitudes to the ethnic community, and by the reputation of the bank in the ethnic community. The branches where the bank manger was prepared to spend time in the ethnic community, to become known, and to get know his customers were rewarded by increasing the amount of bank business. We did find examples of good practice, and examples of managers being involved with the ethnic community. We found, however, examples of less experienced managers and a lack of involvement in the community. We also found a relatively high willingness on the part of the ethnic minority entrepreneurs to change their bank and some considerable dissatisfaction with the bank, often triggered by a change of manager. High turnover of bank staff is all too frequent and we believe it is something that the banks can tackle positively by developing specialized ethnic units for dealing with ethnic minority entrepreneurs. These units could be staffed by bank employees that have experience of dealing with financing proposals from the ethnic minority communities.

We found examples of good practice where bank managers were involved in the local community. Of course, this level of commitment will depend upon the individual manager, but it could still be encouraged by bank policy and through staff development. The level of involvement was found to be distinctly variable and bank managers' perceptions of involvement were also variable.

Even experienced managers based their comments on their experiences of dealing with Asian entrepreneurs and this invariably affected manager attitudes. The low level of participation of African-Caribbeans remains a cause for concern. We might expect that some concern was expressed about low participation rates, especially at strategic managerial levels. The banks, however, did not have any proactive and positive policies towards African-Caribbean entrepreneurs. It is not surprising that grievances and feelings of disadvantage were expressed amongst the African-Caribbean entrepreneurs that we interviewed. These views were confirmed by our more recent study. This only serves to heighten beliefs in the African-Caribbean community that the odds are stacked against them and to lower expectations of success. Targeting of African-Caribbean entrepreneurs by the commercial banks would be one positive measure to increase participation rates and exploit untapped potential.

THE FUTURE FOR ETHNIC MINORITY ENTREPRENEURS

Blackburn (6) points to some problems for the future development of ethnic minority small businesses. He predicts, for example, that ethnic market niches, i.e., the market within their own community, will decline due to the declining links with their country of origin. He concludes that: 'As a result, the notion of "break-out" is central to a study of ethnic-owned businesses' (p. 37).

There is some agreement that the notion of break-out is important for policy makers and support agencies. However, it is a concept that is difficult to target and to operationalize appropriate policies. It is also a topic which is difficult to research. Ram and Hillin (16) were able to overcome some of the operational and research difficulties by adopting a case study approach to their research and we turn now to consider the implications of their research since it illustrates the current issues facing the development of ethnic minority entrepreneurs.

ACHIEVING BREAK-OUT

Ram and Hillin followed the experiences of three Asian firms who were receiving consultancy help as a result of a local authority initiative in the West Midlands. Two of the three firms were heavily involved in their own ethnic community markets, with Asian customers representing 90 per cent of their client base. All three firms relied on word of mouth and personal recommendation for the development of their business and all three firms were experiencing difficulties due to the declining importance of the ethnic client base, which has been identified as a problem by Blackburn (6) above.

Although, achieving break-out will be crucial to the future development of ethnic minority entrepreneurs, as Ram and Hillin illustrate there are a number of difficulties in operationalizing any strategy. Attempts to persuade one of the businesses to re-locate was met with some resistance because of perceived discrimination by potential (white) customers:

> A longer term suggestion was to consider relocation to a more 'up-market' high street position. Cash understood the logic of this suggestion, but he related the experience of one of his competitors, which created a certain ambivalence. RugCo's principal rival—an Asian firm—opened up an outlet in a predominantly white suburban area. Although its merchandise was of a respectable quality and competitively priced, the firm closed down due to lack of trade. Cash believed that the reluctance of white customers to purchase from ethnic minority businesses played a major part in the closure (p. 10).

Ram and Hillin illustrated that break-out has staffing and recruitment strategy implications as well as significance for marketing strategy. In addition, there are training issues that need to be addressed by support agencies and in general:

> Break-out then requires a re-assessment of labour organization practices if the opportunities provided by access into majority markets are to be exploited (p. 13).

The implications of the research of Ram and Hillin and the acceptance of the difficulties of developing strategies that can achieve break-out have important relevance for policy. Ram and Hillin call for better information on ethnic businesses and a re-assessment of funding for business support interventions which they consider needs to be on-going and developmental over a period of time.

Ram and Hillin point to the holistic nature of break-out. Break-out is a concept that has implications for all aspects of an ethnic minority entrepreneur's or small firm's operation and the access to appropriate resources. Ram and Hillin highlight the need to have access to appropriate resources. One resource, that is crucial is access to appropriate sources of finance and to bank finance. Also important to the continued development of ethnic minority entrepreneurs and small firms, as we have discussed above, is the quality of relationships with bank managers.

DEVELOPING GOOD PRACTICE

Although some positive measures have been taken we have indicated, in this chapter, that there is more that could be done to develop the potential of ethnic minority small firms. Banks could develop specialized training and encourage managers to retain their experience of dealing with ethnic minority entrepreneurs' applications. Specialized units for dealing with such proposals could be developed that contain trained staff. At present, deployment of experienced officers is haphazard and is hardly the best use of bank human resources. Such an unplanned policy adversely affects the profitability of the banks as well as the potential of ethnic minority entrepreneurs.

Networking is a key issue between support agencies and other institutions. There is some evidence of specialization by support agencies which in some cases has been supported by home office funding. For example in Birmingham, 3bs concentrates on supporting black businesses in Birmingham. Specialization has been taken further than in the banks, but as yet the extent of networking still needs strengthening and developing, despite the advent of Business Links. Business Link Birmingham was one of the nine pilot Business Links yet there is some evidence that it remains merely a brokering agency for small firm support (17). Some of these issues are discussed in more detail in the following chapter on the work of support agencies and a discussion of the importance of the claimed 'enterprise culture'.

Local authorities have sometimes taken the lead on ethnic minority support, often having specialist counsellors from the ethnic community. However, targeted support for such communities often has low take-up rates because of a lack of awareness. There is more that can still be done to raise awareness.

CONCLUSIONS

A consensus has emerged that the issue of break-out will be crucial to the future development of ethnic minority entrepreneurship and small firms. Future policies will have to appreciate the holistic nature of this concept if ethnic minority entrepreneurs are not to be confined to ethnic niche markets and resources from their own communities. Future practice needs to be geared to developing strategies that can break these barriers. After a decade or more of overcoming barriers, ethnic minority entrepreneurs are more than ever in need of specialized assistance, both from support agencies and the banks.

For African-Caribbean entrepreneurs we find that they do not use bank finance and are more reliant on internal sources than white entrepreneurs. There may be evidence of bias by the banks against African-Caribbean entrepreneurs which partly accounts for the low take-up of bank finance. It is also partly accounted for by expectations of discrimination. Not surprisingly, there is a reluctance on the part of African-Caribbean entrepreneurs to approach the banks for finance.

Finance is perceived as the most important issue and constraint by African-Caribbean entrepreneurs. This will not be solved by current enhancement and promotion of the Small Firms Loan Guarantee scheme, which we found was viewed as a marginal scheme by bank managers; nor by attempts to improve the 'visibility' of business angels.

Learning outcomes

At the end of this chapter you should be able to:

1. Describe the importance of ethnic minority entrepreneurs for the continued local economic development in the UK, especially the inner city areas.
2. Identify the importance of Asian and African-Caribbean entrepreneurs.
3. Describe the untapped potential of development that still exists with black entrepreneurs.
4. Explain why ethnic minority entrepreneurs are dependent on bank finance.
5. Explain why break-out has become an important issue for the future development of ethnic minority entrepreneurs.
6. Discuss policy measures that could be taken to encourage this future development.

Suggested assignments

1. Students compare the tables on the use of finance by African-Caribbean entrepreneurs to tables in Chapter 4. What are the main differences shown by the tables between:
   - African-Caribbean entrepreneurs and mainstream small firm owners
   - African-Caribbean entrepreneurs and Asian entrepreneurs.
2. There has been considerable research effort into understanding the characteristics of ethnic minority entrepreneurs, the issues that they face, and their potential in economic regeneration and recovery. Using material from this chapter, discuss the potential reasons for this attention with Asian ethnic minority entrepreneurs.
3. Why should African-Caribbean entrepreneurs have been neglected as a focus of research on ethnic minorities?

REFERENCES

1. WARD, R. AND JENKINS, R. (eds) (1984) *Ethnic Communities in Business*, Cambridge, London.

2. WALDINGER, R., ALDRICH, H., WARD, R. and ASSOCIATES (1989) *Ethnic Entrepreneurs*, Sage, London.

3. CURRAN, J. and BLACKBURN, R. (1993) *Ethnic Enterprise and the High St Bank*, Kingston Small Business Research Centre, Kingston University.

4. ETHNIC MINORITY BUSINESS DEVELOPMENT INITIATIVE (EMBI) (1991) *Final Report*, Home Office, London.

5. RAM, M. and HILLIN, G. (1994) 'Achieving Break-Out: Developing a Strategy for the Ethnic Minority Firm in the Inner-City', paper presented to the Ethnic Minority Small Firms Seminar, UCE, Birmingham, March.

6. BLACKBURN, R. (1994) 'Ethnic Enterprise in Britain', paper presented to the Ethnic Minority Small Firms Seminar, UCE, Birmingham.

7. DEAKINS, D., HUSSAIN, G. and RAM, M. (1994) *Ethnic Entrepreneurs and Commercial Banks: Untapped Potential*, UCE, Birmingham.

8. DEAKINS, D. and RAM, M. (1994) 'Black Entrepreneurs and Finance', paper presented to the Moss Side and Hulme Business Federation, Manchester October.

9. RAM, M. and SPARROW, J. (1993) 'Minority Firms, Racism and Economic Development', Local Economy, vol. 8, no. 3, p. 117-29.

10. BALLARD, R. and KALRA, V. S. (1994) *Ethnic Dimensions of the 1991 Census*, University of Manchester, Manchester.

11. RAM, M. and DEAKINS, D. (1995) *African-Caribbean Entrepreneurship in Britain*, University of Central England, Birmingham.

12. DEAKINS, D., HUSSAIN, G. and RAM, M. (1992) *The Finance of Ethnic Minority Small Businesses*, University of Central England, Birmingham.

13. CAMBRIDGE REPORT (1992) *The State of British Enterprise*, Cambridge Small Business Research Centre, University of Cambridge.

14. OWEN, D. (1993) *Ethnic Minorities in Great Britain: Economic Characteristics*, University of Warwick Centre for Research in Ethnic Relations, Warwick.

15. JONES, T., McEVOY, D. and BARRETT, J. (1992) 'Raising Capital for the Ethnic Minority Small Business', paper presented for the ESRC Small Business Research Initiative, University of Warwick, September.

16. RAM, M. and HILLIN, G. (1994) 'Achieving Break-Out: Developing Mainstream Ethnic Minority Businesses', Small Business and Enterprise Development, vol. 1, no. 2, p. 15-21.

17. DEAKINS, D. and RAM, M. (1994) 'Comparative European Policies in Enterprise Support: UK, Germany and France', paper presented to the 17th National Small Firms Policy and Research Conference, Sheffield, November.

RECOMMENDED READING

CURRAN, J. and BLACKBURN, R. (1993) *Ethnic Enterprise and the High St Bank*, Kingston Small Business Research Centre, Kingston University.

ETHNIC MINORITY BUSINESS DEVELOPMENT INITIATIVE (EMBI) (1991) *Final Report*, Home Office, London.

WALDINGER, R., ALDRICH, H., WARD, R. and ASSOCIATES (1989) *Ethnic Entrepreneurs*, Sage, London.

WARD, R. and JENKINS, R. (eds) (1984) *Ethnic Communities in Business*, Cambridge, London.

7 Enterprise Support and Government Policy: A Review of Developments

INTRODUCTION

The election of the Conservative administration in 1979, under Margaret Thatcher, coincided with recent growth in, and attention given, to the SME sector of the economy (see Chapter 2 on the importance of small firms in the UK economy). The free market philosophy of this administration fitted the more important role given to entrepreneurship and enterprise. The early years of the Government also took place against the background of the severest recession in the UK since the 1930s. Many large firms were making workers redundant. The small firm and 'enterprise' were seen as the key to reducing unemployment and job creation. At the time, evidence was also beginning to emerge that small firms could be important for future job creation. For example the Birch study (1) claimed that it was small firms (rather than large firms) that accounted for the majority of jobs created.

The advantage of placing a greater role on the small firm and the individual in job and wealth creation was that it avoided large scale state intervention in the economy, through, e.g., state subsidies to large manufacturing concerns. The very tight monetary regime that had been adopted did not permit such public expenditure programmes. Indeed, part of the policy was to actually cut state expenditure, during a period of very severe recession, a decision that caused extreme controversy with over 400 leading economists stating their written objection and opposition to such cuts and state economic policies. The Government turned to supply side measures that were inexpensive and fitted the philosophy that individuals would create their own wealth and hence jobs, if they were given the opportunity and freedom to start their own businesses.

The introduction of the term 'enterprise culture' has been attributed to Lord Young; the belief was that a new enterprise spirit had been regained as encapsulated in the following comment by Lord Young (2) 'The restoration of enterprise in Britain has played a major role in the revival of growth, employment and prosperity' (p. 34).

The Government fostered the idea that before 1979 the UK economy suffered because the culture of society did not encourage enterprise. The standard career was to work for a large firm rather than start your own business. Role models of successful businessmen had not been promoted by the state before. Although they certainly existed they were not promoted. Now the Government did more to encourage the publicity of successful entrepreneurs who had created their own successful businesses such as Alan Sugar and Richard Branson. The belief was, that the environment, both economically and socially, had been inappropriate before 1979. Now the state would take a range of measures designed to create the right environment for successful enterprise and entrepreneurship. Thus, part of the Government's strategy was to foster talk and belief that they were creating a new 'enterprise culture'.

At the heart of these developments were support agencies and in particular the development of the enterprise agencies (or in Scotland enterprise trusts), Training and Enterprise Councils (TECs), and in Scotland Local Enterprise Companies (LECs). Attempts to co-ordinate support provision have recently been attempted with the creation in 1993 of pilot Business Links. This chapter concentrates on the role of these support agencies. They are seen as synonymous with the attempt to create an enterprise culture (3). Despite their role in the creation of the claimed new enterprise culture, research into the role of enterprise agencies has been limited. Like other chapters this chapter draws on the research undertaken by the author through three separate research studies which are utilized to review the development and work of support agencies (4, 5).

In this chapter we examine some of the issues in enterprise support and make comparisons with the alternative model of support through strong chambers of commerce in Germany and France (from research undertaken by the author, in Baden-Württemberg in Germany and the Auvergne region of France). The conclusions compare these different models of support and we find that there are some advantages in having strong chambers of commerce.

THE ROLE OF SUPPORT AGENCIES

Enterprise Agencies (EAs) have mirrored the development of state concern with support for small firms. The first agency was established at St Helens in 1978 and since then they have grown in an *ad hoc* way, with over 300 such agencies currently in the UK. Part of their role has been to nurture the growth of start-up business, to unlock the potential for entrepreneurial activity, and to raise enterprise awareness. This diverse pattern of support agencies has been augmented with the recent establishment of the TECs in England and Wales and the equivalent LECs in Scotland from 1989 to 1991. They may be seen as adding to an already confusing range of alternative agencies, yet they also provide an opportunity to re-think and rationalize the provision of enterprise support. A network of 82 TECs, 13 LECs (funded by Scottish Enterprise), and other LECs in the Highlands of Scotland has now been established.

The *ad hoc* development of the enterprise agency movement means that provision of support, spatially and vertically, is the result of chance and accidents of geography and the economic mix of the environment that happened to exist at the time that different EAs were formed. The agency movement has been criticized for the lack of strategic focus of interventions (3). The movement can also be criticized for its *ad hoc* nature although, to some extent, this gives agencies flexibility to meet local needs. There is some evidence that agencies have a low profile in the small business community (6), and they can be criticized for being reactive in provision rather than pro-active (7).

The delivery of small business advice varies considerably from agency to agency. There are huge asymmetries in the size, staffing, and operation of individual agencies. Some agencies provide merely basic counselling advice for start-ups; others have a full range of training and consultancy services for the SME community. Our first research study revealed that a range of support services was common, such as business clubs, financial support, clerical services, databases, and additional business services. This diversity has led to criticisms of the duplication of support provision. There is an uneven geographical pattern of support and there may be over-provision of support in some areas and under-provision in others. Diversity is illustrated by the operation of agencies in Scotland, which are called enterprise trusts and operate under a rather different environment from those in England and Wales. Also the LECs in Scotland have more powers to intervene in the infrastructure and environment than the TECs in England and Wales.

TECs and LECs also vary in size (and budget) even though they are supposed to be based on local labour markets with populations of 250 000. There have already been a number of studies that have examined the concept and remit of TECs. The most comprehensive of these by Bennett *et al.* (8) argue that the TECs have been given insufficient empowerment:

The key impediments to business development in the UK is that not enough power has yet been given out to redress a century long imbalance that has frustrated Britain's economic growth (p. vii).

Emmerich and Peck (9), however, argue that the TECs are likely to focus on low level skills and that the composition of the board members is too dominated by representatives of large firms rather than representatives from small firms. A study by Topham *et al.* (10) compared the budgets of TECs to social and business needs of their areas. Ranking by budget did not match local needs, the implicit conclusion being that many TECs will not be able to meet local needs. Curran (11) showed that there is still a low level of awareness of local TECs by the small business community and concluded that TECs were unlikely to reach small firms and provide appropriate enterprise support.

It has been argued that agencies need to pro-actively support target groups. For example, a Home Office initiative (12, 13) to bring ethnic minority groups into the 'mainstream' (support) recommended that agencies should have pro-active, targeted policies and that effective networking was needed to unlock untapped potential. It has been suggested that targeted policies of support have potential to help other distinct groups of clients such as high-tech small firms (14). A case study of small firm support in the West Lothian region in Scotland by Turok and Richardson (15) suggested that there are benefits from targeted support.

Discussion of the funding of agencies has been concerned with whether they should be funded from public funds or private sponsorship. For example, Smallbone (16) has suggested a classification for agencies in the London area based on the degree of public sector involvement and funding. This view of EAs as a 'partnership' between the public and private sectors is becoming less relevant as agencies are attempting to increase their degree of autonomy. TECs and LECs have become the fund holders for enterprise support and training. Agencies are now dependent on them for contracts and have to bid for enterprise funding such as running the Business Start-Up Scheme (formerly the Enterprise Allowance Scheme) and enterprise development programmes. Agencies have attempted to make some progress towards financial independence but are still dependent on TEC and LEC funding and therefore indirectly on state funds. This dependency on the TECs for funding was confirmed in a survey by Durham University Business School in 1992 (17) which suggested that 50 per cent of EAs in England and Wales are dependent on TEC funding for the delivery of business counselling services.

Whether agency intervention makes an effective difference to small business development is a moot point. If agencies are to be effective then their role lies in unlocking latent entrepreneurial talent. This is obviously difficult to achieve, but is associated with their effectiveness in raising their profile in the small business community and the extent to which members of the community can be targeted. Since agencies have been criticized for blanket support and their low profile, it is possible to argue they have had little impact on small business development. For example, Casson (18) has argued that empirical evidence suggests that interventions to promote small firm start-ups are unlikely to stimulate entrepreneurship. Business In The Community (BITC) commissioned reports (19, 20) suggest support is effective in creating sustainable businesses but the actual difference that the agency makes is difficult to assess. Moore (21) has suggested that the impact of EAs can vary from 'marginal to 'significant' (pp. 24–5). Another study (22) has suggested their impact has been quite low. A careful recent review of the evidence by Storey (23) suggests that the level of enterprise support is not a significant factor in the development of SMEs. Storey (24) has also argued convincingly for the abandonment of start-up support (25) (the traditional role of EAs) and this has been reflected recently in policy in the move to establish Business Links which are focusing support on existing firms and on business development (see below).

The quality of support in the UK has, so far, been variable. The effectiveness of support is determined by the degree of selectivity, co-ordination, and collaboration of different agencies and the profile of the agency. Our research (25) has suggested that the collaboration and co-ordination between agencies is, as yet, very limited when compared to other levels of networking that take place, for example in Germany. Other studies have supported the view that the links between agencies and other institutions in the infrastructure of support are undeveloped (26). Co-ordination of support between EAs and other institutions has been slow to develop.

RESOURCES OF AGENCIES

Some agencies have been dependent on seconded staff (full time staff seconded from a large company or other organization such as a bank) for the delivery of enterprise support. Our research revealed that the average percentage of support provided through secondees was 16.2 per cent. However, the second stage of the research also showed that secondee support was a declining characteristic of UK agencies. This has been an important characteristic in the development of agencies, but directors revealed strong opinions that temporary secondee support did not necessarily provide the right type of counselling skills (since secondees were often managers from large firms). For example, it created additional training needs of counsellors (to acquire appropriate skills) and prohibits the development of a co-ordinated service since, with full time professional staff, job descriptions can be tailored to agency needs.

Traditionally, agencies have relied on a mixture of sponsorship and central government funding from the LEAGS scheme. (The Local Enterprise Agency Grants Scheme (LEAGS) had provided government grants that matched the agency's ability to raise funds from private sponsorship). Central policy making had diverted funds for enterprise support to the new TECs and LECs by the time our research was undertaken. The TECs and LECs had affected agency policies in a number of ways. In some cases agencies had been forced to combine into a consortium to bid for contracts with the TEC or LEC, in other cases associations had been formed in anticipation of the TEC or LEC being formed. Agencies that had established managed workspace were found to be in the strongest position in terms of their independence from the reliance on contracts from the TECs or LECs for enterprise support provision. The diversity of agency provision was reflected in workshop provision. The average extent was 29 000 sq.ft., but some agencies had over 100 000 sq.ft.

THE ROLE OF BUSINESS LINKS

Business Links have been charged with the role of bringing together the often confusing pattern of support that faces the entrepreneur or small firm owner. We draw upon the example of Business Link Birmingham (BLB) to illustrate the role of Business Links. BLB sees itself as a single gateway for existing firms seeking assistance with their business problems. In general, Business Links provide support in the following areas: marketing, business survival, staff and management training, quality management, corporate and business planning, and European issues and information (27). In BLB's case eight areas have been identified: exporting, sales and marketing, quality, team development, management and finance, legal and regulation, property, and technology.

BLB offers help at three levels. The first level includes information and advice in response to enquiries through an easy to remember phone number. The second level involves the business adviser service. If the client wishes they can be allocated a Personal Business Adviser (PBA) whose role is to carry out a diagnostic check or 'health check' on the business. For example an officer commented: 'It is at that point that we bring the PBA in, which is a free service, which is working with the client anything up to 3 days to assess the real needs of the business.'

The third level involves the referral of the client to an agency who will attempt to carry the PBA's recommendations. This means a continual review by the PBA, which is charged with the responsibility of ensuring that the project is completed successfully.

Although in theory, Business Links are meant to target existing SMEs that employ between 20 and 200 employees, we found in BLB's case that this target had already been revised downwards after six months of operation to include firms that employed five or more. In addition the idea that Business Links could target 'winners', (i.e., the small number of fast growth firms), was not backed by any criteria for targeting such firms beyond a belief that they would be self selecting. In BLB's case it was believed that such firms would select themselves by coming forward for assistance.

SOME ISSUES IN ENTERPRISE SUPPORT

TARGETING OF SUPPORT BY AGENCIES

Our study found little evidence of targeted support to different clients. It was found that the main bases of targeting support were age (26 per cent), gender (13 per cent), prior employment (11 per cent) and ethnicity (9 per cent). It was found that the size of the agency (FTEs) was significantly associated with any targeted support. Larger agencies were significantly more likely to develop some form of policy to different client groups. The second stage of research confirmed that relatively few attempts were made at providing specialized assistance to specific groups of clients. Only a minority of agencies attempted special provision such as Women into Business seminars. Where directors had previously been sceptical of the benefits of such courses, they had changed their views after attending or running such courses.

The creation of Business Links would seem to offer an opportunity both to rationalize support in the UK (by reducing duplication) and to develop some specialization by different EAs. However, we found that, in the case of Birmingham, there was little attempt to do either. Some provision for targeted support to ethnic minority clients was provided, as might be expected, but there was no attempt to encourage specialization beyond that which already existed. For example, the director of BLB was of the opinion that:

> I do not see it (rationalisation) personally as a saving, I see it as an opportunity to spot the gaps . . . and retrain the resource to the gaps which we may well define as a service that is needed.

In Germany, all manufacturing SMEs belong to the Industrie-und Handelskammern (IHK), the local Chambers of Commerce. These institutions are much stronger than UK Chambers of Commerce and play a much more pivotal role in promotion and dissemination of information. There is also a greater diversity of financial institutions. The regional states, the Länder, have considerable independence and power to implement their own investment and funding programmes. In the UK there are no such powerful organizations as the IHK and the regional Länder. In the West Midlands alone there are 10 TECs; with budgets of only £20 million, they are too small to make an effective difference to the level of enterprise support and training.

In Baden-Württemberg the IHK was able to provide specialist support and training for high technology small firms by having a director who specialized in technology. His role was seen as that of promoting the interests of technology based firms, co-ordinating resources and support. Specialized start-up support was available at the Chamber even though their members were small and medium-sized manufacturing firms. The difference in support was the way in which the Chamber could bring its influence to bear on other institutions such as the banks to provide support. The co-ordinating role was more effective than equivalent organizations in the UK. This included providing information and seminars for the local banks as well as venture capital providers. For example, a comment by a representative of one of the local banks was that. 'The IHK, once a year, hold special seminars on advice to small firms, which bank staff attend.'

In Baden-Württemberg there was also a range of special assistance to help different industrial sectors such as high technology small firms. This was in the form of grants, subsidies, guarantees, and soft loans. But beyond industrial sectors there was little in the way of targeting assistance to other categories. Similar to both the UK and France the Chamber provided seminars on specialized help for areas such as exporting, marketing and development. The IHK saw the promotional role as being more important than direct support especially with start-up concerns. In this way it could co-ordinate support such as finance or other requirements of its members.

NETWORKING BETWEEN AGENCIES AND THE CO-ORDINATION OF SUPPORT

Our UK study revealed that different agencies employed counsellors and trainers as generalists or specialists. Although there were attempts by agencies not in formal networks to break away from a generalist approach, it was noticeable that those in a formal network had greater opportunities to break away from the traditional generalist start-up advice that has characterized EA support in the past. The more formal the network, the greater the possibility of developing niche roles for individual agencies with the employment of full time professional staff that have recognized specialist skills and experience in providing support to different categories of clients. Implicit in this development is the cross-referral of clients that may need specialist help and advice. There are other advantages from the efficient use of staff resources. For example, it can be possible to free resources and staff time so that other issues can be investigated. Examples of this included the delegation of responsibility for marketing and public relations for agencies in the network to one individual and responsibility for developing sources of funding to another. Networking places agencies in a stronger position to develop funds for clients. Some of the larger agencies were able to administer their own venture capital funds for clients, including both first stage and second stage funding. If these were administered centrally through networking, it might be possible to widen the benefits of such schemes to more clients where high risk capital is often a problem, to increase the attractiveness of the schemes to potential investors, and to cross-refer clients in the network who may need specialist advice and assistance.

The diversity of the pattern of small business support provided by EAs gives them the flexibility to meet local needs. However, this very diversity can operate as an inhibitor to developing an effective and collaborative network. Asymmetries between agencies in size, resources, sponsorship, personnel, and attitudes can operate to prevent integration. Our research demonstrated a strong independence of agency directors and a desire to retain their own tradition of provision, even though they were prepared to admit that they could see advantages in a more co-ordinated network of support. This means that it can be difficult, even in the more developed networks, to resolve conflicting views and personalities. The harbouring of jealousy of other agencies' roles can inhibit progress and co-operation. The extent of competition for funding affected the ability and propensity of agencies to network, sometimes inhibiting closer co-operation between individual agencies. The impact of TECS and LECs on this extent of networking has been mixed. In some cases the TECs had forced agencies to form a consortium to bid for TEC funding; in other cases the formation of the TEC had cut across agency boundaries and co-operation. TECs and LECs have already been criticized for their lack of accountability, their small scale, and the potential conflicts of interest in board membership (28, 29).

One survey of British and German Chambers of Commerce (30) found that the resources of British chambers were on average only 7 per cent of those in Germany and they had only 17 per cent of the staff. For example, the Germans do not have to bid for contracts like an enterprise agency and their income from year to year can be calculated with relative certainty. This contrasts with the relative uncertainty of funding for local EAs in the UK. When we carried out the interviews with EA directors, some of them were not only unsure what their income would be for the following year, but in some cases were unsure whether they would still be in existence in a year's time.

The certainty of income allows the IHK to plan support, training programmes and counselling. By the nature of provision, the German system also avoids any duplication. Other institutions work with the IHK rather than trying to set up their own support system. For example, local authorities and regional authorities provide schemes that complement the provision of the IHK rather than set up agencies that may be in competition or offer duplication of support from the IHK. The IHK is relatively independent, powerful, and is able, as a result, to employ specialist staff. For example, we were able to interview a director of the IHK responsible for advice and support for technology based firms.

Where other agencies existed they met a specific and identified need and complemented the work of the IHK. For example in Pforzheim, a specialized agency for the jewellery industry existed, the Creditoren-Verein (CV). This agency's role was to provide specific debt collecting for the jewellery industry where debt collection was seen as a specific problem. Again the agency had the characteristics of independence, membership by subscription, and power that was supported by law.

There are similarities between the German Chambers of Commerce and French Chambers of Commerce. The local Chambre de Commerce et D'Industrie is independent, powerful and membership is compulsory. The agencies concerned with support and re-generation in Clermont-Ferrand proved to be atypical for France, because there was special provision due to the need to re-construct and diversify the local economy from its dependence on Michelin as a major employer. However, there was evidence of co-operation between these agencies concerned with enterprise support. For example, a director from the Chambre commented: 'We work together (with the Development Commission) but . . . there is some competition.' This point was developed by an officer from the Comité D'Expansion Economique (of the Puy de Dôme Department). He considered that the relationship with the Chambre was:

> A sort of partnership, yes. The success depends on the relationship between the entrepreneur and the Chambre. If things are going well between the entrepreneur and the Chambre, then they will stay with the Chambre. If not, they will come here and vice versa.

In addition, there were some smaller Chambers for shopkeepers and smaller firms—the Chambre de Métié. There was one Chambre de Métié in the Department (the Puy de Dôme). The services of this smaller Chamber, however, were distinctly different from the main Chambers of Commerce. The main Chambers of Commerce have members whose employment varies from 10 to 100 employees, whereas the Chambre de Métié is more likely to serve the 'petite de commerce', the self-employed and skilled trades people. Thus there was some competition, but co-operation also seemed to be effective between different support institutions.

The level of collaboration that exists in Germany between support agencies and financial institutions means that better quality start-ups are ensured. It may be more difficult to establish a new business because informational requirements are higher, but the quality of those start-ups is also higher (25). One of the problems in the UK is that the extent of new small firm creation has been subject to much volatility (31, 32).

SUPPORTING GROWTH FIRMS

In the UK, Business Links has been established with the aim of targeting support at enterprise development. Comparisons with France and Germany are borne out with the emphasis on firms that employ 10 to 100 employees. However, the methods for reaching such firms are not clear beyond marketing a series of 'events' such as workshops and business development programmes. Business Link Birmingham (BLB) attempts to achieve this aim of targeting growth firms. In the original prospectus BLB was to target existing businesses that employ 20 to 200. In practice they have been operating with firms that employ 10 to 200 and we have mentioned before that this has now been adjusted downwards to include those employing five or more.

However, although BLB has a clear policy of providing support through PBAs to existing firms the criteria for supporting growth firms were admitted to be unknown. As the director also commented:

> I can't offer a solution to that point. Clearly picking winners in my City Council's minds would be a different formula from my DTI requirements and arguably from the TEC.

(BLB is funded by three different bodies, DTI, Birmingham TEC and Birmingham City Council.)

At the same time, the Business Start-Up Scheme has been phased out with an accompanied reduction in schemes of blanket support. Although there is a powerful argument for switching resources away from start-up support, the criteria for selecting growth firms have not been developed. 'Picking winners' has been advocated yet we are still no nearer developing criteria that will identify so-called 'fast-track' firms. As another officer has admitted: 'We don't know what the answer is (to picking winners) . . . at the end of the day it comes down to self-selection.' Growth firms will hopefully phone into BLB for advice and support with their business development. There has been some evidence to show that start-ups can achieve more success where different skills are identified and developed through a 'team start' (33).

A further issue arose with the potential conflict with the provision of a quality service that is required to give support for fast growth and developing firms, yet at the same time meet quantitative indicators of support provided to meet targets set (in BLB's case) of three different funders. As the director of BLB commented: 'I have to do both. All the grant schemes that I have, have quantitative indicators and output related activity to get the money.'

The interviews with EA directors also revealed that there was some complacency in developing quality indicators. Most directors were content to monitor counselling sessions through quantity indicators such as records of enquiries but there was relatively little in the way of developing quality indicators such as whether value has been added to the firm. This dilemma exists in the UK because the current provision of support is targeted through Business Links or

TECs. These are not independently funded and will have to meet quantitative criteria of supporting 'X' number of firms. This conflicts with any attempt to provide quality support to a small number of fast growth firms.

In Germany there is some selectivity of support. The IHK by its nature will tend to direct support more to existing firms and respond to the needs of existing firms rather than start-ups. Seminars tend to be provided not for start-ups or to raise enterprise awareness but for re-training, technology, or exporting. The programme tends to be a series of support seminars and training that is geared at existing firms and at Germany's famous Mittelstand, the medium-sized firm, of 50 to 200 employees.

In France, a similar emphasis on developing firms rather than directing aid at start-ups was more normal. Start-up clients were more likely to go to the Department agency, the Comité D'Expansion Economique. For example, the officer concerned considered that of his clients:

> One third are people who want to start a new business; one third are clients who want to develop an existing business and one third were people who were facing difficulties.

The director of the Chambre considered that his typical client was a 'medium-sized firm' and that he wished to develop a long term relationship with these medium-sized firms although he did provide advice and support for the creation of new firms.

There are distinct parallels with the development of One-Stop Shops in the UK and some of the work and emphasis of French and German Chambers of Commerce. In the UK there are the beginnings of the development of longer term relationships with existing firms, providing support more in response to firm needs, when it is required, rather than some policies which have been seen as top-down and 'off the shelf' by some commentators (11).

ADDITIONAL ENTERPRISE INITIATIVES

There are a number of state initiatives designed to encourage small firm start-up and growth. At the same time, set in the background to these initiatives has been a general withdrawal of the state from the production and provision of goods and services. The extensive programme of privatization and other major economic changes, such as changes in income taxes and corporation taxes, cannot be discussed here but they form the background of general state measures designed to increase and promote the opportunities for private sector enterprise and development. Specific state measures designed to encourage small firm formation and growth are much more limited. They concentrate on relieving perceived constraints on small firm formation and growth. As such they tend to concentrate on funding and other resource constraints. The main schemes are identified below; we merely list and describe them briefly before turning to an examination of whether there has been any significant change, as result, in our culture.

1. The creation of enterprise zones. These were created in a limited number of areas designed to provide special conditions that would foster the growth of new businesses. They represented a special 'tax free' zone where the firm did not have to pay local authority rates. Each zone was created for 10 years. The most famous enterprise zone has been the Isle of Dogs since it attracted the Canary Wharf investment and development. The Isle of Dogs illustrates the major problem with enterprise zones: they have attracted large scale firms and funding which it is arguable would have been invested anyway but in other areas where firms would have more long term viability. In addition the Enterprise Zones do not have the infrastructure to support long term growth and viability. The Isle of Dogs, for example, has continued to suffer from poor transport links compared to the City of London and it has never attracted the amount of office space that it needed to establish itself as a major centre of re-generation. Amin and Tomaney (34) in a study of the North East, are critical of the creation of Enterprise Zones, investment has gone into property development rather than into manufacturing.

2. The Enterprise Allowance Scheme (EAS), designed to encourage unemployed people to start their own businesses. The original requirement, that an individual had to be unemployed for a period of up to six months, has now been dropped and as administered by the TECs, unemployment status need not be a qualification to enter the scheme. Like other funding schemes this has been discussed in Chapter 5. As explained there, it provides a start-up grant during the first year of operation. The actual level of grant can vary since the scheme is now administered and controlled by the TECs. Like the pattern of UK support, discussed above, there is diversity in this support. There can, for example, be different levels of enterprise training and requirements under the scheme depending on the TEC responsible. In general, however, the EAS has been criticized for creating businesses that may not be viable, for subsidizing inefficient businesses, for creating unemployment since other businesses may be forced to stop trading through 'unfair competition', and for not tackling the problem of the long term unemployed for which group it was designed to help (35).

Official evaluation reports can often paint a rosy picture. For example, one MSC Report (36) claimed survival rates of 74 per cent after 18 months for businesses on the scheme. However, such crude survival rates tell us little about the effective quality of such start-ups. The repeated criticism of the EAS is that jobs and businesses were being created at the expense of others. Official reports tend to ignore such opportunity costs.

Some TECs still operate this scheme in a modified form as the Business

Start-Up scheme but some TECs have also phased it out, reflecting the greater emphasis on existing firms through the Business Links. Again this illustrates that the level of enterprise support varies throughout the UK and that the level of support, for an individual entrepreneur, often depends on the geographical area that they are located in and the policy of their local TEC.

3. The Small Firms' Loan Guarantee Scheme (SFLGS). Finance was seen as a potential constraint on individual enterprise. This scheme was designed to relieve problems that might exist in raising finance for viable ventures that lacked security. As discussed in Chapter 4, the problem with this scheme is that the bank has to put forward a venture to qualify and the banks have not been enthusiastic supporters. Compared to similar schemes, in Germany, take up rates have been only at 10 per cent of such levels (37). Yet the continued importance of the scheme to the Government was demonstrated in the Budget of 1993, when the then Chancellor, Norman Lamont, increased the incentives under the scheme.

Evaluation reports can give misleading impressions of the effectiveness of such schemes. A Department of Employment Report (38) showed that out of 106 firms enrolled on the scheme in 1986, two years later, 100 firms were still operating. However, this report failed to give any indication of how the scheme could be better marketed, e.g., by the banks, so that the disappointingly low take-up rates could be improved.

As discussed above, the extent and level of networking is one of the reasons for the higher take-up of an equivalent scheme in Germany. The role of institutions such as the IHK means that the promotion and subsequent take-up of such a scheme is on a far higher level. The low take-up in the UK reflects, in part, the lack of collaboration and effective networking between the banks and external support agencies.

4. The enterprise initiative, a Department of Trade and Industry (DTI) scheme which offers help to small businesses to get professional advice and consultancy. Launched in 1988, it was part of the Government's switch from specific help with funding to more emphasis on advice and consultancy. It was designed particularly to help existing small businesses to expand by providing financial assistance for small firms to employ consultants. It represented a scheme targeted at perceived management constraints that face small businesses. The main component of the initiative was the Consultancy Initiatives (CI) programme, which provides assistance for consultancy in defined areas such as marketing, design, and business planning. The enterprise initiative and CI scheme seems to have had some significant impact although it can be argued, as with other schemes, that take-up rates are low (39). The main problem with the scheme seems to have been lack of adequate follow-through on implementation by firms and the perception that the scheme was more suited to medium-sized firms rather than small firms.

5. The Business Expansion Scheme (BES), intended to help existing

businesses with expansion plans seeking additional equity. The relative failure of this scheme to attract additional sources of equity for small firms is indicated that it is being withdrawn in 1993. The problem with the scheme was not that it failed to provide equity finance. According to Mason *et al.* (40), between 1982 and 1988 £700 million of equity capital was invested under the scheme but, as they point out, much of the equity raised went into property firms in the South East rather than manufacturing concerns. Like many of the other schemes it has failed to tackle the problem that it was aimed at solving.

It has been replaced by the *Enterprise Investment Scheme (EIS)*, designed to encourage potential investors to invest in small amounts of equity. It has been dubbed 'son of BIS' and it is be hoped that it does not fail in the same way as its predecessor—so far it is too early to attempt any evaluation.

6. A number of other semi-official schemes were established, all designed to encourage small firm start-ups. For example, in some areas funding is available under British Coal redundancy schemes. British Steel also has similar schemes; and there is the role of Task Force Funding in inner city areas. City Challenge, designed to revitalize inner city areas, also adds to the wide range of potential assistance.

When added together, the combination of these different enterprise initiatives and the background of the broadbrush government economic changes in taxation and privatization provide the basis for claims that the Government have created an 'enterprise culture'. However, this is a much more difficult concept to evaluate. To some extent, there has been a debate about whether there have been sufficient changes in society to talk about the creation of an enterprise culture. We briefly consider some of the contributions to the debate.

THE ENTERPRISE CULTURE: DOES IT EXIST?

We concentrate on whether the Government (since 1979) has been successful in its aim to create a new enterprise culture in the UK. Obviously implicit in this claim is that there has been some change in the attitudes and beliefs of society since 1979. To claim that there has been this change it is necessary to show that society, in 1979, was different in perceptions and attitudes. Before 1979, it is claimed that society did not provide an environment that fostered entrepreneurship and enterprise development; that enterprise skills were insufficiently rewarded; that there was insufficient motivation and reward to start your own business; and that existing businesses were stifled for lack of opportunity and the right climate for development and growth. It is claimed that the development of enterprise skills, whether in large or small organizations, was not fostered by the culture and environment that existed in 1979.

Lord Young and subsequent government ministers have claimed that there were sufficiently significant changes in the attitudes and environment of society to claim the existence of such changes by the mid-1980s. There has been a subsequent academic debate about whether this enterprise culture does exist. The claim is that the spirit of enterprise has been freed (41).

The debate has drawn comments from a wide academic background; contributions have ranged from theologians (42), sociologists (43), economists (44) and politicians (45). Advocates of the existence of the enterprise culture have been enthusiastic in their claims. For example, Bannock (46) has gone so far as to call this a 'sea change' in social attitudes in the 1980s.

Claims for the creation and existence of an enterprise culture suffer from a number of problems. Firstly, it is difficult to define precisely what is meant by the term 'enterprise culture'. It is a term which is full of ambiguities and has led to different attempts at definition (47). MacDonald and Coffield (48) have compared the term 'enterprise' to 'Heffalump'—the mythical creature of supposed vast importance that no one has ever seen.

Secondly, as pointed out in this chapter, evaluation reports on the effectiveness of state initiatives give misleading impressions of their effectiveness and impact. Mills (49, commenting on the EAS, says:

> The rhetoric of the EAS claims to create an Enterprise Culture and encourage the growth of entrepreneurs in Britain. In practice it seems to have been a means of reducing the unemployment statistics (pp. 93).

Thirdly, it is very difficult to assess the much more tenuous question of whether there has been any noticeable change in the culture of society. For example, Amin and Tomaney (34), in their study of the North East, assess the impact of enterprise initiatives and comment that it has been the: 'expressed aim of the Conservative administration to foster an entrepreneurial culture and to use this as a main plank for local economic generation' (p. 479).

This study is critical of the government initiatives (such as enterprise zones) and the gradual run down of state regional grant aid. Even the creation of the Nissan plant in the region comes in for criticism as being a relatively costly investment. Other initiatives are criticized for encouraging investment in property rather than manufacturing, such as the Tyne and Wear Urban Development Corporation.

Fourthly, there have been long term changes that have been taking place in the structure of the UK economy. For example, the decline of traditional industries and structural change involving a shift out of manufacturing were in evidence long before 1979. Similarly economic and social changes were under way before 1979, e.g., increased economic activity rates by women.

It is likely that forces for change in society's attitudes are much more complex and if changes have taken place they have been started by forces in society that were changing before 1979. It may be that the enterprise initiatives introduced by the Government have given these changes a boost and brought them forward. However, many of the claims for the impact of these initiatives must be treated with caution. The more exaggerated claims, such as the creation of an enterprise culture do not bear up to close scrutiny and examination.

CONCLUSIONS

In the 1980s, the development of a support network of 300 enterprise agencies and 82 TECs and 22 LECs has seen a large private and public sector investment in supporting enterprise development of new and small businesses. Whether this investment will ever be adequately evaluated is doubtful. At present, the level of support is confusing and suffers from a number of inadequacies. Attempts to create Business Links may help to rationalize this support, however, if past UK experience is any guide, it is more likely that there will be inadequate collaboration by different agencies. We are still a long way from the German model of effective intervention, collaboration, and networking that supports the creation of viable and high quality small businesses.

Business Links are a move in the right direction in terms of re-focusing enterprise support. However, the development of the EA movement has left the UK with an unplanned and confusing mixture of public and independent support that owes more to historical accidents of provision and individual promotion than any policy of consistent and planned support targeted to areas and firms that need the support. Duplication of support provision remains a problem in the UK. TECs, although arguably too small, have in some cases been beneficial in acting as a catalyst to force agencies to work together. However, limited co-operation still remains a problem. Business Links will not solve this problem; they may re-direct some enterprise support through the referral of business development cases, but they will not improve the co-ordination of support.

State enterprise initiatives have met with limited success. But often the true cost of these initiatives is not appreciated (or admitted), e.g., there are many people who would not be in business if more jobs were available. Wider criteria need to be applied to evaluation of state schemes, i.e., the quality of jobs created, longitudinal criteria (how long do the jobs last for?), assessment of the externalities of the schemes, and suggestions for improvement of the schemes.

Too often little account is taken of whether the right type of people are being encouraged into business. The associated suffering of families of those who are encouraged to start their own businesses, that later fail, is ignored. Often these business failures, which have been at record levels in the recession, are accompanied by the loss of personal equity, property, and homes. Families which may have enjoyed a good standard of living can, in some cases, be left destitute and with large personal debts. The social costs of this greater concern with the enterprise culture are too often ignored. The 'downside' aspects of running a small business are often not appreciated by the people who are encouraged to start their own businesses due to an emphasis on success and achievement. The associated social costs of such success are conveniently ignored, e.g., strains on married life and family relationships, long hours of work, and the lack of fringe benefits such as non-contributory pension schemes.

Learning outcomes

At the end of this chapter students should be able to:

1. Appreciate the range and diversity of government enterprise initiatives designed to encourage and foster the development of the enterprise culture.
2. Discuss the roles of support agencies and the present inadequacies of UK support provision.
3. Describe the advantages of networking between agencies and other institutions involved in the support of new ventures.
4. Compare UK levels of networking to the German and French experience and the role of German and French Chambers of Commerce.
5. Discuss criteria that can be used to evaluate state schemes.
6. Appreciate and discuss problems with the term 'enterprise culture'.
7. Recognize the contribution of official studies and independent writers when assessing the development of an enterprise culture.
8. Appreciate both negative and positive aspects of the attempt to create an 'enterprise culture'.

REFERENCES

1. BIRCH, D. L. (1979) 'The job generation process', *MIT study on neighbourhood and regional change*, MIT, Boston.

2. LORD YOUNG (1992) 'Enterprise Regained' in HEELAS, P. and MORRIS, P. (eds), *The Values of The Enterprise Culture: the moral debate*, Routledge, London.

3. SEGAL QUINCE WICKSTEED, (1988) *Encouraging small business start-up and growth: creating a supportive local environment*, HMSO, London.

4. DEAKINS, D. and SPARROW, J. (1990) *Enterprise Agencies Survey: policies and practices in targeting post start-up support for new businesses*, Birmingham Poltechnic, Birmingham.

5. DEAKINS, D. (1993) 'What Role for Support Agencies? A case study of UK Enterprise Agencies', *Local Economy*, vol. 8, no. 1, pp. 57–68.

6. CARSWELL, M. (1990) Small firm networking and business performance, *Proceedings of the 13th National Small Firms Policy and Research Conference*, Harrogate.

7. SMALLBONE, D. (1990) 'Success and failure in small business start-ups', *International Small Business Journal*, vol. 8, no. 2, pp. 34–47.

8. BENNETT, R. J., WICKS, P. J., and McCOSHAN, A. (1994) *Local Empowerment and Business Services: Britain's Experiment with TECs*, UCL Press, London.

9. EMMERICH, M. and PECK, J. (1992) *Reforming the TECs: Towards a New Training Strategy*, Final Report of the CLES TEC/LEC Monitoring Project, CLES, Manchester.

10. TOPHAM, N., PADMORE, K., and TWONEY, J. (1994) *English TECs: Ranking, Requirement and Resources*, Salford University, Salford.

11. CURRAN, J. (1993) 'TECs and Small Firms: Can TECs Reach the Small Firms Other Strategies have Failed to Reach?', paper presented to the House of Commons Social and Science Policy Group, Kingston University, Kingston.

12. EMBI (1991) *Ethnic minority business development team final report*, Home Office, London.

13. EMBI (1991) *Assisting ethnic minority businesses: good practice guidelines for Local Enterprise Agencies*, Home Office, London.

14. OAKEY, R. (1991) 'High technology small firms: their potential for growth', *International Small Business Journal*. vol. 9, no. 4, pp. 30–42.

15. TUROK, I. and RICHARDSON, P. (1989) Supporting the start-up and growth of small firms: a study in West Lothian, Strathclyde Papers on Planning, no. 14, University of Strathclyde, Glasgow.

16. SMALLBONE, D. (1990) 'Enterprise Agencies in London—a public private sector partnership?', *Local Government Studies*, September/October, pp. 17–32.

17. FULLER, T. and HANNON, P. (1992) 'Information Technology and Business Networks; navigation systems, theory and practice', in *The Entrepreneur in the Driving Seat*, Proceedings of the 22nd European Small Business Seminar, Amsterdam.

18. CASSON, M. (ed.) (1990) *Entrepreneurship*, Edward Elgar, London.

19. BUSINESS IN THE COMMUNITY (1985) Small Firms: survival and job creation, the contribution of enterprise agencies, BITC, London.

20. BUSINESS IN THE COMMUNITY (1988) The future for enterprise agencies, BITC, London.

21. MOORE, C. (1988) 'Enterprise Agencies: privatisation or partnership?', *Local Economy*, vol. 3, no. 1, pp. 21–30.

22. CENTRE FOR EMPLOYMENT INITIATIVES (1985) *The impact of Local Enterprise Agencies in Great Britain: operational lessons and policy implications*, CEI.

23. STOREY, D. J. (1994) *Understanding the Small Business Sector*, Routledge, London.

24. STOREY, D. J. (1993) 'Should we Abandon Support for Start-Up Businesses' in CHITTENDEN, F., ROBERTSON, M. and WATSON, D., *Small Firms: Recession and Recovery*, Paul Chapman, London, pp. 15–26.

25. DEAKINS, D. and PHILPOTT, T. (1993) Comparative European Practices in the Finance of Small Firms: UK, Germany and Holland, University of Central England, Birmingham.

26. COOPERS AND LYBRAND DELOITTE AND BUSINESS IN THE COMMUNITY (1991) *Local support for enterprise*, BITC, London.

27. CUTLER (1994) 'Gearing Up for Business Link', *Local Economy*, vol. 8, no. 4, pp. 365–8.

28. BENNETT, R. G., McCOSHAN, A., and SELLGREN, J. (1991) 'TECs and VET: the practical requirements of organisation and geography', *Regional Studies*, vol. 24, no. 1, pp. 65–9.

29. PECK, J. and EMMERICH, M. (1993) 'Training and Enterprise Councils: Time for Change', *Local Economy*, vol. 8, no. 1, pp. 4–21.

30. BENNETT, M. J., KREBS, G. and ZIMMERMAN, H. (1993) *Chambers of Commerce in Britain and Germany and The Single Market*, Anglo-German Foundation, Poole.

31. DALY, M. and McCANN, A. (1992) 'How Many Small Firms?', *Employment Gazette*, February, pp. 47–51.

32. DALY, M., CAMPBELL, M., ROBSON, G., and GALLAGHER, C. (1991) 'Job Creation 1987-89: The Contributions of Small and Large Firms', *Employment Gazette*, November, pp. 589–596.

33. VYAKARNAM, S. and JACOBS, R. (1993) 'TEAMSTART, Overcoming the Blockages to Small Business Growth' in CHITTENDEN, F., ROBERTSON, M., and MARSHALL, I. (eds), *Small Firms: Partnerships for Growth*, Paul Chapman Publishing, London, pp. 192–205.

34. AMIN, A. and TOMANEY, J. (1991) 'Creating an Enterprise Culture in the North East? The impact of Urban and Regional Policies of the 1980s', *Regional Studies*, vol. 25, no. 5, pp. 479–87.

35. GRAY, C. (1990) 'Some Economic and Psychological Considerations on the Effects of the Enterprise Allowance Scheme', *Small Business*, vol. 1, pp. 111–24.

36. SIMKIN, C. and ALLEN, D. (1988) *Enterprise Allowance Scheme Evaluation: second eighteen month national survey – Final report*, MSC, London.

37. CHARLES BATCHELOR (1993) *Financial Times*, 23 March.

38. NATIONAL ECONOMIC RESEARCH ASSOCIATION (1990) *An Evaluation of the Loan Guarantee Scheme*, Department of Employment, London.

39. SEGAL QUINCE WICKSTEED (1989) *Evaluation of the Consultancy Initiatives*, HMSO, London.

40. MASON, C., HARRISON, J., and HARRISON, R. (1988) *Closing the Equity Gap? An assessment of the Business Expansion Scheme*, Small Business Research Trust, Milton Keynes.

41. MORRIS, P. (1991) 'Freeing the Spirit of Enterprise', in KEAT, R. and ABERCROMBIE, N. (eds), *Enterprise Culture*, Routledge, London, pp. 21–37.

42. MORRIS, P. (1992) 'Is God Enterprising? Reflections on enterprise culture and religion' in HEELAS, P. and MORRIS, P. (eds). *The Values of the Enterprise Culture: the moral debate*, Routledge, London, pp. 276–90.

43. ABERCROMBIE, N. (1991) 'The privilege of the producer' in KEAT, R. and ABERCROMBIE, N. (eds), *Enterprise Culture*, Routledge, London, pp. 171–85.

44. RICKETTS, M. (1987) *The Economics of Business Enterprise*, Wheatsheaf Books, London.

45. LAWSON, N. (1984) *The British Experiment*, Fifth Mais Lecture, H.M. Treasury.

46. BANNOCK G. (1991) *Venture Capital and the Equity Gap*, National Westminster Bank, London.

47. RITCHIE, J. (1991) 'Chasing Shadows: Enterprise Culture as an Educational Phenomenon', *Journal of Education Policy*, vol. 6, no. 3, pp. 315–25.

48 MacDONALD, R. and COFFIELD, F. (1991) *Risky Business: Youth and the Enterprise Culture*, Falmer Press, London.

49. MILLS, V. (1991) 'Review of Some Economic and Psychological Considerations on the Effects of the EAS', *International Small Business Journal*, vol. 9, no. 4, pp. 91–4.

RECOMMENDED READING

For a summary of government policy measures affecting small firms see:

STANWORTH, J. and GRAY, C. (1991) *Bolton 20 years On: The Small Firm in The 1990s*, Paul Chapman, London, Chapter 2, pp. 16–39.

For a careful discussion of the criteria which might be used to identify growth firms see:

STOREY, D. J. (1994) *Understanding the Small Business Sector*, Routledge, London, Chapter 5, pp. 112–59.

For the debate on the enterprise culture two collections of contributions to the debate are recommended:

HEELAS, P. and MORRIS, P. (1992) *The Values of The Enterprise Culture: The Moral Debate*, Routledge, London.

KEAT, R. and ABERCROMBIE, N. (eds) (1991) *Enterprise Culture*, Routledge, London.

Other reading on the enterprise culture:

AMIN, A. and TOMANEY, J. (1991) 'Creating an Enterprise Culture in the North East? The impact of Urban and Regional Policies of the 1980s', *Regional Studies*, vol. 25, no. 5, pp. 479–87.

MACDONALD, R. and COFFIELD, F. (1991) *Risky Business: Youth and the Enterprise Culture*, Falmer Press.

RITCHIE, J. (1991) 'Chasing Shadows: Enterprise Culture as an Educational Phenomenon', *Journal of Education Policy*, vol. 6, no. 3, pp. 315–25.

8 *Innovation and Entrepreneur-ship*

PREVIEW

Like Chapter 6, this chapter has been influenced by the main speakers and contributions from delegates at a UCE/ISBA seminar on Innovation and Entrepreneurship held at the Birmingham Centre for Manufacturing in May 1994. In particular, it contains material from two entrepreneurs concerned with innovation who prepared material for this seminar. The author has also had a number of discussions and interviews with the two entrepreneurs concerned. Both entrepreneurs drew upon their differing experience of the innovation process to provide material that served as case study material. In addition, both entrepreneurs have valid comments about the environment for small firms that are involved with the innovation process in the UK, and about how that environment can be improved.

Material from both their cases is drawn upon for illustration in this chapter. The full case study concerning Eco-Wall Ltd follows in Chapter 9, written by the entrepreneur, Joe Wilson. This book has been dedicated to his memory and I hope that in a small way the material in this chapter and Chapter 9 will influence sufficient people to improve the environment for entrepreneurs concerned with the innovation process in the UK.

The contention that such entrepreneurs are critical to the performance of the UK economy and therefore need to be able to succeed in the UK is undoubted. The second entrepreneur, Ray Davies, is also quoted in this chapter. His company, Rialtec, was a classic example of technology transfer from scientific research in Aston University to a commercial company located in Aston Science Park. Yet Rialtec, has been re-located abroad, at least in part because of an insufficiently supportive environment in the UK. As we observe, such a re-location is disturbing. This, combined with other observations, currently means that there is considerable concern that the environment in the UK is insufficiently supportive for entrepreneurs involved with the innovation process. This concern is not just based upon two case studies, but on the contributions of other delegates to the seminar and with a number of interviews and discussions that are on-going with high technology based entrepreneurs in both the West Midlands and in Scotland. As we will see in this chapter, despite government White Papers that continue to point to the importance of innovation management and best practice we have as yet to establish the infrastructure of support (in the widest sense) to ensure success.

Contribution to this chapter also comes from Professor Ray Oakey, Peter Ives (Technology Unit, National Westminster Bank), Peter Sturrock (Profit-through-People, Aston Science Park), together with Nigel Bottomley and Barry Caiden from the National Association of Mutual Guarantee Schemes at Altrincham.

INTRODUCTION

Innovation and entrepreneurship is potentially a vast topic, and for the purposes of this chapter we concentrate on issues that face the small firm entrepreneur who is engaged in some form of innovation. Innovation, itself, is a tricky concept to pin down—writers often consider the high technology based small firm when discussing entrepreneurs concerned with innovation. Yet innovation can occur with low technology as well as high technology based firms. It may simply involve 'managing change'; the entrepreneur may find a novel method of changing the process of production as well as the product. The product is loosely defined here to include services; innovation in services can occur through new variations in the service provided which are often called new 'products'.

In order to illustrate the elusive nature of the concept of innovation and entrepreneurship, consider a small craft manufacturer making earrings. Let us assume he/she is skilled and finds that he/she is able to use new material that has been developed elsewhere, say in the aircraft industry by a major manufacturer. He/she is taking technology that has been developed elsewhere and applying it to an everyday use. The question is whether he/she is an innovative entrepreneur? There is no R&D—it can be merely an application or incremental change to existing technology. For the purposes of this chapter, he/she is an innovative entrepreneur, having found a way of applying technological change in a new way, perhaps from the commercialization of technology developed elsewhere.

Thus the innovative entrepreneur is more than just the pure scientist, he/she has to have the additional skills and abilities that we met with Schumpeter in Chapter 1, i.e. they need to have the ability to recognize the commercial application of technological advance. The next chapter provides a case study of that process. Of course to get to the commercialization stage, a marketable product, there may be further R&D that is necessary.

Having defined our terms of reference, we can then identify particular issues: e.g., whether small, innovatory firms can successfully raise finance; whether entrepreneurs can successfully manage technological change; whether entrepreneurs can protect their investment and ideas through the patent system; whether a specific support infrastructure (such as a science park or incubator) can successfully nurture and develop innovatory small firms. All these questions have attracted some interest. It is assumed that we can identify innovatory entrepreneurs as a distinct group and that their characteristics are sufficiently different from (non-innovatory) other entrepreneurs. In reality, there are differences within innovatory small firms, e.g., we might want to distinguish between *high technology* small firms and *new technology* small firms. New technology may be novel but not necessarily high technology and in many developing countries new technology solutions to areas such as irrigation may involve alternative technology as well as new technology.

What is different about the entrepreneur engaged in the innovation process? It can be argued that such entrepreneurs and small firms are worthy of special study and interest because of a number of characteristics as follows.

1. They have different and special financing requirements, illustrated in Figure 8.1. These arise because of the need for *seed capital*. The R&D process can take some time before the firm has a marketable product. During this period there is no return for the investor. It is sometimes argued that innovatory entrepreneurs

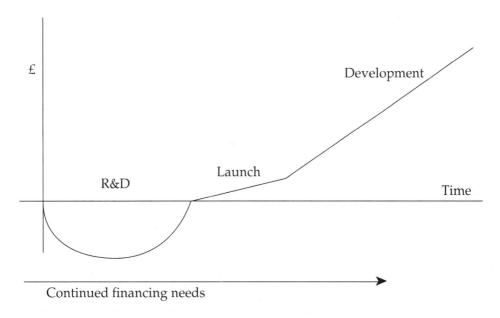

Figure 8.1 The financing requirements of high technology small firms

will have greater needs for venture finance and long term capital. In the development of the technology there will be a further need for *development capital*. When we discussed Schumpeter's definitions of innovation we saw that there were three distinct phases: invention, innovation, and diffusion. The diffusion stage requires the development of the technology so that it can be applied in different uses and adopted throughout the economy.

2. The entrepreneur will require distinct and different managerial skills. The management of innovation requires a combination of technical and managerial ability that is different from other small firms. For example, the R&D process can be modelled as a time decision making problem. Timing of decisions such as the taking out of patents can be crucial. Scherer and Ross (1) have modelled technological development within firms as a trade-off between development costs and market revenues and demonstrate that there are considerable *first mover* advantages in the innovation process. It can often be more advantageous to be first on the market with a new product rather than be first with a patent. This is particularly true for leading edge technology where suppliers may be sufficiently influenced to follow the market leader rather than necessarily the best technology. This has happened, for example, with the suppliers of software for IBM type PCs. IBM has become the market leader even though it could be claimed that Apple MacIntosh had superior technology.

3. Further problems arise with *technology transfer*, which involves the commercial application of research carried out in a different environment such as a science laboratory in a university. It is argued that innovatory entrepreneurs have different support needs. For example, special environments may need to be created to facilitate successful technology transfer, e.g., from pure scientific research in universities to production techniques in firms. Hence the establishment of some science parks attached to universities in the UK and the network of Business Innovation Centres (incubators) that have now spread across the EU countries. Business Innovation Centres, however, tend to be more generally based than science parks.

4. It has been claimed that high technology small firms require a network or *cluster* of like firms to be successful, the most famous example being Silicon Valley in the USA. In addition, the Massachusetts model of successful high technology development of small firms as spin-outs from the university has led to attempts to re-create that success here in the UK through the establishment of science parks attached to universities in the UK. The most successful of these has been the Cambridge Science Park, sometimes identified as the *Cambridge Phenomenon* (2)—the spin-off from technical developments in scientific research carried out at Cambridge University. To begin with firms were closely dependent on research carried out at the university.

5. Finally, it can be argued that such firms are worthy of study because they are crucial to the development of the regional and national economy. Solow (3) first

identified the importance of innovation for economic development. Over 60 per cent of all economic growth is due to technological advance rather than through improvements in labour productivity. A number of official reports such as the 1993 White Paper on Science and Technology (4) have identified the potential from the encouragement of entrepreneurs that are engaged in innovation or technical change and the need to transfer technology successfully. Unfortunately, the author concludes at the end of this chapter that the UK does not contain an environment that fosters entrepreneurs who are engaged in the innovation process. The classic scenario for the UK still exists that we are good at ideas (invention) but poor at the commercialization of ideas (innovation and diffusion).

SOME DEFINITIONS

For our purposes, innovation can be defined as all those activities that give rise to a new product or process of production (5). These can include:

1. Basic research which generates new knowledge without necessarily a specific use intended.
2. Invention which includes the application of knowledge to achieve a specific end, such as the building of a prototype model (Schumpeter's invention stage incorporates 1 and 2).
3. Development which involves refinement of the prototype model into the final product or process (Schumpeter's innovation stage).
4. Wider take-up and absorption of the technology into society (Schumpeter's diffusion stage).

Definitions of innovation include those of Freeman (5): 'The first commercial application or production of a new process or product.' The OECD (6) defines innovation as: 'The transformation of an idea into a new or improved saleable product or operational process in industry or commerce.' Innovations may be categorized into product innovation and process innovation. The adoption process by which firms take up and apply new technology is a central feature of the overall innovation process.

IDENTIFYING THE ENTREPRENEUR CONCERNED WITH INNOVATION

To identify entrepreneurs who are concerned with innovation is a problem that is not easily overcome for researchers or for our purposes in this chapter. One way that has been adopted is to identify high technology small firms by industrial sector and hence assume that they will include the entrepreneur who is concerned with R&D. This approach assumes that the key entrepreneur can be identified.

It has been suggested by Butchart (7) that high technology small firms can be classified according to industrial sector. Butchart defines high technology according to the intensity of R&D to turnover and science based industries. There are only certain industrial sectors that will meet Butchart's criteria. These will tend to be science based manufacturing or engineering industries and services connected to those industries.

There are a number of problems with this approach:

1. Firstly, it will exclude industrial sectors where the management of technological change and adoption of such change will still be important.
2. It is difficult to measure the intensity of R&D, e.g., it could be on the basis of expenditure or number of employees in R&D.
3. R&D is a less than perfect measure of innovatory activity, e.g., R&D spend does not necessarily correlate with how innovative a firm is, nor does it correlate with the number of patent applications lodged by firms.

Any approach to define high technology or new technology small firms is fraught with difficulty. Further, because technology itself is rapidly changing, using industrial sector definitions can become out-dated quite quickly. Researchers have tried to get around these problems by concentrating on specific industries such as bio-technology or on specific locations such as science parks.

ISSUES IN INNOVATION AND ENTREPRENEURSHIP

1. ARE ENTREPRENEURS AT A DISADVANTAGE IN THE INNOVATORY PROCESS?

The contributions of Schumpeter and Galbraith would suggest that entrepreneurs and small firms are at a disadvantage, compared to the larger firm, in the innovatory process. Schumpeter (8) was more concerned with the effect of market structure. However, we have already seen in an earlier chapter, that he considered that the entrepreneur was an innovator. The role of the entrepreneur was crucial in economic development. For Schumpeter, the entrepreneur was a person who created new ways of fulfilling currently unsatisfied needs or created more efficient ways of satisfying those needs. The act of entrepreneurship sets the innovation process in motion. The reward is extraordinary profit, but this is eroded by imitation. More competition increases the likelihood of imitation and hence the reward for innovation is reduced. From this Schumpeter argued that oligopolistic or monopolistic market structures were necessary to provide the rewards for entrepreneurial innovation. Perfect competition would stifle innovation because there is no motive from profits to innovate.

As developed by Galbraith (9), large firms were seen to have distinct advantages in the innovation process. Large firms were essential to the process of technological advance, but we can see that there was an inherent conflict in the Schumpeter view. This conflict is contained in the view that entrepreneurs are the movers of technological change but monopolistic structures were necessary to provide the motives (of profit) to innovate. Galbraith argued that the costs of invention could only be undertaken with the resources at the disposal of the large firm. In addition, economies of scale existed in R&D which meant that large firms could develop new products more cheaply than small firms.

Phillips (10) has also developed the Galbraithian view into a technology 'push' hypothesis. This hypothesis states that the research staff of a firm are the main instigators of innovation. Basic scientific advances are brought forward to the main organization for commercial development. The larger a firm's research staff the more it can benefit from this technological push.

An alternative hypothesis is associated with 'demand pull'. The main driving force behind technological innovation comes from the marketing staff of the firm, who in dealing with customers identify problems and engage the research staff to solve the problems.

The evidence from market structure suggests that there are advantages with oligopolistic firms, but the rate of successful R&D falls with monopoly. Despite the disadvantages faced by small firms there is evidence that the small firm is more efficient in the technological and innovatory process. Robson and Townsend (11), for example, have produced evidence to suggest that SMEs have increasingly provided a greater share of the number of innovations in the UK over the period 1945–83. They also show that SMEs have increased their innovative efficiency over this period (the ratio of innovation share and employment share).

2. INNOVATIVE ENTREPRENEURS FACE DISADVANTAGES IN RAISING FINANCE AND OBTAINING OTHER RESOURCES

In theory, entrepreneurs and small firms concerned with the innovation process face disadvantages with bank finance. This is due to a number of factors:

1. Banks are primarily concerned with short term finance. They will not be prepared to lend seed capital.
2. Banks face increased problems in risk assessment due to increased uncertainty associated with new or high technology (12). In the UK the National Westminster Bank have introduced 'technology managers' whose role is to specialize in the assessment of new technology applications. If a technology manager receives an application it can be referred to consultants for

assessment. However, we have found that the extent of training of such technology managers is only 'two to three days' (13).

3. Entrepreneurs and small firms may not be able to protect their investment through patents or other means. Hence this can increase the difficulties they face in obtaining funding.

4. The tradition in banks that managers are generalists means that they will not have the skills to assess high technology applications.

5. Banks do not place any value on R&D in the balance sheet, because it is an intangible asset.

6. Entrepreneurs with a high technology small firm may be reliant instead on venture capital. However, recent research suggests that there has been a retreat of the venture capital sector in the UK from funding the high technology small firm (14).

7. Government schemes designed to relieve some of these funding problems are relatively small scale and are not easily available or promoted. For example, SMART and SPUR (see Chapter 4) have relatively small budgets and the size of their awards will not cover the financing needs of entrepreneurs that do qualify. By definition, the SMART award scheme rewards entrepreneurs who have been successful in the innovatory process anyway, it can completely ignore those entrepreneurs facing financial problems or who have difficulties getting their technology accepted.

3. ENTREPRENEURS FACE DIFFICULTIES IN PROTECTING INTELLECTUAL PROPERTY RIGHTS (IPR)

The IPR system in the UK and worldwide can operate against the successful protection of IPR by entrepreneurs and small firms, due to the time involved and the legal complexities of the system. Although the legal system offers the entrepreneur concerned with the innovation process a method of enforcement of patent (or other IPR) rights, it is a veritable minefield of regulation. Registration of IPR can be a lengthy and expensive process since the entrepreneur will often have to engage special legal experts.

Main methods of protection of IPR

- Patents system
- Copyright
- Trademarks
- Others (see below).

(a) Patents

A patent is a monopoly right to the exclusive use of an idea or invention within the geographical boundaries specified. In the UK it can last for 20 years. Note that this is the normal period in most countries since it follows the guidelines of the Paris Convention of 1898 where all the leading industrial countries signed the convention and the time period for patents to apply. Given that technological advance is now much more rapid (in every five year period we have doubled our knowledge), there is a strong case for the time period of patents to be reduced. However, agreement on the optimum time period for a patent is much more difficult to achieve since the reward for the entrepreneur needs to be balanced against the need for society to diffuse the technology.

Machines, products, or processes are patentable if they are:

- New
- Inventive
- Capable of industrial application.

Sometimes individuals choose not to patent an invention but just try to protect the idea with a 'know how' or confidentiality agreement.

(b) Copyright
The author of a work is the person who creates it and he/she or his/her employer owns the copyright which will last either 50 years after the author's death or 50 years after it was created.

(c) Trademarks
Trademarks give goodwill or reputation belonging to a firm which attaches to its products or services. The trademark needs to be registered to secure legal protection.

(d) Others
These include 'know-how' which can be protected with a special agreement, design right, and registered designs.

All of these forms of IPR are like any other form of property in that they can be traded, bought or sold. Often firms will come to an agreement to license the production of their new product or service by another firm, perhaps in another country. Royalties are then paid to the entrepreneur or firm that holds the patent or copyright.

One of the problems with the patent system for entrepreneurs and small firms is that the geographical areas that are covered by the patent can be quite limited. For example, until recently a firm would have to take out patents in separate European countries to protect an invention in different European countries. This has become easier with the European Patent Office of the EU, but the extent of legal protection is still limited.

Patents can be difficult to enforce. Copying and imitating products is quite common. Often products do not infringe the patent right if made abroad and imported into the UK. In addition, they may just imitate the product and be marketed as a different product.

The high technology entrepreneur or small firm has the problem that registering for patents is expensive, complicated, takes time, and still does not guarantee protection. It is not surprising, therefore, that the evidence suggests that the take-up of the patent system is low among such entrepreneurs and small firms (15). In Chapter 1 we discussed recent research by the author which indicated that there was a very low take-up of IPR protection cover through insurance from a sample of high technology based entrepreneurs (16). This would seem to indicate that entrepreneurs do not take out patents or other forms of IPR protection because they find such protection too difficult or expensive to obtain.

We have met the concept of moral hazard in Chapter 4. The operation of the patent system also contains a moral hazard problem. In theory, the patent system may be viewed as a race with the winner taking all (17). Moral hazard arises because other entrepreneurs or small firms that have engaged in R&D lose out and potentially gain nothing, since under the patent system there is only one winner, however imperfect that patent protection may be. As we have stated before, it pays an entrepreneur to be first on the market, rather than first to patent. Thus the entrepreneur and small firm may be more concerned with being first rather than acquiring legal protection of their invention or new product.

4. ENTREPRENEURS AND SPECIAL SUPPORTIVE ENVIRONMENTS SUCH AS SCIENCE PARKS AND INCUBATORS

Segal (2) highlighted the supportive network of a cluster of high technology small firms with the study of firms that had developed technological spin-offs from Cambridge University. An extraordinary growth in the number of new high technology small firms developed around Cambridge, using the infrastructure and network of contacts he termed the 'Cambridge Phenomenon'. It is possible to point to other clusters of high technology new firms that have developed spontaneously, the most famous being at Silicon Valley in California.

Science parks have been established, in some cases linked to universities, to create a favourable environment for the development of high technology based entrepreneurs. It is assumed that new technology small firms need the contacts and network of support that may be provided, perhaps relating to the more favourable treatment by financial institutions, use of skilled labour, and support services attracted to the park. There is little direct evidence, so far, however, that science parks provide any more benefits than could occur through the natural networking of such firms as occurs, for example, in the Thames Valley. A study by Warwick SME Centre (18) comparing firms on and off science parks found little difference in performance.

In Germany we have found from our own research that some success has been achieved by targeting assistance at special centres. The Länder are powerful regional bodies that have considerable independence to invest money in their own schemes. Thus in Baden-Württemberg we found that special assistance had been provided for new technology firms through grants and soft loans. The advantage in Germany was the extent of promotion of such schemes by the Chambers of Commerce.

Cambridge provided the first science park in 1973; the second was established at Heriot-Watt in 1979; and by 1989 there were 39 science parks in the UK. Despite the growth in the science park movement during the 1980s, the evidence suggests that the provision of a special environment makes little difference to the networking abilities of the entrepreneur and the high technology small firm. Mitra (19) has shown that there was little evidence of networking between firms on science parks. Entrepreneurs are often dealing with firms some distance away and recent evidence suggests that we have overrated the importance of networking in the past, especially its importance for the innovative entrepreneur. Curran and Blackburn (20) have shown that for service sector firms, local economic networks are not important.

PERFORMANCE OF ENTREPRENEURS CONCERNED WITH INNOVATION

While it is accepted that innovative small firms and entrepreneurs provide added value to the local economy, they appear to perform little differently from other small firms, at least in the UK, e.g., Oakey (21) comments: 'analysis of the growth performance of high technology small firms in the UK during the 1980s . . . has been unimpressive' (p. 2).

As well as overall performance, if we examine at the UK micro-level individual firm performance, there is little evidence of fast growth, despite the evidence from the USA, in areas such as Silicon Valley, where impressive growth has been recorded (5). In some cases this spectacular growth has led to the view that the high technology small firm or the innovative entrepreneur could be a panacea for some of the UK's problems of industrial re-structuring. The classic Segal *et al.* study of the 'Cambridge Phenomenon' mentioned before (2) also seemed to hold out the growth of the small innovative firm in clusters of networking, exploiting technology transfer in specially created environments such as science parks. Yet, as Oakey points out, by the time European Governments were attempting to foster the growth of such firms, the narrow window of opportunity had been closed. The result in the UK is that the high technology small firm entrepreneur has never been able to deliver the hoped for growth even in special environments.

The result, is that the entrepreneur still faces the same if not higher constraints than 10 years ago, resulting for the UK, according to Oakey, in 'a lost decade' (21). This loss of potential for entrepreneurship and innovation has been reflected in the performance of the venture capital industry. In the early 1980s, venture capital supported small innovatory firms. By the end of the 1980s, most of the funds from venture capitalists went into well-established firms as management buy-outs or management buy-ins. As Oakey also comments:

> Now, at the beginning of the 1990s, the UK venture capital industry. . . has virtually abandoned new technology-based firm (NTBF) start-ups as too risky and unrewarding . . . (and) . . . the conditions for innovation and growth in NTBFs are probably bleaker now than was the case in 1980 (p. 5).

This lost opportunity for the UK may have many causes—an over-optimistic assessment of the potential of small innovatory small firms; short-termism on the part of investors; lack of the right support from Government and other bodies; and insufficient infrastructure of risk taking venture capitalists to support high tech small firms or entrepreneurs and innovation, an infrastructure that does seem to exist, for example, in Massachusetts in the USA.

Whatever the reason, innovative entrepreneurs face tremendous barriers to development. If we consider that R&D periods are often long, resources are scarce, equity will be exhausted, and patents are expensive, then we can appreciate that the innovative entrepreneur faces special and acute barriers and problems. An entrepreneur may face ten years developing their product, and even after development there are marketing and promotion problems; there are continued development problems after prototypes have been produced. Despite the occasional special assistance, these problems are often insurmountable.

To consider these special problems in more detail, it is useful to consider how they operate in a case study. A classic example is provided in the next chapter which illustrates, from the perspective of an entrepreneur, some of the problems faced by such entrepreneurs, especially in the UK.

Given the difficulties that have been outlined above that face the entrepreneur concerned with the innovation process we argue that there must be 'innovative' support mechanisms. For the remainder of this chapter we focus on some of the support measures that could be taken or developed to realize and develop some of the (lost) potential from entrepreneurs concerned with the innovation process.

SUPPORTING THE INNOVATIVE ENTREPRENEUR

1. INNOVATIVE FUNDING MECHANISMS

We have identified some of the problems that high technology based entrepreneurs face. It is possible to argue that the funding problems are also faced by low technology applications—any innovatory process requires some R&D and it is this stage of the process that requires support. However, funding is only one aspect of this support, and we will see later that a holistic approach needs to be taken. Philpott (22) has shown from his research that there are information and funding gaps with innovatory entrepreneurs. Clearly, despite the improvements that have been made by some of the clearing banks such as the National Westminster Bank (23), which does have a coherent policy for supporting technology, we cannot expect existing funding to close the funding gap for innovatory entrepreneurs. It requires state support, perhaps a state investment bank that has frequently been called for along the lines of the German state investment bank, KfW.

It is clear that normal commercial banking principles preclude the banks from any heavy investment in high technology at the R&D stage. However, the current lack of such a state policy towards high technology means that an investment bank of this sort is unlikely in the near future. Also, given the Government's desire to promote self-help schemes it would seem that Mutual Guarantee Schemes (MGSs) have far more potential in the UK, especially when one considers that technical advance is often incremental, i.e., a firm will make a small advance on existing technology, perhaps by applying it to a different application. In these circumstances, particularly in the UK, MGSs possess enormous potential not just for high technology based small firms but for all SMEs engaged in innovatory product and process development.

Mutual Guarantee Schemes (MGSs)

MGSs have operated on the mainland of Europe for some time. They originated in France over 100 years ago. Between the two world wars, they were adopted more widely in France and then later in other countries, particularly after 1945. An indication of their importance today is that there are some 736 schemes operating in the EU countries (24) yet there are none in the UK. Of course, MGSs can benefit any type of SME but they are considered here because, given the special nature of the funding problems for innovative SMEs, they remain potentially of most benefit to particular sectors, especially to the funding requirements of innovative small firms.

The principle behind MGSs is relatively simple (as with many of the best schemes). SMEs join a self-help society which provides a fund. This association is used to bargain with a major bank or other financial institution which lends to the society at favourable interest rates. There are savings to the financial institution in reduced administration (and reduced bad debts) and the benefits to the firms are that finance is available at low interest rates, long term. This simple model has a powerful economic argument. Society members are able to increase their bargaining power with the major banks and the banks reduce their transaction costs. There are potential additional benefits to the economy depending on the way that the MGS is administered by the participating firms. Certainly in theory it should be possible to improve business development of at least some of the participating firms through the operation of the MGS. In the UK, for example it may be tied into the operation of a business support organization such as a TEC, LEC, or Business Link.

It must be stressed that MGSs are totally different in concept from state loan guarantee schemes and they do not contain some of the disadvantages of such schemes. They are effectively demand driven; there is no attempt to impose them on unwilling and unsupportive financial institutions. Indeed, financial institutions should welcome them, since it will permit the institution to operate at greater efficiency.

The firms in the MGS mutually guarantee each other through their business assets. No personal guarantees are involved, but the MGS has the advantage (for the lending institution) that if one firm does default the other firms are liable, through their asset base, for the debts. Thus for the banks it is a no loss situation and strengthens the bargaining hand of the MGS.

The National Association of Mutual Guarantee Schemes (NAMGS) claim the following advantages for MGSs (25):

- More appropriate funding methods
- Lower interest rates
- No personal guarantees
- A more secure operating base
- Increased employment prospects
- Better trained management
- Expert management assistance available for small firms
- A marketing tool for TECs, LECs, and Business Links.

In theory there should be no reason why MGSs should not work in the UK. The significance for innovative small firms and entrepreneurs is that both seed and development capital could be raised through the MGS. Funding, as we have argued above, is particularly difficult to raise. Firms often develop products in an incremental way, technical advances are not huge, and major breakthroughs are relatively rare. They are often carried out by existing firms and entrepreneurs, firms that are suited to developing an MGS. The only thing that seems to be lacking is the commitment on the part of the Government to support such schemes. We can only re-echo the opinion of Oakey (26) that a technology policy is long overdue in the UK, a policy that would support schemes such as MGSs.

2. NETWORKING BETWEEN EXTERNAL SUPPORT AGENCIES AND FINANCIAL INSTITUTIONS

Davies (27) has provided an example of an innovative entrepreneur who, having attempted to develop in the UK, decided to move his business to the more supportive environment of South Africa. His business applied new technology to materials to develop them for alternative uses with contractors such as the Ministry of Defence. Despite establishing the business through defence and other contracts, Davies found that he was unable to attract the support in terms of funding and other support required to develop and expand his business. This led to the decision to re-locate the main business in South Africa.

The experience of Davies illustrates the importance of effective networking for the development of support for the innovative entrepreneur. Here we are considering the full network, or infrastructure, of support for the innovative entrepreneur. The more common use of support organizations would refer to enterprise support agencies such as enterprise agencies and TECs in England and enterprise trusts and LECs in Scotland. Yet support for the technology based entrepreneur also includes the banks and other funding agencies, the DTI, local government, Chambers of Commerce, the EU, higher educational institutions, and consultants. As we have argued before in Chapter 7, despite the introduction of Business Links, these support organizations do not work in a co-ordinated manner.

We claim that the much heralded Business Links are in danger of becoming mere referral agencies for clients seeking support (28). After the compulsory 'health check' the client is moved on to another support agency. There is little of the effective networking that takes place in Germany where powerful local Chambers of Commerce (with compulsory membership) have the ability and 'clout' to bring help as it is needed. Our research has shown that this can be particularly beneficial to the innovative entrepreneur and the high technology small firm since the German Chamber of Commerce often has a technical specialist whose expertise lies in co-ordinating support from agencies, banks, universities and state support for the technology based entrepreneur. Claims that the use of Chambers of Commerce for more focused support will not work in the UK (UCE/ISBA seminar (29)), miss the point that it is because the membership is compulsory that they are able to target support and co-ordinate that support. What is more they are able to respond to small firms' needs; support is 'bottom-up' rather than 'top-down'.

Davies (27) comments that the bank considered his business on the same basis as 'that of a corner shop'. He considers that the financial climate in the UK does not favour or encourage the development of innovation within the small firm/entrepreneur. His firm has been located in South Africa because the funding regime does not provide the right type of support. Banks still suffer from short termism and are pre-occupied with collateral (30). Venture capitalists have withdrawn from funding the high technology small firm. State sponsored schemes, such as SPUR, SMART and even the SFLGS, are inadequate to plug the support gaps that exist due to a lack of any effective networking between support agencies and financial institutions in the UK. As Davies (27) comments: 'The aim should be to get small and medium-sized technology-based firms to *thrive*, not just *survive*' (p. 7).

3. THE ROLE OF THE DTI

Broadwith (31) has shown that the DTI recognizes that: 'innovation is critical for sustainable wealth creation' (p. 2). The DTI/CBI study has shown that there are critical success factors that determine whether entrepreneurs are able to exploit technology. The emphasis of the DTI, however, seems to be on regional delivery through the spread of best practice. The Austrian School principle of force of competition is quoted as providing the spur to innovate and develop. Unfortunately, market competition can be haphazard in the selection of best practice. In the face of severe competition, the innovative entrepreneur faces particular competitive disadvantages and we have argued that these disadvantages are serious enough to warrant special support through a coherent technology policy. Identification of best practice and successful role models can be encouraged as through the SMART awards. However, these schemes miss the crucial point that such entrepreneurs are by definition winners anyway. Support should target potential in the UK for the development of entrepreneurs in innovation and there is considerable evidence provided by the DTI itself that we are not achieving that potential.

CONCLUSIONS

This chapter has attempted to synthezise and present some of the issues that surround entrepreneurship and innovation. We have concentrated on the issues that are important for small firm entrepreneurs, and we have attempted to suggest some policy measures that could be taken to encourage the important function of the entrepreneur in terms of innovation. However, it is a salutary fact that the two examples given in this and the next chapter both represent entrepreneurs that had 'given up' the uneven struggle for entrepreneurs concerned with innovation and R&D in the UK. The Government's own White Paper on Science and Technology (4) recognized the untapped potential that still exists from our failure to commercialize inventions and capitalize on British technology. One of the reasons for this failure must be the inhospitable environment faced by the innovative entrepreneur.

To tackle this failure we need a radical change of policy and thinking. No amount of tinkering with the support system will make much difference. Business Links will not make more than a superficial change in the networking abilities and the evidence already is that they add yet another layer to the confusing range of support faced by small firm entrepreneurs. There are some signs of the beginnings of specialized targeted support, yet to make any significant impact, changes are required in all the institutions concerned with the support infrastructure. This infrastructure includes banks, Chambers of Commerce and local authorities. Even universities need to be more entrepreneurial in their outlook. Comparing the UK to an area that is successful, such as Massachusetts in the USA or Baden-Württemberg in Germany, we can see that a radical change in the infrastructure is required, if the UK innovative entrepreneurs are ever to compete on equal terms with their North American and German counterparts. This situation will only change if the Government abandons its *laissez-faire* attitude to innovative SMEs. Policies that could be implemented quickly include:

1. A state-supported MGS for innovative or high technology based small firms and entrepreneurs.
2. A state-funded investment bank to provide long term seed capital and additional support for innovative entrepreneurs.

Learning outcomes

At the end of this chapter the students should be able to:

1. Appreciate and discuss the problems faced by small firm entrepreneurs in the innovation process.
2. Understand the concept of innovation as a process.
3. Recognize that innovation can take many forms and may involve low technology as well as high technology.
4. Discuss the value of creating special environments such as science parks.
5. Understand the concept of MGSs and their potential for the small firm entrepreneur.
6. Appreciate the value of full external networking by the support infrastructure for entrepreneurship and innovation.

Suggested assignments

This chapter should be read in conjunction with the following chapter which involves a full case study.

REFERENCES

1. SCHERER, F. M. and ROSS, D. (1990) *Industrial Market Structure and Economic Performance*, 3rd edn, Houghton Mifflin, Boston.

2. SEGAL, QUINCE *et al.* (1985) *The Cambridge Phenomenon*, Segal Quince Wicksteed.

3. SOLOW, R. M. (1957) 'Technical Change and the Aggregate Production Function', *Review of Economics and Statistics*, vol. 39, pp. 312–90.

4. WHITE PAPER ON SCIENCE AND TECHNOLOGY (1993) *Realising Our Potential: A Strategy for Science, Engineering and Technology*, HMSO, CMND-2250, London.

5. FREEMAN, C. (1982) *The Economics of Industrial Innovation*, Frances Pinter, London.

6. OECD (1980) *The Measurement of Scientific and Technical Activities*, Frascati Manual.

7. BUTCHART, R. L. (1987) 'A New Definition of High Technology Industries', *Economic Trends*, vol. 400, pp. 82–9.

8. SCHUMPETER, J. A. (1942) *Capitalism, Socialism and Democracy*, Harper, New York.

9. GALBRAITH, J. K. (1967) *The New Industrial State*, Hamilton, London.

10. PHILLIPS, A. (1966) 'Patents, Potential Competition and Technical Progress', *American Economic Review*, vol. 56, pp. 301–10.

11. ROBSON, M. and TOWNSEND, J. (1984) *Trends and Characteristics of Significant Innovations and Their Innovators in the UK since 1945*, Science Policy Research Unit, University of Sussex.

12. VYAKARNAM, S. and JACOBS, R. (1991) 'How Do Bank Managers Construe High Technology Entrepreneurs', paper presented to the 14th National Small Firms Policy and Research Conference, Blackpool, November.

13. DEAKINS, D. and PHILPOTT, T. (1994) 'Comparative European Practices in the Finance of New Technology Entrepreneurs: UK, Germany and Holland', in Oakey R. (ed.), *New Technology-Based Firms in the 1990s*, Paul Chapman, London.

14. PRATT, G. (1990) 'Venture Capital in the UK', *Bank of England Quarterly Review*, vol. 30, pp. 78–3.

15. BAIN AND CO REPORT (1990) *Innovation in Britain Today*, Bain and Co.

16. DEAKINS, D. and BENTLEY, P. (1993) *The Small High Technology Firm, Risk Management and Broker Provision of Insurance*, Enterprise Research Centre, University of Central England, Birmingham.

17. KAUFER, E. (1988) *The Economics of the Patent System*, Churchill, Harvard.

18. WESTHEAD P. and COWLING, M. (1994) 'Employment Change in Independent Owner-Managed High Technology Firms in Great Britain', paper presented to the 2nd High Technology Small Firms Conference, Manchester, September.

19. MITRA, R., COOLEY, C., and LAKIN, J. (1993) 'Science Parks and the Growth of Small Firms' , paper presented to the 16th National Small Firms Policy and Research Conference, Nottingham, November.

20. CURRAN, J. and BLACKBURN, R. (1994) *Small Firms and Local Economic Networks: The Death of the Local Economy*, Paul Chapman, London.

21. OAKEY, R. P. (1994) 'New Technology-Based Firms: A Review of Progress', paper presented to the UCE/ISBA seminar, Innovation and Entrepreneurship, Birmingham Centre for Manufacturing, Birmingham, May.

22. PHILPOTT, T. (1994) 'Information Exchange Between the Banker and the High Technology Small Firm', paper presented to the UCE/ISBA seminar, Innovation and Entrepreneurship, Birmingham Centre for Manufacturing, Birmingham, May.

23. IVES, P. (1994) 'The Nat West Bank and Technology Policy', paper presented to the UCE/ISBA seminar, Innovation and Entrepreneurship, Birmingham Centre for Manufacturing, Birmingham, May.

24. AECM (1992) European Mutual Guarantee Association.

25. STURROCK, P. (1994) 'Innovation and Entrepreneurship: Developing Support, The Potential of Mutual Guarantee Schemes', paper presented to the UCE/ISBA seminar, Innovation and Entrepreneurship, Birmingham Centre for Manufacturing, Birmingham, May.

26. OAKEY, R. P. (1991a) 'Government Policy Towards High Technology: Small Firms Beyond the Year 2000', in CURRAN, J. and BLACKBURN, R., *Paths of Enterprise*, Routledge, London.

27. DAVIES, R. (1994) 'Innovation and Entrepreneurship: Developing Support', paper presented to the UCE/ISBA seminar, Innovation and Entrepreneurship, Birmingham Centre for Manufacturing, Birmingham, May.

28. DEAKINS, D. AND RAM, M. (1994) 'Comparative European Policies in Enterprise Support', paper presented to the 17th ISBA National Small Firms Policy and Research Conference, Sheffield, November.

29. UCE/ISBA (1994) Comments of participating delegates at the UCE/ISBA seminar, Innovation and Entrepreneurship, Birmingham Centre for Manufacturing, Birmingham, May.

30. DEAKINS, D. and HUSSAIN, G. (1991) *Risk Assessment by Bank Managers*, Birmingham Polytechnic, Birmingham.

31. BROADWITH, B. (1994) 'Supporting Innovation: DTI Policy', paper presented to the UCE/ISBA seminar, Innovation and Entrepreneurship, Birmingham Centre for Manufacturing, Birmingham, May.

32. SHUTT, J. D. and BRADSHAW, N. (1994) 'The Design and Delivery of a Range of Management Support Services to Support SME Growth through Innovative Product Development and Technology Transfer', paper presented to the 2nd High Technology Small Firms Conference, Manchester, September.

RECOMMENDED READING

OAKEY, R. P. (1984) *High Technology Small Firms: Innovation and Regional Development in Britain and the United States*, Frances Pinter, London.

OAKEY, R. P. (1991a) 'Government Policy Towards High Technology: Small Firms Beyond the Year 2000', in CURRAN, J. and BLACKBURN, R. *Paths of Enterprise*, Routledge, London.

OAKEY, R. P. (1991b) 'High Technology Small Firms: Their Potential for Rapid Industrial Growth', *International Small Business Journal*, vol. 9, no. 4, pp. 30–42.

9 Innovation and the Perspective of the Innovative Entrepreneur: a Case Study

Book author's note and tutors' note: This case study attempts to achieve more than just providing material for the development of a case study. It has been written by the entrepreneur, Joe Wilson, and was first presented to a seminar at the University of Central England in May 1994. It has the advantage of being written from the perspective of the entrepreneur and is not written by an academic who has put his/her own perspective on the case study.

The case study represents some of the problems that entrepreneurs face in innovation. The product had been about ten years in development without receiving financial backing from commercial banks or other potential investors at any stage. Joe had been involved in very large personal and financial commitment in order to get the product to the stage at which it could be applied in the building of new super-ferries. The case study illustrates a number of other points, including relationships between large and small firms. Entrepreneurs and small firms are often at a bargaining disadvantage with large firms when negotiating contracts, a factor which was to prevent Joe from securing a contract with the ferry company. The case study concerns the supply of a special lightweight material that had been developed by Joe over a period of time which could be applied to the building of ferries because of exceptional load bearing qualities combining strength with light weight and fire retarding properties.

There are a number of questions for discussion given at the end of the case study. However, the case study may be used in a number of ways by students. Suggested assignments include the following:

1. Small group discussions of points given at the end of the chapter.
2. Role play assignment. Two groups of students take on the role of the small and large firm. They raise issues that would arise in negotiation and bargaining.
3. Students are required to complete a written report that discusses the main issues in entrepreneurship and innovation. Students are required to develop the policy implications of these issues.

AIMS

This case study aims to:

1. Illustrate some of the problems faced by the small firm entrepreneur in the development of an innovative product using new technology.
2. Identify some of the environmental factors in the UK, affecting innovation and hence economic development.
3. Discuss the factors that affect the research and development process.
4. Demonstrate how the principles of the innovation process can be explained with a real example.

INTRODUCTION

This case study is concerned with the research and development process and getting the problems of converting the Schumpeterian 'invention' stage to 'innovation' (1). Schumpeter considered that the distinguishing characteristic of entrepreneurs was that they were innovators yet he also recognized that they face disadvantages in the R&D process. This case study illustrates some of the pitfalls facing the entrepreneur in the R&D process and in dealing with large firms.

In the context of this case study, it is felt important to mention the development process. It has been recognised in recent literature that new technology based entrepreneurs face development problems which require special funding such as seed capital and involve themselves in considerable risk of failure at some point during the innovation cycle. To illustrate this, Figure 9.1 shows a typical product life cycle.

During the development process, the entrepreneur's equity capital is very likely to be exhausted, thus reducing their ability to raise development capital (2, 3). Marketing, for instance, is in the final phase of the innovation cycle when firms

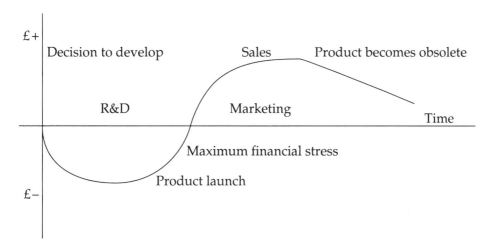

Figure 9.1 Typical product life cycle

have a tendency to underfund or omit this important aspect of the product development. A survey (2) has shown that 46 per cent of UK and US based small firms have no sales staff. Insurance is another aspect of the innovation process that firms tend to underfund or omit from their business plan. At a seminar held at UCE (4), a number of insurance companies stressed the fact that they felt that a small firm with a turnover of less than £250 000 was uneconomic in terms of commission for a broker to be involved. Clearly, when viewed in the context of Figure 9.1, small entrepreneurial firms do not receive adequate insurance advice and support at the time when they need it most, in the R&D phase. The levels of insurance needed for patent protection and product liability are so high that not accounting for them in the business plan could lead to early business failure when the product is launched and the firm is at its highest point of financial stress.

The estimation of the period of lead-time to develop a product is a critical ingredient of the business plan since it determines the point at which external investment can begin to be reduced and profits produce a return on investment. Clearly, an investor will be easier to attract if the lead-time is three years than would be the case if it was eight years. Market sectors, such as biochemistry, with long lead-times in the development of a product have been experiencing a steady decline in popularity as targets for investment (3).

The most common problem encountered in the innovation process is the transfer of product ideas from the laboratory well before the time when they are ready for commercial exploitation. As this literature suggests, after a development period which has lasted just under ten years, the problems that have been encountered in raising development finance have been enormous with the seed capital stage being funded from personal resources, and development capital being almost impossible to find. This has been mainly due to the period of recession that the UK has experienced over the past four years, coupled with the financiers' views of the construction sector risk. The typical response from both banks and equity capital institutions has been that:

> The business plan is excellent, the product is excellent but head office is not interested in investing in this sector at this time. However, come back with a firm order and we will consider the proposition again.

All that is needed to win a major order for an innovative product coming to the market is a letter of offer from a funder stating that, subject to certain conditions, the finance will be made available to be able to manufacture and supply the product. Unlike our European counterparts, the UK financial institutions are only interested in funding a product once a supply contract has been secured. This leaves the innovative small firm in a Catch 22 situation of having to give financial guarantees for their products before they can secure the order. This was the reason why the main contract outlined in this case study went, not to the lowest UK bidder but to a Finnish company with financial guarantees from their Government. All of these factors combine to bring about a position of having a revolutionary, commercially viable product with insufficient funding to further develop and market it.

BACKGROUND

The subject of this case study centres around the battle between the international ferry companies and the Channel Tunnel project to win the favour of the travelling public and, more importantly, the commercial haulage contractors. The concern of the author of this case study was in securing an order from Stena Sealink, one of two major ferry operators who have been making large investments in new, large capacity ferries in anticipation of increased competition and a changed environment once Eurotunnel is operational.

In 1993, Stena AB, a Swedish company, placed an order for two massive high-speed ferries of its new design. The order went to the Finnyards shipyard in Rauma, Finland and the total investment was calculated at approx £130m. The first of the ferries in Stena's Highspeed Sea Service (HSS) is due for delivery in 1995 and will be put into service on a Stena Sealink route operating from the United Kingdom. Stena have the option to charter a second HSS, due to be delivered in 1996 and two further orders to be delivered later this decade.

Stena's HSS is unique for a number of reasons, apart from its size and loading capacity. For the first time ever it will allow a high speed ferry to carry Roll On Roll Off vehicles, trailers, and coaches as well as passengers and private cars. Being the biggest high-speed ferry in the world, the HSS will cruise at 40 knots, twice the speed of a traditional ferry. It will carry 1500 passengers and 375 cars or 50 trucks and 100 private cars.

THE PROBLEM AND SCENARIO

By far the biggest technical innovation and development was in the design and construction of the aluminium hull. The ship tank model had been tested in the facilities of the National Experimental Shipbuilding Tank in Gothenburg and it was determined that the ability of the ferry to perform commercially was critically affected by the weight of the vessel. The low weight obtained was attributable to the new aluminium hull design which was patented by Stena. However, the choice of the lightweight aluminium metal for the hull led to further technical considerations regarding its safety and performance in fire, especially in view of the number of vehicles being carried daily and the number of passengers whose lives could be affected by the effects of an on-board fire.

These fears, accelerated by recent cross-channel ferry disasters (Zeebrugge and Roscoff), have also led to new marine legislation being drafted by SOLAS, the International Organisation for Standardization. Under this new legislation, any materials used in the construction of high-speed ferries must exhibit high fire-retardant properties, low smoke emissions, low toxic fume emissions, and be able to withstand the marine environment. The choice of aluminium for the hull presented a problem in this respect, with its low temperature melting point and poor performance in fire. Stena needed an innovative technical solution for protecting the aluminium hull from combustion and subsequent toxic emissions while maintaining the weight advantage afforded by the lightweight hull construction. As there were no suitable materials commercially available, they sought a firm in the R&D process capable of meeting the technical specifications necessary for the new craft.

THE SOLUTION

Faced with the problem of protecting the aluminium hull, essential for its weight, Stena approached Brunner Mond Ltd in the United Kingdom who were marketing under exclusive licence, a British invention called CEEPREE which claimed exciting and new fire retardant properties. Brunner Mond Ltd referred Stena to the inventor of CEEPREE, Geoffrey Crompton of Crompton Garland Ltd, for a technical solution to their problems. Stena liked what they heard; Crompton Garland Ltd had technology which was far reaching in the fire-safe arena. Crompton Garland Ltd, however was a very small company with limited resources albeit with much larger international sized companies licensed to use their products.

In early 1993, both the technical director and naval architect responsible for the hull design wrote to Crompton Garland Ltd encouraging their development of a fire-safe lining for the hulls of marine vessels outlining in no uncertain terms the potential market including their own ferry building programme.

At this point Crompton Garland Ltd was faced with a commercial dilemma: the development could either be done for Stena on a technical consultancy basis, as no product existed at the time which could match the exacting technical specification, or do the work at risk with the carrot of a large supply contract at the end of the development. Either route chosen would be financially rewarding but a third scenario which the company did not consider was that they would be participating in a purely academic exercise with financial ruin a distinct possibility.

Faced with the situation and Stena's reluctance to advance any development fees, Crompton Garland Ltd decided to take the commercial risk route, confident in their belief that they could uniquely meet the technical brief presented to them by the design team for the vessel.

Eco-Wall Ltd became engaged in providing further development of an existing technical product in an applied way that would meet the demands of Stena and would provide financial and marketing skills in the development of this new product.

THE INNOVATIVE PRODUCT

With Eco-Wall Ltd, Crompton Garland Ltd undertook 12 months of design and testing costing in the region of £75 000 in time, materials, and expenses. A finely tested panelling system that surpassed the specifications, made even tighter by Stena as time went on, was developed and produced as a prototype. Eco-Wall Ltd contracted to supply the shipyard at a price they confirmed was highly competitive. Indeed, at a pre-contract meeting in Finland the company were asked to increase their square metre price to cover for eventualities.

The new product surpassed all tests that were required. For example, a fire test, required at very short notice, known as the cone calorimeter test, carried out by Warrington Fire Research, showed the product to perform 95 per cent better than the specification from the shipyard. In the specification provided by the shipyard to the company it was stated that:

> Due to the essential requirement for the lightweight materials for this type of vessel, the insulation and lining of the hull could be considered to be carried out by types of panels of composite materials, but the weight of the solution will be the main parameter when selecting the solution.

At meetings with the company and Stena's naval architect and the head of interior design for the shipyard in the third quarter of 1993, it was stressed by both the client and contractor and minuted that the innovative solution being offered would not reflect on the choice of supplier for the contract. Both Stena and Finnyards stated that the problem that they were trying to resolve needed a technically innovative solution and that Stena, being innovators themselves, were very keen to promote such solutions.

THE OUTCOME

After written confirmation to both the client and the shipyard that the product could be delivered 16 per cent below the specified weight, 95 per cent better than the toxicity and contribution to fire requirements, and at a further reduced price, the company were informed that the contract had been awarded to a company familiar to the shipyard who had used them before but at a specification that had not been proven by testing.

The shipyard asked whether the company would be interested in providing technical solutions in small crucial areas of the vessel which their selected sub-contractor was not able to meet. Eco-Wall Ltd successfully overcame technical system problems in the latter 12 month development period, providing a commercial solution, and yet were defeated by a political decision.

Four months after being informed that the supply contract had been awarded to a local firm, Eco-Wall Ltd was told by Stena that the local firm had not met their technical specifications and that they had informed the shipyard that a reduction in specification was not acceptable. Subsequently negotiations have reopened with the shipyard for the supply of the contract. The author is assured that the publication of this case study had no bearing on the decision by Stena to insist on the local company meeting the technical specification laid down at the commencement of the bidding for the contract.

POSTSCRIPT

Book author's note: At the time of writing, Stena are still negotiating with the current directors of Eco-Wall Ltd to provide a solution that has not been solved by local suppliers. The requirements of providing a lightweight yet fire-retardant material are still the driving force behind these continuing negotiations. This illustrates how political decisions to use local suppliers will not necessarily work in areas where product development is led by technological advances and the feasibility of technical solutions.

Learning outcomes

At the end of this case study chapter you should be able to:

1. Describe the difficulties faced by entrepreneurs when developing new and newly applied technology to new developments in products.
2. Discuss the difficulties of supplying such developments overseas for UK entrepreneurs concerned with innovation.
3. Describe the resource requirements in the development phase of the innovation process.
4. Explain why small firm entrepreneurs are at a disadvantage in the innovation process.
5. Describe the value of networking between entrepreneurs/small firms who are engaged in technical development and the innovation process.
6. Discuss ways that state involvement can relieve some of the constraints faced by such entrepreneurs and small firms.
7. Describe how support mechanisms might take account of some of the constraints and problems faced by entrepreneurs in the innovation process.

Suggested assignments

1. Students prepare notes for discussion in groups on the following points:
   (a) Can innovative entrepreneurs be successful with new technology in the UK?
   (b) The UK is a world leader in technical innovation but continues to suffer from low investment and low technology applications. We need to break into the virtuous circle of high investment and high technology.
   (c) Small new technology based firms also have problems with the patent system designed to protect their ideas due to the high cost of litigation.
   (d) The initial contract for the construction of the two ferries went to a Finnish company despite a lower price being tendered by a British company shortlisted by Stena.
   (e) The Finnish Government underwrote the construction costs of the project with the client paying in turn-key fashion when the ferries are delivered.

(f) This project would have secured employment for the ailing British shipyards given some similar financial support.

(g) Technical innovation in the UK is both a minefield and a recipe for financial disaster for individuals and firms involved with it.

2. A small group of students are required to prepare a presentation on the major constraints facing innovative entrepreneurs and discuss potential solutions to barriers to technical development.

3. Students are required to research local support for new product development or innovation including any specialized support such as science and technology parks. A report is required indicating the strengths and weaknesses of such support.

REFERENCES

1. SCHUMPETER, J. A. (1942) *Capitalism, Socialism and Democracy*, New York, Harper.

2. OAKEY, R. P. (1984) *High Technology Small Firms*, London, Frances Pinter.

3. OAKEY, R. P. (1991) 'Government Policy towards High Technology: Small Firms beyond the Year 2000', in CURRAN J. and BLACKBURN R., *Paths of Enterprise*, London, Routledge.

4. DEAKINS, D. and BENTLEY, P. (1993) *The High Technology Small Firm, Risk Management and Broker Provision of Insurance*, University of Central England, Birmingham.

10 *Entrepreneurial and Growth Firms: Management Issues*

INTRODUCTION

There is a basic distinction between the person or entrepreneur who wishes to go into self-employment to pursue their own interests (and perhaps enters self-employment because there is no or little alternative) and the person or entrepreneur that enters small business ownership because they have desires to develop their businesses, to achieve growth, expand employment, and develop into a medium-sized or a large firm. The former type of small business owner has very different managerial objectives from the latter type. Objectives of the first type will be concerned with survival and maintenance of lifestyle, whereas objectives of the second type will be concerned with growth and expansion with the entrepreneur eventually owning several companies.

Many people who have been made redundant due to 'downsizing' of traditional manufacturing firms in the 1980s have entered self-employment as small business owners. They are normally sole traders, employ few or no people, and their major objectives are likely to be concerned with survival and maintaining sufficient income to ensure that the business provides them and their family with sufficient income. These small businesses, which are the overwhelming majority of small firms in the UK, are sometimes called 'lifestyle' businesses. In other words the owner-manager is only concerned with maintaining a lifestyle that he or she may have been accustomed to in a previous form of employment. A minority of small firms may be called 'entrepreneurial firms', their owners will be concerned mainly with the managerial objective of achieving growth, and will often go on to own more than one firm.

There has been much speculation about whether such 'entrepreneurial firms' can be identified *ex ante*, i.e., before they achieve growth rather than *ex post*, i.e., after they have achieved growth. This presents a problem for researchers and policy makers and for investors such as venture capitalists who will want to identify high growth and high performing firms. It is a classical adverse selection problem created by uncertainty and limited (if not asymmetric) information. Despite the inherent built-in difficulties of identifying such growth firms, this has not stopped policy makers from establishing support agencies such as the Business Links that have been established to support existing small- and medium-sized firms which have the potential for growth as we have described before in Chapter 7. This inherent problem has also not stopped researchers from attempting to identify the characteristics and features of such growth firms and their entrepreneurs.

There is no agreement on exactly what measure to use to distinguish a high performing firm, e.g., should performance be measured on the basis of employment created, or by some other criterion, such as profits, turnover, or financial assets? Attention has, nonetheless, focused on identifying growth firms rather than identifying constraints which may block the growth potential of many entrepreneurs and small firms. The inherent problem for policy makers, however, is that environments that favour the expansion of some firms may not remain stable.There are only certain windows of marketing opportunity that can lead to success of entrepreneurs and to growth firms. The right timing has proved to be crucial in many circumstances, even if other factors, which can be equally crucial, might be in place. We saw with the Eco-Wall Ltd case that the right product may not lead to growth and success if the timing is wrong and the environment has not been supportive. Even very successful entrepreneurs such as Bill Gates (Microsoft) may not be able to re-create their success. There may, however, be a unique combination of circumstances and perhaps the right combination of people that produce the high growth firm.

We have seen before, in Chapter 1, that over 97 per cent of all firms employ less than 20 people and that the majority of the growth in the numbers of small firms in the 1980s came in the micro-firms that employ less than 10 people. Indeed there was a sharp distinction between firms that employ less than 10 people, who have had a large increase in numbers, and those that employ 10-50 whose numbers have remained largely stable in the UK in the 1980s. There are obviously human resource management and control issues for entrepreneurs that wish to grow beyond employing 10 people. These issues involve constraints that are not easy to overcome. The small number of potential growth firms has been pointed out by Storey (1). As we have discussed before in Chapter 2, Storey considers that if we take a sample of 100 new firms, only three or four will be responsible for the majority of any growth in employment creation over a period of time.

There is, of course, a difference between those small firms and entrepreneurs that achieve growth and those that may wish to grow but face constraints which may exist in the form of access to finance or other resources, or (in the case of ethnic minority firms) barriers to achieving breakthroughs into wider markets. For example, taking evidence on face value that firms have remained small and therefore do not wish to grow can be misleading. At the time of writing, our research with African-Caribbean entrepreneurs is demonstrating that over 50 per cent of entrepreneurs wished to grow but faced barriers in access to finance and insurance.They were often located in ethnic market niches in the inner city, and so faced barriers in making inroads into white mainstream markets. Thus identifying growth firms may not be as valuable as recognizing and lifting barriers which may account for the limited potential of many small firms.

In addition, making assumptions that the only high performing entrepreneurs and small firms are those that achieve high growth rates can also be misleading. For example, again our research with African-Caribbean entrepreneurs is showing that strategies adopted for survival and coping with what is often an inhospitable and marginal socio-economic environment can be as successful and efficient, in these terms, and as high performing as a growth firm in a much more conducive environment.

It is the *potential* 3-4% of all new small firms that may be high growth performing firms that support agencies, such as the Business Links, wish to identify and provide special assistance for. We stress the word 'potential', because there is a belief that many entrepreneurs and small firms may have the potential for growth. It is these potential growth firms rather than the real growth or fast track firms that the agency should wish to identify so that the firm can be assisted to overcome the barriers to growth, such as the availability of long term finance or appropriately skilled staff and managers. The contention of Storey, that only a small percentage of new firms will be responsible for the major gains in employment, contrasts with that of Reid (2) who has analysed a database of 73 small Scottish firms helped by Scottish enterprise trusts between 1985 and 1988 and considers that:

> One of the most notable aspects of the SBEs (small business enterprises) is that they are typically subject to rapid growth, whether one looks at this in terms of growth sales, assets, or employment . . . with full time employment almost doubling (p. 187).

After a multivariate econometric analysis and after correcting for simultaneity effects, Reid concludes that there is evidence of vigorous growth of small firms after financial inception with a significant proportion of 'super growth' firms. These contrasting views can be reconciled if one considers that Reid is dealing with a database that involves relatively young start-up small firms (the average age of Reid's firm was 3.5 years). However, it also illustrates the danger of believing that only a very small handful of entrepreneurs or small firms are capable of growth which is a commonly expressed view.

The underlying logic behind such principles of supporting existing firms, that have the potential for growth, cannot be disputed. If assistance can be targeted at growth firms, then this will make much more difference to economic performance than the equivalent support made available to all small firms as blanket coverage. However, the problem lies in identifying such firms so that support can be targeted. We have also seen before, in Chapter 7, that although business links have been established to target growth firms, the director of one business link admitted that he did not have any clear criteria for identifying growth firms beyond a belief that they would be self-selecting (that is they would come forward of their own accord).

IDENTIFYING GROWTH FIRMS

Despite the problems that have been discussed above, a number of writers have attempted to identify characteristics of growth firms. These characteristics tend to be associated with the management of the firm. Rather than the particular personality characteristics of the entrepreneur, it is management skills that are crucial to achieve growth in the firm. Unless the entrepreneur is able to delegate and to motivate staff, then the firm will not successfully grow. The Advisory Council on Science and Technology (ACOST) Report of 1990 (3) on barriers to growth in small firms, identified management skills as one crucial factor and noted that a different set of management skills in small firms (compared to large firms) was necessary for entrepreneurs to succeed. In other words, a manager with a successful track record in a large firm, did not guarantee success if the manager attempted to transfer skills and establish his/her own business. A manager in a large firm, is likely to have a set of specialized skills and knowledge that may not easily transfer to the context of a small firm. The manager in a large firm, in addition, will have had access to resources and other specializations that are unlikely to be available in a new small firm such as computing knowledge and skills.

Successful entrepreneurs and high growth firms often start from an experienced manager that has pursued a successful career with a large firm or other forms of employment. The case of Peters and Co., discussed in Chapter 5, could be regarded as a classic example of a start-up (high growth) small firm, where the three entrepreneurs concerned had all pursued different careers with different organizations, two of whom had successful careers with a large private sector organization. However, once an experienced manager leaves, he/she will have to employ a range of skills that will test their resourcefulness:

1. Strong negotiating and selling skills.
2. The ability to sell their business idea to potential funders.
3. The ability to manage the accounts of the firm, deal with buyers, deal with tax forms, register for VAT, etc.

All of these duties require skills and advice that they may not have needed before. In addition to these management skills, the firm will need the right product/service at the right time and perhaps be located in the right area. It is not surprising, when considering all of these factors, that Storey is able to observe that only 3–4 per cent of all new firms will be the major creators of employment; the high growth firms.

Although there has been considerable research effort to identify growth firms, as Storey (4) points out much of this research has been based on univariate analysis. Studies have concentrated on examining the impact of individual variables on the growth of small firms, when in practice there will be many factors that will interact and be responsible for growth. In fact it is doubtful whether it is possible to isolate individual factors. However, we discuss below some of them that are likely to impact on the growth potential of any firm. We are not saying that these will be crucial or even necessary for growth, but they are likely to be sufficient factors behind growth firms.

1. CHARACTERISTICS OF THE ENTREPRENEUR

Despite the difficulties of identifying personal characteristics of the entrepreneur and the criticisms of the 'characteristics approach' (see Chapter 1), there will only be certain individuals that have the management skills and resourcefulness that have been discussed above. Barkham *et al.* (5) have claimed that the age of the entrepreneur is important—in fact the younger the entrepreneur the more likely the entrepreneur is to start a growth firm. They also note that the founder of a growth firm is more likely to be a member of a professional association and is ambitious. Measurement of entrepreneuruial characteristics is fraught with difficulty and is often confused with management abilities. For example, Barkham *et al.* consider that being part of a management team is an entrepreneurial characteristic but more accurately this factor reflects the need to have a range of management skills for the firm to develop its potential as a growth firm.

2. MANAGERIAL SKILLS

We have mentioned that firms founded by teams of entrepreneurs are more likely to grow than firms founded by a single entrepreneur. A team start-up will not only have a higher level of capitalization but, as in the Peters and Co. case study, if the entrepreneurs can bring complementary skills then the individual entrepreneurs will not be over-stretched by the demands of launching and running a small business. It is important that the management team bring different skills to the business and that duplication is avoided.

One managerial skill which will be important, yet is difficult to measure is the ability to delegate. For many entrepreneurs, their business is often 'their baby' and they are reluctant to delegate responsibility for decision-making to members of their staff and other managers. From the author's observations associated with the research programme in the West Midlands, the problem of delegation and loss of control cropped up with entrepreneurs who had the potential for growth yet their own reluctance to delegate was a significant constraint in preventing further expansion. This ability to delegate is important and contributes to the importance of forming a management team that can share decision making, yet it is not a factor that will be identified by many research surveys.

In addition for any growth firm, human resource management skills are going to be important. Again these are skills that cannot be measured objectively. Growth firms will involve entrepreneurs that have the ability to motivate and stimulate their staff to achieve high performance. This will be particularly important as the firm grows and the entrepreneur is forced to delegate and rely on staff to ensure, for example, growth in sales and growth in production while maintaining quality.

Training can be important to unlock the potential of growth, yet recent research by Barclays (6) showed that nearly 80 per cent of businesses surveyed do not undertake any form of management training in the UK. It is hardly surprising that there are so few growth firms. They comment that:

> . . . the research reveals that some of the key hurdles to growth for small businesses could be overcome (at least partly) by taking appropriate training and acting upon advice (p. 23).

There has been some debate, in the literature, about the nature of human relations in small firms. The Bolton Report in 1971 (7) claimed that small firms have advantages that produce harmony in industrial relations. Entrepreneurs when founding firms have advantages in having loyal employees and can ensure that industrial relations are harmonious. If a firm achieves growth, the implication is that it will be difficult to maintain harmonious human relations. More recently this view has been challenged by Rainnie (8) who shows that relationships are more complicated and may involve exploitation of the workforce through 'sweated labour' with autocratic relationships between the workforce and the entrepreneur. This particularly applies in certain industrial sectors where Rainnie claims competitive conditions influence the state of relationships between the owner-manager or the entrepreneur and the workforce, such as the clothing industry where workers can be exploited in 'sweated labour' conditions. Ram (9) has also shown that in the clothing industry, relationships can be complicated and in family controlled firms can lead to 'negotiated paternalism' where the workforce negotiates the conditions and responsibilities that form part of their working conditions. Ram shows that the identification of conditions that have been responsible for growth in the family owned clothing small firms is complicated and depends on factors such as family relationships, the ability to maintain a skilled labour force, and negotiation skills. All of these factors are subjective and, hence, difficult to identify yet are important factors in successful small firm growth in the clothing industry. In fact for many small clothing firms, as Ram points out, a successful managerial strategy is one that ensures survival in a highly competitive environment. A firm that can survive and adapt to changing market conditions can be just as successful as a firm in a different industrial sector that is able to achieve growth.

Curran *et al.* (10) in a study of 81 owner-managers and entrepreneurs and their employees in the service sector found that employment relations were 'generally good', with 80 per cent of the entrepreneurs' perceptions good or excellent and higher proportions among their employees, but with little trade union representation in the workforce.

The importance of human resource management skills has been underplayed, since they are difficult to identify. Additional skills may be easier to identify, such as ability in marketing or in finance. For example, whether a firm undertakes market research is an objective variable that can be measured. Barkham *et al.* (5) have identified the ability to undertake market research as an important factor determining growth. However, there are also likely to be subjective factors that will determine the success of the entrepreneur.

In the following chapters we stress the importance of careful research and planning and the adoption of an appropriate competitive strategy for the success of the entrepreneur. In the last chapter, following Porter (11), we mention the importance of identifying the competition and carrying out some competitive analysis before adopting a competitive strategy that is appropriate to the competitive environment facing the firm. These skills are associated with strategic management. Strategy is often only discussed in regard to large firms, yet planning and strategy can be just as important to small firms and their growth potential.

3. EXPORTING

Storey (1), among others, has indicated that exporting firms are more likely to be associated with growth. We can hypothesize that the ability of the entrepreneur to seek new markets abroad will be important for securing continued growth, particularly if the firm is concerned with manufacturing. There are obviously some limits to local markets and most indications are that most firms that do achieve growth do so through markets outside their local areas and abroad (12).

Again a different set of management skills are needed, although there is considerable assistance now for firms to break into export markets, either from support agencies or direct government assistance. Even with willingness to export, resources can be a problem and we have found that additional resources and insurance requirements can prevent a potential growth entrepreneur from exporting. For example, there may be specialized insurance requirements for exporting to the USA due to the greater cost of litigation. These finance and insurance barriers can be significant in preventing exporting and hence the growth of a firm.

4. SECTOR

The industrial sector can affect the likelihood of growth. Of course, firms across a range of different sectors will still achieve growth but, not surprisingly, a number of studies have suggested that high technology small firms and entrepreneurs perform better and have better rates of growth than other small firms (13, 14). However, as we have discussed before in Chapter 8, a high technology entrepreneur may face greater barriers to growth. A high technology entrepreneur will have different funding requirements due to the sunk costs involved in R&D and additional associated costs will be higher, such as insurance.

5. ENTERPRISE SUPPORT

We have suggested in Chapter 7 that the impact of support for entrepreneurs and small firms can be variable and that the overall effectiveness of such support can be questioned. Yet there is evidence that is emerging in the UK that the level of support may make a significant difference on a regional basis. For example, Hart *et al.* (15) compare manufacturing firms in Northern Ireland to the Republic of Ireland and Leicestershire during 1986 to 1990. They have found that the Northern Ireland firms grew much faster than their counterparts in either Leicestershire or the Republic, leading them to conclude that one of the factors that may account for this difference in performance is the higher level of assistance and support in Northern Ireland.

Until quite recently there has been a sceptical view of the difference that enterprise support may make, with a belief in some quarters that successful entrepreneurs will be successful anyway whether enterprise support exists or not. This has been combined with a generally accepted view that there was a low level of awareness of assistance by entrepreneurs and small firms. However, this view is probably now changing. Greater levels of awareness, combined with qualification requirements for funding in agencies (attendance on training courses to qualify for funding) mean that it is more likely that successful and growth entrepreneurs will have come into contact with enterprise support at some point.

6. PROFITABILITY AND RE-INVESTMENT

It may seem obvious, but unless a small entrepreneurial firm is relatively profitable, then there will be insufficient funds available to re-invest and to finance growth whatever the objectives of the entrepreneur and whatever the opportunities that are available to the firm. By 'relatively profitable' we mean that the firm is able to meet commitments and have a significant surplus after withdrawals and payment of creditors. If the entrepreneur withdraws profits rather than re-invests them in the business, this will obviously limit the potential for growth since long term finance has often been identified as one of the most important barriers to growth in small and entrepreneurial firms (3, 16, 17).

7. AGE OF THE FIRM AND LIFE CYCLES

A number of studies have suggested that the age of the firm is a significant determining factor in growth rates with relatively younger firms achieving higher growth rates than older firms. For example, Reid (2) concludes from his sample that there is:

> . . . strong confirmation of a life cycle effect for SBEs (small business enterprises): younger SBEs grow faster than older SBEs; smaller SBEs grow faster than larger SBEs (p. 206).

The Barkham *et al.* (5) study also shows that the smaller the firm the greater the subsequent growth rate.

The hypothesis that the growth rate of a firm is related to the age and life cycle of the firm is based upon the view that all new firms will go through distinct stages of growth, of which the most rapid growth rate will be shortly after formation. This view has been best expressed by Churchill and Lewis (18) in their model of the five stages of small firm growth which is analogous to the life cycle model of products. As developed by Churchill and Lewis the five stage model is

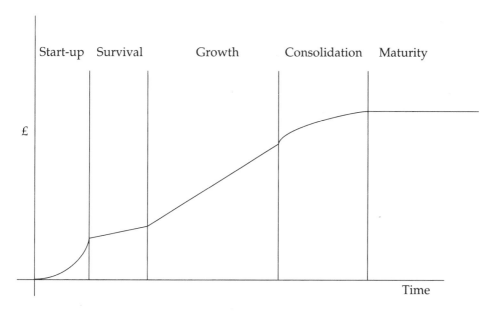

Figure 10.1   Life cycle model of small firm growth

best expressed in a diagram which is shown in Figure 10.1. The five stages may be given different names but they include the following.

(i) Start-up/inception
During start-up the firm will be constrained by liquidity and other resources, markets are limited, and the firm may be involved in small niche markets with limited numbers of customers. Management style is individual and entrepreneurial.

(ii) Survival
As the firm develops, it achieves a situation of survival. Growth begins to develop but the main objective may be survival at this stage.

(iii) Growth/success
In the growth stage the firm reacts quickly to opportunities and achieves its maximum rate of growth by quickly responding to new oportunities.

(iv) Consolidation/take-off
As growth slows down, the firm consolidates its position. The firm may not be as entrepreneurial. Risks taken may be fewer and the firm is slower to respond to market opportunities.

(v) Maturity

As opportunities decline for the firm, growth becomes negative, the firm sheds labour and to complete the cycle the firm may eventually die.

The limitations of growth models have been discussed and criticized by a number of different writers (1, 19), although no acceptable alternative explanation of small firm and entrepreneurial growth has been developed. Growth is probably more complicated than that suggested by a simple life cycle approach. It is probably more incremental than that suggested by smooth curves, with growth (if it does occur) coming in disconnected jumps and surges. In addition, firms may enter growth at different times, then enter decline and re-surge later, more in keeping with business and trade cycles. North and Smallbone (20) have shown that growth can be just as likely in well established manufacturing SMEs as in new and recent firms. This leads to the hypothesis that growth depends at least as much on the economic trade cycle and environment than on the inherent characteristics of the firm such as age or characteristics of the entrepreneur. As Storey (1) points out growth is rarely incremental and 'the models describe rather than predict' (p. 122).

8. ECONOMIC ENVIRONMENT

The general state of the economic environment will affect the ability of firms to achieve growth. Differences in regional economies also seem to affect the ability and potential for firms to achieve growth. In a study of regional differences in high technology firms in the UK, Keeble (21) concludes that there is a North-South divide in the performance of high technology small firms and entrepreneurs with firms in the growth 'corridors' of the South East much more likely to achieve growth than their equivalents in the North, the West and Scotland. Barkham *et al.* (5) in their study conclude that: . . . 'whatever the characteristics of the entrepreneur . . . a strong influence on the performance of the firm is the growth of the market'.

9. ABILITY TO NETWORK

It has been suggested that the ability to network is a significant factor in small firms growth especially that of the high technology small firm (22). In general, however, the importance of networking for small firm growth rates has probably been overrated. In a careful analysis of their service sector firms, Curran and Blackburn (12) argue that (local) networking is relatively unimportant to the success of service sector firms.

10. THE LEGAL AND REGULATORY ENVIRONMENT

It has been claimed that entrepreneurs need freedom from regulation in order to achieve potential growth. The success of entrepreneurial and small firms in the

1980s may have been encouraged by reductions in direct taxation to levels that are equivalent to those paid by other (larger) firms. However, it is more likely that similar changes would have taken place with different taxation levels and a different regulatory environment. There is actually no evidence to support the view that taxation levels have a direct effect on effort or willingness to enter entrepreneurship or self-employment. It is sometimes argued that high taxation levels may remove incentives for entrepreneurs to achieve growth and increased profits.

Theoretically, the effect of taxation on effort can be shown to be ambiguous. Without going into detail, it is possible to use economic theory either to support or not support arguments for reduced taxation. In principle, if direct taxation is reduced (either on income or profits), the entrepreneur may decide to take the increased real income in the form of increased leisure time, rather than say work harder to increase profits which are now taxed at a lower rate. The effect will depend on the value placed on leisure time by the individual entrepreneur; if leisure is highly valued then this will be substituted for income as taxation rates are cut. Empirical evidence on the effect of direct tax changes is conflicting, with some evidence (particularly in the USA) that suggests that changes in direct taxation rates can have positive effects. However, recent work involving research on the self-employed by Rees and Shah (23) in the UK, suggests that changes in taxation have negative effects on the work effort of the self-employed. Rees and Shah found that cuts in direct taxation have resulted in the self-employed taking more leisure time and working less hours.

Generally changes in regulation, unless they are major changes, will have only marginal effects on the potential of entrepreneurs and small firms to achieve growth. The acceptance of European Union regulations, which has often been a subject of complaint by small firm lobby groups, including recent concern over giving part time workers the same rates as full time workers, needs to be balanced against the opportunity offered by the free European market of the Union which vastly outweighs any trade-off on increased legal and social regulations. As stated above the size of potential markets is a significant factor that affects the potential of entrepreneurs to achieve growth.

CONCLUSIONS

Growth in small firms is a complex process. It is not a linear continuous process, nor does it depend upon a limited number of factors. Growth occurs from a complex interplay of factors that will include variations in all the market and managerial elements that have been discussed in this chapter. Barriers to small firms' growth have been examined in two official reports: the ACARD (16) (which later became ACOST) and ACOST (3) reports on barriers to small firms' growth. While both of these reports recognized the importance of the availability of financial and other resources, they stressed the importance of having managers and management skills that can adapt to and cope with change, the ability to develop staff, the ability to exploit new opportunities, the ability to cope with increased information, and the ability and flexibility to cope with changing environments in which the firm operates. Barber *et al. (17)* also point to the importance of management techniques and skills in achieving growth:

> Some of the most difficult problems facing the growing firm will relate to its management needs. The monitoring, co-ordination, and control of the activities in a growing firm will require the utilisation of increasing amounts of information, placing an increasing burden on management (p. 17).

The implications are clear for support agencies. Interventions at significant times in entrepreneurial and small firm developments need to be geared to improving the management skills of entrepreneurs so that they can exploit opportunities and cope with the increased pressures on resources that growth brings.

We still know very little of how entrepreneurs are able to react and the process of change involved in growth. This paucity of knowledge and lack of understanding is a reflection of the focus of previous research, which has been quantitative, attempting to identify factors that influence growth. Since growth is a complex process, involving the application of subjective management skills and a learning process for the entrepreneur, we cannot begin to understand this process without further information obtained from qualitative research methods. There is a need for longitudinal and preferably ethnographic research that tracks entrepreneurs, firms, and their growth patterns over a number of years. For example, we do not know the extent to which entrepreneurs are able to learn from their experience, how they adapt to changes, and what strategies are adopted to achieve growth.

In addition, many interventions by support agencies are not designed to encourage entrepreneurs to learn from their experiences to cope with problems that will enable them to unlock potential and to achieve growth. Support agencies themselves are often constrained by having to achieve basic quantitative indicators such as the number of entrepreneurs that enroll for a particular scheme. Evaluation of these schemes in turn is based on survival rates, not on the value of the scheme for the entrepreneurs in terms of achieving growth and increased performance. This can only be measured by longitudinal research that tracks the performance of such firms and entrepreneurs to examine the effectiveness of support. Support often consists of task-orientated help. Basic courses are often concerned with skills such as book keeping, taxation, or debt collection. While the value of these courses for new entrepreneurs cannot be disputed, there is need, as we have suggested above, for the continuation of support and for this to concentrate on the processes of management, including human resource management, rather than basic business and financial skills.

The very small number of entrepreneurs that achieve growth or high performance reflect the barriers that new small firm entrepreneurs face, rather than willingness or even ability to grow. Our research with African-Caribbean entrepreneurs has illustrated the importance of constraints that such entrepreneurs face located in the inner city and ethnic niches and that there is often a desire for growth. Survival and coping with problems in such environments is often as successful as achieving growth in a more favourable environment.

We have spent some time in this chapter on the importance of human resource management skills and employment relations in the small firm, because they are often the key factors for the entrepreneurial firm to achieve growth. The difference between those firms that can grow and adapt to conditions and those that do not must lie in the management skills of the entrepreneur. Too often, the importance of these management skills are ignored through concentration on marketing or the personal characteristics of the entrepreneur.

In addition, an entrepreneur who wishes to achieve growth will need to adopt business planning methods and analyse competition and the market before deciding on the best strategy to exploit an opportunity and achieve growth. We turn to these business planning methods in the final two chapters. It is known that many entrepreneurs are concerned with survival and short term planning horizons, operating on day to day decisions. If growth is to be achieved, it is necessary to examine the direction and market position of the firm. It is not surprising that there are only a few entrepreneurs that can achieve significant growth. For some it is difficult to delegate managerial decision making and undertake research into market opportunities and their competitors. However, unless entrepreneurs stumble on opportunities through good luck, it will be necessary to consider market analysis techniques and business planning methods that can plot a growth course for a business and optimum strategies over long term planning horizons of several years. To undertake such strategic planning, whether a new or existing entrepreneur, it is necessary to undertake careful and appropriate research using a variety of different techniques that will underpin strategic planning through a business plan. We examine such research methods in the next chapter and then in the final chapter the purpose and value of business plans.

Learning outcomes

At the end of this chapter you should be able to:

1. Identify and describe some of the important factors that affect growth in small firms.
2. Describe some of the barriers that will face entrepreneurs who have the desire to grow.
3. Explain how entrepreneurs might be able to overcome some of the barriers to small firm growth.
4. Describe the importance of understanding the growth process for support agencies.
5. Understand the importance of human resource management and good employment relations for entrepreneurs who wish to achieve growth.
6. Explain why the effect of tax changes will be ambiguous for small firm growth.

Suggested assignments

Students are allocated into small groups and have to identify through contacts established by the university/college an entrepreneur who has been concerned with growth, perhaps owning more than one company. Students are required to:

1. Draw up an appropriate interview questionnaire based upon the topics and barriers to growth discussed in this chapter.
2. Interview the identified entrepreneur and record the interview. The interview should concentrate on problems and barriers experienced by the entrepreneur.
3. Report their findings and present them to a class session. Comparisons are made in class between the experience of different entrepreneurs.

REFERENCES

1. STOREY, D. J. (1994) *Understanding the Small Business Sector*, Routledge, London.

2. REID, G. C. (1993) *Small Business Enterprise: An Economic Analysis*, Routledge, London.

3. ACOST (1990) *The Enterprise Challenge: Overcoming Barriers to Growth in Small Firms*, HMSO.

4. STOREY, D. J. (1993) 'The Growth of Small Firms', paper presented to the International Seminar on Small Business, Parma, September.

5. BARKHAM, R., HANVEY, E., and HART, M. (1994) 'Growth in Small Manufacturing Firms: An Empirical Analysis', paper presented to the 17th National Small Firms Policy and Research Conference, Sheffield, November.

6. BARCLAYS BANK (1994) *Bridging the Skills Gap*, Barclays Bank.

7. HM GOVERNMENT (1971) *The Committee of Enquiry on Small Firms (Bolton Report)*, HMSO, London.

8. RAINNIE, A. (1989) *Industrial Relations in Small Firms*, Routledge, London.

9. RAM, M. (1993) *Managing to Survive: Working Lives in Small Firms*, Blackwell.

10. CURRAN, J., KITCHING, J., ABBOTT, B., and MILLS, V. (1993) *Employment and Employment Relations in the Service Sector Enterprise*, Kingston Small Business Research Centre, Kingston University, Kingston.

11. PORTER, M. (1990) *Competitive Strategy: Techniques for Analysing Competitors*, Free Press, New York.

12. CURRAN, J. and BLACKBURN, R. (1994) *Small Firms and Local Economic Networks: The Death of the Local Economy?*, Paul Chapman, London.

13. ACS, Z. J. and AUDRETSCH, D. B. (1987) 'Innovation, Market Structure, and Firm Size', *Review of Economics and Statistics*, vol. 69, no. 4, pp. 567–574.

14. ROTHWELL, R. (1994) 'The Changing Nature of the Innovation Process: Implications for SMEs', in OAKEY, R. P., *New Technology-Based Firms in the 1990s*, Paul Chapman, London, pp. 13–21.

15. HART, M., SCOTT, R., GUDGIN, G., and KEEGAN, R. (1993) *Job Creation and Small Firms*, NIERC, Belfast.

16. ACARD, (1986) *Software: A Vital Key to Success*, HMSO.

17. BARBER, J., METCALFE, J. S., and PORTEOUS, M. (eds) (1989) *Barriers to Growth in Small Firms*, Routledge, London.

18. CHURCHILL, N. C. and LEWIS, V. L. (1983) 'The Five Stages of Small Firm Growth', *Harvard Business Review*, vol. 6, no. 3, pp. 43-54.

19. O'FARRELL, P. and HITCHENS, D. (1988) 'Alternative Theories of Small Firm Growth: A Critical Review', *Environment and Planning*, vol. 20, pp. 1365–82.

20. NORTH, D. and SMALLBONE, D. (1994) 'The Contribution of Established SMEs to Regional and Local Economic Development', paper presented to the 17th National Small Firms Policy and Research Conference, Sheffield, November.

21. KEEBLE, D. (1994) 'Regional Variations in High Technology Small Firms' in Oakey, R. P. (ed.) *New Technology-Based Firms in the 1990s*, Paul Chapman, London.

22. SEGAL QUINCE AND PARTNERS, (1985) *The Cambridge Phenomenon*, Segal Quince Wicksteed.

23. REES, H. and SHAH, A. (1993) 'The Characteristics of the Self-Employed: The Supply of Labour', in ATKINSON, J. and STOREY, D. J. (eds), *Employment, The Small Firm and The Labour Market*, Routledge, London.

RECOMMENDED READING

ACOST (1990) *The Enterprise Challenge: Overcoming Barriers to Growth in Small Firms*, HMSO.

REID, G. C. (1993) *Small Business Enterprise: An Economic Analysis*, Routledge, London.

STOREY, D. J. (1994) *Understanding the Small Business Sector*, Routledge, London.

11 Sources of Information and Research Methodology

INTRODUCTION

This chapter should be read as an introduction to Chapter 12 on Business Plans. It examines some of the research methods which may be necessary as background preparation to provide information for either a feasibility study or the strategic business plan. In addition, we mention briefly some of the secondary sources of information which are now commonly available. One of the problems that entrepreneurs face is that often they do not have sufficient time to research market opportunities. Obviously, entrepreneurs will not have either the resources or the time to spend on collecting extensive data. At Birmingham, we went some way to resolving this problem by setting students assignments with local entrepreneurs which involved some of the research methods discussed in this chapter. Assignments are given at the end of the chapter with suggested guidelines and outlines of requirements. For entrepreneurs who wish to carry out research to write their own business plans there are still a lot of sources that can be accessed quickly and even if some primary market research can be undertaken this will improve the assumptions and market forecasts used for the business plans and be more likely to influence potential funders in a positive way.

This chapter aims to provide some guidelines only for carrying out basic research for a business plan. It does not attempt to provide a comprehensive survey of research methods. There are adequate books which can be examined on research methodology and we cannot do justice in the confines of this chapter to a full discussion. However, it is probably true to say that the majority of business plans are put together with either no research or very little research and, in consequence, this will affect the information in the business plan, the way that it is presented, and the way it is received by potential funders.

For students, if you can provide a methodology section for the business plan (or feasibility study), then its quality will be improved. It is important to give some attention to the methodology adopted to carry out research. It is insufficient to explain methodology in terms of either secondary or primary sources of data. Research methodology is concerned with whether you have used quantitative methods, how you analysed these, and whether you used qualitative methods. If you can use a mixture of both quantitative and qualitative survey methods, as well as secondary sources of data where these are relevant, then this will improve the quality of information that is presented in the business plan. It may not be appropriate, however, to use both quantitative and qualitative methods, although a section on methodology should explain why you decided to adopt one or both methods.

Research methodology is dealt with in more detail later; we begin with a brief survey of some secondary data sources that you may wish to consult.

THE IMPORTANCE OF INFORMATION

Any organization operates in conditions of uncertainty. There will always be only a limited amount of information about competitors, the price of their products or services, strategic decisions of competitors, preferences of customers, and costs of operation. However, uncertainty can be reduced by obtaining information. This will reduce the possibility of making mistakes regarding crucial business and strategic decisions. The entrepreneur and small firm can be at a disadvantage because they do not have the same resources as large firms to enable the firm to carry out information gathering, particularly where this might involve getting primary data. Nevertheless, much information can now be obtained through secondary sources and the availability and content of these sources continues to grow.

A business is often at its most vulnerable when launching because it will not have the same knowledge or information as its competitors. It will need to establish a range of contacts with suppliers and buyers, its credit rating will inevitably be low, it may not be aware of what credit it can take advantage of, and what are the best sources of advice. There may also be shortages of skilled labour and it will still have its reputation to establish. These problems can at least be reduced if a new business takes advantage of the wide range of sources of information that are now available. The purpose of this chapter is to examine some of these sources briefly. There is such a wide range of secondary sources that we will only provide brief notes on these.

Information and technology note: The acquisition of information becomes particularly important for firms that employ high technology or are engaged in fields in which technology is rapidly changing. Thus, the importance of successful R&D becomes crucial to the success of firms in high technology fields. Recent studies have pointed out that R&D itself may be carried out by firms merely to gain information and knowledge. See in particular, Cohen and Levinthal (1).

SECONDARY DATA SOURCES

Sources of information are conveniently classified as either primary or secondary information sources. All secondary information sources include officially published data provided by the Government or their agencies or by other institutions, such as banks, CBI, trade unions, local authorities and Chambers of Commerce.

What follows are some brief notes on the main official publications of the Central Statistical Office (CSO). These are conveniently classified as either general or (more) specific sources.

GENERAL SOURCES

1. *National Income and Expenditure Year Book*

The so-called *'Blue Book'*. It contains the main components of national income and expenditure in the form of summary tables. It is useful if you want to know national or regional data on output, incomes, wages, or prices.

2. *Annual Abstract of Statistics*

Again this is a comprehensive source of secondary data, containing summary tables on population, national income, and the labour force. It is more comprehensive than the blue book, containing details on regional characteristics and financial data.

3. *Census*

The national census is the ultimate secondary data source and the most comprehensive demographic information source. For businesses, it represents a valuable potential data source for their marketing campaigns and data on potential markets. It will contain a lot of socio-economic data on standards of living, material possessions, and lifestyles. The census data is analysed in and published in a more useful form through separate publications on particular demographic features of the population. For example, Ballard and Kalra (2) have published a breakdown of ethnic minority demographic data.

As we have mentioned these sources are only indicative; in practice it is more likely that you will need and use more specific sources that provide detailed information on specific topics, e.g., the proportion of women who are under 25, married, with children, in socio-economic category B. More recent information will be required because there is an inevitable time lag with the publication of general sources of information. The following sources could be included in this category.

SPECIFIC SOURCES

4. Monthly Digest of Statistics

An up-to-date survey of the main components of national income, including wages and prices. This is less comprehensive than the general sources above but has the advantage of being relatively recent.

5. Economic Trends

Summaries of the main economic indicators with articles on changes and forecasts where appropriate. This is a monthly publication and is a useful indicator of future trends in the economy and is thus one of the more useful of the official sources for businesses.

6. Regional Trends

Similar to Economic Trends but with the emphasis on regional variations with indicators of differences in standards of living between the regions. This could be a valuable source of information for a small business seeking to obtain regional data on employment, income and market trends.

7. Population Trends

Up-to-date demographic data with articles on birth rates, death rates, etc., and their implications for the future characteristics of the UK population.

8. Financial Statistics

Contains the main financial indicators including money supply and dealings in the security markets, bank and building society advances, data on non-bank financial intermediaries, interest rates, and data on the wholesale money markets.

9. Bank of England Quarterly Bulletin

Money supply data but including the balance sheets of the banks and the Bank of England.

10. New Earnings Survey

An annual publication that gives detailed information on earnings, hours worked, overtime, holidays and general labour force information including unemployment and job vacancies. The detail in the survey can be quite valuable for businesses. For example, it gives wage rates by occupation for men and women and the hours that they work.

11. Business Monitors

The business monitors are a valuable source of reference for entrepreneurs wishing to start a new business or expand an existing business. They provide valuable information on particular business sectors and can be obtained from many of the larger reference or university libraries (or possibly through inter-library loan). They contain output data on industries and sales. It will give information on output in the industry and thus some information on competitors. Business monitors are a very good reference source for general trends within an industry, e.g., on the car industry a business monitor will provide recent information on production, sales of different models, output levels, exports and imports, and market share of the main producers.

Thus, business monitors will often be a first source of reference when compiling information for a business plan and any entrepreneur on researcher is encouraged to consult the appropriate business monitor for their industry/business sector.

12. Census of Production

Output figures and tables, including concentration measures. This publication also contains the Standard Industrial Classification (SIC) which is periodically up-dated in the Department of Employment's *Employment Gazette* and is a useful reference for researchers.

13. Employment Gazette

A monthly publication that often contains articles of interest to small businesses. For example, it gives periodic articles on the number of new firms (and deaths). It contains details of labour force statistics, including earnings, unemployment, and hours worked.

ON-LINE DATABASES

Many of the official sources above are now available as databases accessed by computers. For example, the universities are usually subscribers to 'JANET' giving access to databases held in other universities, most significantly a CSO database held at Manchester University which holds data from most of the CSO publications.

One of the advantages of using these 'on-line' databases is that the full, time series data can be downloaded onto a micro or for analysis straight into a statistical package if students are working on researching feasibility studies and business plans at the university and hence statistical analysis can be carried out easily and immediately

EXSTAT provides micro-level data on individual companies including profit levels, turnover, asset size, shareholdings, and general financial/accounting data. These EXSTAT databases are a development of the EXTEL cards which used to be available in a published form in some libraries. These, effectively, are brief summaries of an individual company's financial and trading record. Obviously for entrepreneurs and small businesses they are a potentially valuable source of information on the profitability and performance of existing competitors. However, they only provide information on limited companies so cannot include information on very small 'micro-businesses' which are partnerships or sole traders.

A number of commercial databases are now available where information at the micro-level can be obtained for a fee to the commercial company that compiles and markets the database. These databases include DATASTREAM, which contains detailed financial and share price information, and KOMPASS, a powerful pan European database containing detailed information on companies throughout Europe.

CD/ROM DATABASES

Most libraries now have databases using CD disks that store basic statistical data as a database on a CD disk. These may be databases of literature, journal articles or statistical and financial information. The development of these databases has made things like 'literature searches' far easier and there is nowadays an increasing amount of information and basic data which is available on CD/ROM.

An example of one financial database which is available in some libraries is FAME, which is a financial database on CD, and after a little practice it can be used as a valuable source of financial data on the SME sector and the performance of firms.

There are many additional secondary sources of information, e.g., local authorities often publish useful local economic reports. These may also be available from other agencies such as the Training and Enterprise Councils (TECs) in England and Wales and the Local Enterprise Companies (LECs) in Scotland. They will often be a valuable source of local 'intelligence'.

It is impossible to list or discuss all that is available in the confines of this short section. The quality and value of this information will also vary from one area to another. It is often freely available, although to obtain some information, e.g., on CD/ROM may either involve a fee or the purchase of the database itself. We would encourage the researcher to seek out what is locally available and if not always published, on enquiry local breakdown of economic information is often made available.

One source of secondary data that may be either overlooked or underrated is the appropriate trade and industry journal for the business sector appropriate to the business proposition. Again the value of these publications is variable, but they can be an important source of market intelligence.

TRADE AND INDUSTRY PUBLICATIONS

Apart from commercially available on-line databases, there are a number of private sector publications that can be useful to entrepreneurs and small firms which need to research new market opportunities and assess existing or potential competition. There are trade periodicals, providing *qualitative* information on prospects and performance of companies in their industry. This is often quite useful and provides an alternative to the *quantitative* information that is available through the secondary sources given above. For example, an interview with a managing director in a trade publication can often give an insight into the strategic decisions and planning of the company. These publications may also be useful for names of who to approach when dealing with a company. Occasionally, more detailed quantitative information may be published through their own survey of subscribers, perhaps through a questionnaire survey.

MINTEL REPORTS

If either access to a good library is available or one can afford the fee then there are the valuable Mintel reports, providing market intelligence reports on particular products or sectors. They use market research methods to provide information on competitors' products and sales figures. They are very valuable for potential or existing entrepreneurs and if resources are not a problem, then they can provide information that would otherwise be difficult to collect. However, the Mintel reports are expensive (because large firms and libraries can afford to pay for them) and for the vast majority of small firm entrepreneurs it is more likely that they will have to rely on primary sources of data and research in order to obtain market research information.

OTHER SECONDARY SOURCES

A number of agencies operate an intelligence service and databases specifically designed to provide information for small firm entrepreneurs. These databases may cover, for example, sources of finance or sources of assistance. The quality and availability varies from region to region and may be affected by institutional arrangements in any one area. For example, local government re-organization can affect the range and quality of sources of information available from the local authority.

Institutional arrangements will vary from region to region, but there are also Euro-Information Centres in selected localities which provide a range of information on European funding and assistance.

This area is rapidly changing and with the development of on-line databases, more information is becoming available, although there is often a fee to use some of the services. For example, some centres now provide a Patent Database that allows potential users and entrepreneurs to search the database for existing patents in a particular product/field, but there is a fee for using such databases.

PRIMARY SOURCES

Although there is a vast range of secondary sources of information, it will be appreciated that they often do not provide the right combination of data or perhaps the data is incomplete. There are many situations when this is going to happen with requirements of entrepreneurs for specific information regarding products and potential demand. If you are an entrepreneur who is considering launching a new product, the only way to find out information concerning potential demand is to carry out your own market research using survey techniques and questionnaires. For these reasons, we will concentrate on some of these survey techniques.

There are a number of ways that primary information can be obtained, the most obvious being through the use of questionnaires using an alternative variety of methods including postal, telephone, and face to face interviews. However, data may also be obtained by observation, e.g., traffic surveys; by interview over a long period of time (longitudinal research) to establish whether there are changes in social attitudes; or by records of respondents, e.g., purchases of families recorded by the Family Expenditure Survey. A brief survey of some of the methods that can be used to obtain primary data is given below.

SURVEY METHODS

In the feasibility study and/or subsequent business plan, you may wish to organize a survey of potential customers for yourself or your client using a survey method. There is a danger that these surveys will be done superficially, often containing questionnaires that only reveal the most basic information. You will need to aim for high quality information and that can only be achieved if your questionnaire and survey is well designed. Since the information obtained from any survey is going to form the basis of conclusions and recommendations in the final business plan the quality of this plan is going to depend crucially upon the research techniques used and the design of your questionnaire. Past experience has found that entrepreneurs that carry out their own research pay insufficient attention to the design of questions and the survey method to be used. Some careful consideration to the design of questions and survey method will improve the quality of analysis that can be subsequently carried out in either a feasibility study or business plan.

Survey methods include questionnaire based surveys (normally postal and telephone) and interview based surveys which may be more open-ended.

1. POSTAL SURVEYS

Although postal questionnaire surveys can be carried out more cheaply than interviews and can be used where a large survey might be required relatively quickly, they suffer from a number of disadvantages which means that they are better avoided unless there is no alternative. However, in conjunction with a smaller interview based survey they can provide useful basic data.

The disadvantages of postal surveys are that:

1. Response rates are usually very low (even with incentives provided for respondents).
2. Replies may be unreliable.
3. Consequently samples are biased. Responses will be self-selecting, those that do respond will probably have particular motives to reply.
4. The extent of questions that can be asked is limited and the questionnaire must be constructed very carefully to avoid misinterpretation by respondents.
5. Some responses may be incomplete making analysis quite difficult.

However, these disadvantages need not necessarily rule out postal surveys in appropriate circumstances. For example, if a mailing list is obtained of the members of a particular association, you may wish to test how many of the members might buy a new product or service. The mailing list may consist of several thousand names and a postal questionnaire may be the only option which will allow you to survey the full membership.

Note: However, it is stressed that great care should be taken on the use and design of postal questionnaires. Get advice from someone that has had experience of using this research method. Use reply paid envelopes and pilot the questionnaire beforehand. Use incentives to encourage replies if at all possible and do not rely solely on this survey method. Combine it with interviews of a small sample of the population which will provide more reliable data and provide a check on the value of the postal survey data. Use 'closed' questions rather than open-ended questions as described below.

2. TELEPHONE SURVEYS

Telephone surveys can be used where time is of the essence and you wish to ensure that the response rate is reasonable. However, telephone surveys still contain many disadvantages which include:

1. The range and type of questions are severely limited since replies are given over the telephone, although the questions can be posted in addition to phoning so that the respondent has them available when you phone.
2. Some people object to answering questionnaires over the phone.
3. The respondent has little time in which to consider replies and this limits the type of question that can be asked.

4. If data is required the respondent may not have this easily available, which can lead to incomplete responses.

Telephone surveys probably suffer from more disadvantages than any other method. They are useful occasionally, however, and should not be ruled out, e.g., in situations where you need to obtain some basic and limited data quite quickly. They can also be used in conjunction with a more comprehensive postal survey.

3. INTERVIEWS

Face to face interviews have the advantage that issues can be explored in more depth. They can be used to provide qualitative data on values and opinions of respondents as well as the more basic quantatitive data. However, interviews can be difficult to carry out and the researcher needs to have some method of recording responses. For full in-depth interviews a small tape recorder is normally the only way to record all the information provided by the respondent. Face to face interviews are therefore desirable but they still have a number of disadvantages that include:

1. Interviews are subject to the personal bias of the interviewer. Questions need to be carefully designed and even then the interviewer can affect the outcome by placing his/her own interpretation and explanation on the results.
2. The survey will by its nature be limited in the coverage of respondents and unless they are chosen carefully this can provide a further source of bias. Without access to unlimited resources the number of interviews that can be carried out is going to be relatively small.
3. If the interview is open-ended and assuming that some acceptable method of recording is found, there is still the problem of adequate analysis and categorizing of responses.

4. FOCUS GROUPS

A focus group involves the selection of a small number of respondents that meet together with the interviewer and opinions are provided in an unstructured way to promptings from the interviewer/facilitator. They have the advantage that they can avoid bias on the part of the interviewer but their disadvantages include:

1. They can be difficult to arrange and organize with a group that is representative.
2. It is difficult to get a balanced group that will not be dominated by one or two individuals. If focus groups work they have to have synergy, that is, the group (or sum) contribution should be greater than the individual people (or parts).

3. It is difficult to record the outcomes of the group in a coherent way. As a result, analysis of outcomes can be difficult.

Focus groups can be a useful method to obtain additional qualitative data and are often used in market research to research customer opinions and preferences about particular products.

Any survey method will depend, for accurate and coherent subsequent analysis, on the research design which will include the questionnaire design. It may be acceptable to combine these different survey methods, for example short interviews of a reasonable sample may be combined with more in-depth material with a small number of respondents. In-depth interviews are designed to obtain qualitative information whereas larger surveys are designed to obtain quantitative information. This combination of methods can overcome some of the inherent disadvantages with each method and is sometimes called a *triangulation* approach.

RESEARCH DESIGN

The research design and survey method used will depend on the aims and objectives of the research. For example, a full feasibility study undertaken in advance of a business plan will aim to provide both quantitative data and analysis and more in-depth qualitative information so that a combination of methods will be appropriate. A brief survey required by an entrepreneur to prepare a business plan will need a quick response survey and may involve a mere telephone survey

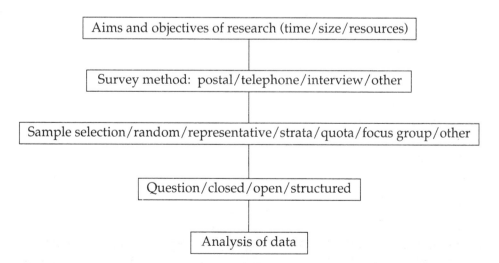

Figure 11.1 Research design

of potential clients. Whatever, the objectives of the research, however, some attention should be paid to research design, sampling method, and questionnaire design.

1. RESEARCH DESIGN

Research design involves the selection of the appropriate survey method(s), the sample, and the design of appropriate questions. It involves matching the survey method or combination of methods to the aims of the study and research. Good research design and some thought to the survey method used will pay dividends later in analysis and the production of the final business plan. This is shown in diagrammatic form in Figure 11.1.

2. SAMPLING METHOD

Some attention should be paid to how you are going to chose your sample. The sampling frame may be provided such as the provision of a membership list of an association; you may then decide to survey the whole membership, the population, or choose a sample. How this sample is chosen will affect the interpretation that can be placed on the final results.

The sample will be drawn from some sampling frame such as *Yellow Pages*, a membership list, or the electoral roll in a local area. Samples may be of the following types:

1. *Purely random.* To select a true random sample each member of the population must have the same chance of being selected. One way to choose a random sample is to generate random numbers using a computer program. You use the numbers to select respondents from your sampling frame.
2. *Representative sample.* A representative sample contains a microcosm of the features of the population in their appropriate proportions. Thus if you are surveying firms, you may wish to have representations of different firm sizes in true proportions to their numbers in the population of all firms. That is, 95 per cent of your sample should employ less than 20 employees. The extent to which your sample can be representative will depend on having information about the population. Samples can only be representative if features of the full population are known such as the proportion that earn less than 'X' per week, or the proportion that are male/female, married/not married, and so on.
3. *Stratified sample.* A stratified sample attempts to break down the population in a coherent manner using one or two criteria. One example might be size of organizations which are respondents. The sample is not representative in having true proportions but you use the criteria of say, size of the firm, as a way of ensuring some representation is included from each group or 'strata' of

the population. Samples may be chosen randomly from each strata if the sampling frame permits this.

4. *Quota sampling.* Quota sampling is a commonly used technique in market research where a characteristic of the population (often age/sex) is used to provide quota numbers for interviewers to ensure a minimum number of respondents is identified in each category. In contrast to stratified sampling this method is often used where no sampling frame is available.

Given limited resources and time the entrepreneur may have little scientific basis for the selection of the sample. A small amount of research will pay dividends, however, and prevent the business plan appearing as though it has been 'thrown together'. A short methodology section in the business plan (or feasibility study) will indicate that some thought has gone into the research behind the plan and that assumptions are well founded, have a good basis and the strategic plans and projections are not haphazard or just 'dreamt up' by the entrepreneur. This can make a tremendous difference and also affects the confidence in which you can present a business plan to any potential funders. Good research will not leave any 'holes' that can be picked upon by potential backers of the proposition.

3. QUESTION DESIGN

As before some care devoted to question design will pay dividends when analysing the results of any research. There are some simple rules which can be found in any statistical textbook, e.g., questions should be:

- Unambiguous
- Relatively short
- Not be biased or leading in some way
- Achieve the objectives of the research
- May be structured/semi-structured or open-ended, but open-ended are generally avoided with postal questionnaires.

It is desirable to have some method of *coding* questions. This enables analysis to be carried out with, preferably, a statistical package on computer or using a calculator.

CODING QUESTIONS: EXAMPLE

An example best illustrates the value of coded questions. Suppose you were carrying out some research into customer preferences when buying a product/service. You could ask a question in the following way:

Please indicate which of the following factors is important to you when buying 'X'. Please tick box as appropriate:

(a) Price ☐

(b) Quality ☐

(c) After sales service ☐

(d) Speed of delivery ☐

The problem with this question is that it does not allow for the respondent to distinguish between each of the factors that might be important when buying 'X'. A better question would ask the respondent to rate the importance of each factor on some scale. For example the question could also be worded in the following way.

Please indicate the importance of the following factors to you in buying 'X' according to the scale provided. Please indicate importance in the box provided:

	Most important	Least important
Scale	1——————————————10	

(a) Price ☐

(b) Quality ☐

(c) After sales service ☐

(d) Speed of delivery ☐

The advantage of the coded response is that responses can be entered in a numerical way and it is easy to calculate the average score for each response and percentages in each category.

There are a wide variety of acceptable questions that can be used including the standard yes/no questions which are sometimes called *filter* questions. The less categories that are used, however, the more we are forcing the respondent into a pigeon-hole of our own choosing. Although such closed questions are desirable, their limitations mean that we would want to combine any analysis from these questions with more open-ended questions that can be used in an interview situation or interview based research.

Open-ended questions should still aim to be neutral and avoid bias. It is often difficult to do so and therefore it is strongly recommended that some time should be spent on *testing and piloting* the questionnaire. Questions can then either be omitted or re-designed in the light of the pilot test. Of course, piloting does take time and resources and such techniques may not be possible due to time or resource constraints. Even if you have not the time to do piloting, it is worth mentioning, again in the methodology section, that this was at least considered.

ANALYSIS

Having taken some care with the research design that underpins the eventual business plan (or feasibility study) it is important to pay some attention to the analysis of research and, more important, to the presentation of that analysis. The analysis stage will directly affect the quality of and presentation of your final feasibility study and the business plan. If the research design is strong then this will be reflected in good analysis and presentation. If too many yes/no type questions are used or insufficient probing is carried out on respondents in the survey, then this will be reflected in the quality of material that can be presented in the final business plan.

We are not looking for sophisticated statistical analysis; there is a danger that blinding people with science may put off potential investors. However, good presentation of basic analysis such as percentages and averages will go a long way to persuading readers that the research is serious behind the business plan but it is not presented in a way that leaves the reader baffled.

Thus for the analysis stage the student or the entrepreneur should aim to ensure, in a relatively simple way, that the reader can understand basic data, percentages, and assumptions behind the income forecasts that are used for the cashflow forecasts. If a computer package can be used for analysis, then it will be relatively easy to produce bar charts and pie charts that illustrate for the reader the basic data that lie behind the projections in the cashflow. Depending on the design of the research, you may have quantitative and/or qualitative analysis.

1. QUANTITATIVE ANALYSIS

Statistical measures which are presented include the arithmetic means, medians or mode. These measures often mean very little on their own and it is useful to present them in conjunction with the standard deviations, where these are easily available from a standard computer package. Yet standard deviations can tell us much more about the characteristics of the sample of respondents than the arithmetic means. They indicate the degree of variance behind a statistical measure. Using the example above of the coded question on factors affecting purchase, if the standard deviations are known as well as the arithmetic means this will enable some knowledge of the degree of variance of respondents' replies. If price has a high mean score (of importance) but a high standard deviation this would mean that there are some respondents that do not think that it is important and it would be worth investigating in more detail with them why that is the case.

For students, this information should also be written up as part of your methodology section in the feasibility study and the business plan. The methodology section will include the sources of information that you used (e.g., secondary) as well as the survey methods that you have used.

2. QUALITATIVE ANALYSIS

Small sample sizes of less than 30 respondents may be used for qualitative analysis. This form of analysis is often powerful and of much more use for the entrepreneur or potential funder. Qualitative analysis aims to look at the process and causes of actions. For example:

> Why do respondents buy or not buy a particular product or service?
> What do respondents think of the service or product provided by the client?
> Do they have any complaints?
> How do they think that the service or product could be improved?
> If they buy a different service or product then why?
> You may want to ask questions about the range of provision, e.g. can they obtain the product?, are opening times suitable?
> What do they think about the quality of the product?

By the nature of the investigation, qualitative analysis usually (but not always) involves open-ended questions. The interview will last for a lot longer, e.g., 30-60 minutes is typical, and you must have some method of recording the interview.

RECORDING INTERVIEWS

Recording the interview provides the basis for the analysis and again affects the quality of your feasibility study and the final business plan. A useful methodology is to carry out a quick quantitative survey for the feasibility study and then carry out a more in-depth qualitative survey for the business plan. You may wish to hold interviews with existing customers as well as potential customers. There are two methods of recording interviews.

1. If you are working as a team and carrying out the interviews together you can afford to have one member making notes and another member of the team asking the questions. A third member of the team can be used to record other information such as the reaction of the respondent to certain questions, the nature of the surroundings, and how these might affect the interview. All this information is valid for qualitative analysis.

2. A better method is to record the interview with a small tape recorder. This allows one member of the team to carry out the interview and enables all the information to be recorded. Nowadays tape recorders can be purchased which are relatively unobtrusive. However, permission of the respondent should always be obtained first. Respondents are not always agreeable to having their interview recorded.

ANALYSIS OF INTERVIEWS

Qualitative analysis should not be unstructured. There needs to be some purpose to the questions and if they are structured this will allow for meaningful analysis afterwards. One or two short quotes are sometimes a powerful way of backing up the quantitative analysis; however, do not overdo this since more than minimal use of quotes from the interviews will tend to obscure the principal factors that you wish to emerge in the overall analysis of the research.

CONCLUSIONS

The final business plan is only as good as the research that underpins the projections. The purpose of this chapter has been to ensure that research undertaken is not undertaken on a haphazard basis. Research should have a sound methodology. While any investor will not be looking for a full research study with a full explanation of research methodology and sophisticated analysis, he/she will expect that assumptions used for forecasts have a sound basis. If this basis is rooted in appropriate methodology and survey methods and you can demonstrate that some original (primary) research has been carried out, then the confidence of both you as the entrepreneur and the investor will be that much better. This can be particularly important if the business plan is going to a venture capitalist or perhaps a business angel for funding where they will be much more concerned (than say a banker) with the extent of primary research and the way in which that research has been carried out.

The value of the research to the entrepreneur is that apart from making projections in the business plan more accurate it can provide the following advantages:

1. It gives increased confidence in the presentation of the business plan to potential funders/investors.
2. It can provide revised calculations of the potential success of the business or the market opportunity.
3. It provides basic calculations which will serve as a planning document with which to measure performance of the business over a number of years into the

future. Without sound methodology and research this will not be possible or will be extremely unlikely.
4. It can provide a database of potential customers which can be returned to later to carry out further market research on extensions to the business or research into the viability of new products.

We have tended to favour small qualitative surveys as being a valuable method of research. However, we do not wish to be prescriptive. The survey or research method used will depend upon the objectives set by the entrepreneur and by the nature of the business proposition. A small self-employed tradesman who wishes to start his own business and borrow £1000 will not require a sophisticated research study. However, even for a small business proposition some time spent on a small amount of research will pay dividends by improving forecasts and make the business plan an accurate and workable document.

Learning outcomes

At the end of this chapter entrepreneurs/students should be able to:

1. Appreciate the range of secondary sources available to entrepreneurs and small business owners and the SME sector.
2. Carry out a research study involving the use of structured questionnaires.
3. Discuss the potential of on-line databases for information gathering.
4. Evaluate the role of information in reducing uncertainty.
5. Evaluate the potential of primary and secondary sources of information for potential entrepreneurs and small firm owners.
6. Realize the importance of different sources of information for carrying out a feasibility study.
7. Appreciate the importance of carrying out both quantitative and qualitative research for both a feasibility study and a business plan.
8. Realize the importance of qualitative research for the business plan.
9. Understand the important statistical measures in quantitative analysis.
10. Appreciate the range of secondary sources of information.
11. Understand the concept of on-line databases.
12. Be willing to record and undertake interviews as part of the research for a feasibility study or business plan.
13. Be willing to revise cashflow forecasts in the light of research undertaken.

Suggested assignments: feasibility study

Students are allocated into groups to research and produce a feasibility study for an existing firm/entrepreneur. The feasibility study may involve a new market opportunity or a change of strategy perhaps involving diversification from existing markets. The firm will be local and identified as a potential client by the university/college. Students work as consultants to the client entrepreneur and are required to:

1. Negotiate and agree terms of reference with the entrepreneur.
2. Use appropriate research methods including market research with an appropriate questionnaire.
3. Identify and analyse existing and potential competition.
4. Identify the additional costs/resources that will be required to exploit the opportunity.
5. Examine the local labour market as appropriate if additional staff are required.
6. Produce a written feasibility study as a written report with sections that include: introduction/terms of reference, research methods, findings, conclusions, and recommendations.
7. Interim presentation. Present the findings to the entrepreneur and obtain feedback.

Note: This assignment should be coupled with a follow-up business plan as suggested at the end of the final chapter.

REFERENCES

1. COHEN, W. M. and LEVINTHAL, D. A. (1989) 'Innovation and Learning: the two faces of R & D', *Economic Journal*, vol. 99, pp. 569–96.

2. BALLARD, R. and KALRA, V. S. (1994) *Ethnic Dimensions of the 1991 Census*, University of Manchester, Manchester.

RECOMMENDED READING

WONNACOT, T. H. and WONNACOT R. J., (1984) *Introductory Statistics for Business and Economics*, 3rd edn, John Wiley and Sons.

PREECE, M. (1990) *Qualitative Research Methods*, Sage, London.

12 Business Plans: Design and Implementation

INTRODUCTION

Designing and writing the business plan should be seen as the outcome of a careful research process and subsequent planning procedure—it should be regarded as part of that procedure but not as the end of that process. The business plan is part of the on-going process of strategic planning for the entrepreneur and small business, whether produced for a start-up business or for an existing business. It can have several purposes: it may be produced to raise funding from banks, venture capitalists, or perhaps it may be required to obtain grant funding from an agency such as a TEC or a LEC; or the business plan may serve as a strategic planning document for the entrepreneur, a plan to guide the business and serve as a basis for taking strategic decisions, and also to serve as a subsequent monitoring device.

Nowadays there are many guides produced by banks, enterprise agencies, accountants, and published books on this on-going planning process (1). This chapter does not attempt to replicate these guides which are often excellent summaries of the essential first steps in starting in business for new entrepreneurs. These guides are often a framework for organizing ideas and formulating a skeleton business plan. Many agencies and bankers would say that most new business start-ups are now required to produce an elementary business plan. This is a major advance on what might have existed only 5 or 10 years ago, when a person with a business idea could talk it over with a bank manager and produce some rough 'back of the envelope' calculations and walk out of the bank with a start-up overdraft. The majority of start-ups and even expansions of existing businesses are still planned on the basis of some cashflow forecasts with a few introductory pages of explanation. Although, there have been major improvements, partly as a result of the expansion of the agency movement discussed in Chapter 7, there remains tremendous variety in the standard of business plans that are produced with many that are severely limited in scope. There is, as yet, no research into the quality and effectiveness of many business plans that are produced. There is an oft quoted statement that a business plan is 'out of date as soon as it is produced'; yet if a business plan is to be effective this should not be the case. This chapter aims to explain how a business plan can be used effectively as an on-going monitoring and strategic planning document which, although it may need revision, should be effective for several years as a strategic planning tool for the entrepreneur. After all, if considerable effort has been expanded on research, as recommended in the previous chapter, then this should have some pay-off in the future planning and monitoring of the business.

One problem, when designing and writing a business plan, is that different funding bodies can have different requirements. We have seen in Chapter 4, that even among different bank managers there were considerably different expectations in terms of what was expected and required from entrepreneurs when producing a business plan for a start-up business (2). In addition, venture capitalists will require a much more detailed business plan and perhaps more market analysis than a bank manager will, for the obvious reason that the venture capitalist will not be able to take security to safeguard his/her investment. An enterprise agency or a TEC/LEC will also vary in their requirements if a business plan is required to secure grant-aided funding. Thus the advice to potential and existing entrepreneurs before writing the business plan is to seek to determine what format is preferred by the potential funder in terms not of content but of presentation. This will avoid unnecessary re-writes of the business plan or changes to the presentation. It is best to have a full business plan that you are satisfied with and will serve you as the entrepreneur when taking strategic decisions for the business. Remember that the business plan should be produced for yourself, not for the potential funder, it can be modified, shortened, summarized or extended for different potential funders (or users) and you should be prepared to make these changes. Some additional hints on the presentation of business plans are given at the end of this chapter.

NEW DEVELOPMENTS

As well as extensive guides that can be purchased or are easily available, it is strongly advised that you have access to or purchase a modern PC (preferably with laser printer). This will make a tremendous difference to the quality of the final printed version of the business plan, making it easy to produce forecasts on a spreadsheet or to produce illustrations of market research through bar charts (as recommended in the previous chapter). In addition, there are software packages available that provide a full business planning package. These will provide the essential sections and help you to produce financial forecasts. One package that is recommended is the Business Architect software which can be operated on any PC, is relatively inexpensive, and provides a detailed dialogue to enable users to navigate their way through the various sections of a comprehensive business plan. Of course, any amount of software cannot replace the basic planning process that requires adequate research. A business plan, however well produced and presented, will only be as good as the quality of data and information inputted into the software that is being used. Obtaining impressive software should not blind the entrepreneur or user (if a student or consultant) to the need to provide good quality research and reliable data that will be processed by the software into a business plan that will serve the business as a valuable planning tool for a number of years.

DESIGNING THE BUSINESS PLAN

There are a number of standard sections that would normally be included in any business plan. These should include sections on aims and objectives, competitive analysis, marketing strategy, and SWOT analysis. However, the sections required for the business plan will vary depending on the nature and sector of the business. A manufacturing business requires a different business plan from a service sector based business. An exporting firm requires a different business plan from a components supplier who relies on large UK customers. A small start-up concern requires a different business plan from a medium-sized firm that is planning an expansion into different products. This is one of the problems faced by software packages that aim to provide a standard package that can be used by any business. A business plan has to be flexible and it is impossible to be prescriptive since every business plan will be different and will be produced for different requirements. Having said that it is impossible to be prescriptive, there are certain sections and guidelines that can be discussed and we attempt to do this below. We attempt to discuss what might be expected from any business plan, although you may not wish to include all of the sections—not everyone will have the time or resources to produce a full and detailed business plan. However, some thoughts given to the following suggestions will help to plan for possible different scenarios, competition, and future changes that will be faced by the entrepreneur. Some thought given at the research and design stage will improve the process of decision making which is one of the main purposes of any business plan.

The following sections are recommended when designing the content of the business plan. As stressed above, these sections are not prescriptive and can be modified to suit the purposes of individual entrepreneurs and business plans.

1. EXECUTIVE SUMMARY

If your plan is carefully researched, constructed, and written, then an executive summary will be very useful to the users of the business plan, which may be potential funders or partner entrepreneurs in the business. Although the executive summary should be the first section, it is likely to be the last section to be written and it can be the most difficult because you have to summarize the main contents of the business plan. You will find it useful to build the executive summary around the competitive strategy.

2. INTRODUCTION

A short introduction should give some background to the business, the key people, and an introduction to the nature of the business and the industrial sector. This section can be used to give the main aims and objectives of the business. In this section you will need to explain the purpose of the business plan. Is it to map out an expansion plan for the business? Or is it to provide a strategy for the launch of a new business? The aims and objectives could be placed in a separate section. You can also use this section to explain the rationale for the business and the business plan. Deciding how to differentiate between what are aims and what are objectives of your business can be difficult. A general guide is that aims can be considered to be quite broad and less specific than objectives. Objectives should be written in terms of specific outcomes. For example, an aim of a five year business plan would be to:

- Provide a strategic planning process to become a major competitor in the industry.

Whereas an objective of the same business plan might be to:

- Achieve a fourfold growth in sales within five years.

In the introduction you can provide additional information such as the nature of incorporation if a start-up, whether the company is registered, whether you have registered for VAT, in which case a VAT number should be quoted, starting employment levels, resources, and whether there is a need for recruitment of staff and personnel.

3. MARKET ANALYSIS AND RESEARCH

In this section you can report the findings of market research that might have been undertaken, if primary research has been undertaken along the lines suggested for this section. You should avoid the temptation to give too much information, although, as suggested before, illustrations of the main findings can be quite useful for presentation purposes and for potential readers of the plan. However, those readers will not want to wade through a large amount of information and data. If the questionnaire that has been used as the basis for the research has been well designed, then it should be possible to present the information and analysis in the form of summary tables with brief comments on the significance and importance of market analysis and summaries of the potential total market and market share.

Some of the software packages that were mentioned above will give a market opportunity analysis. For example, Business Architect will provide a useful market opportunity matrix which gives a score and an interpretation of the value of that score for the importance of the market opportunity. Additional analysis provided by such software can be a useful way of impressing any potential funder.

This section should be used to explain the assumptions behind income generation in the cashflow statements. Are the income levels based upon the market research findings? Or perhaps based on other factors such as seasonality? State of economic levels of activity? Capacity levels if a manufacturing concern? Other factors should also be included such as the basis of payment; income may be generated on the basis of commission, fees or sales. If sales of products and services are involved, then some form of normal credit period will be assumed. Standard practice is, of course, 30-day credit periods between the sale taking place and income shown in the cashflow. If your business is subject to strong seasonal factors, such as high sales in the Christmas period, then this should be shown in the income statement of the cashflow with allowance made for any credit period.

You may wish to consider outlining a brief marketing and distribution plan. This can be contained within the business plan, or if distribution is a major part of the firm's operations, then it is recommended that a separate document is produced. The marketing plan effectively sets out how sales are to be achieved. It may include all aspects of the so-called 'marketing mix':

- Pricing policy
- Promotion (advertising and other forms of promotion)
- Production. The outlets and marketing strategy should reflect the production capabilities of the business. It is important to get these aspects of the business integrated, so that distribution channels and outlets do not overburden the production process and capabilities and that the outlets are appropriate to cope with production capacities.

An example is illustrative. A small firm had produced a new form of hanging basket bracket that was produced to a new design and to a high quality. Yet the marketing strategy adopted bore no relation to production capabilities. The hanging bracket was marketed through a major chain gardening store and as soon as one order was placed the firm could not cope with the production quantities required by a major retailer and chain store. These problems of matching production to outlets and distribution channels cannot always be resolved, but planning for different outcomes in the business plan can help to resolve these problems if they do arise and a separate marketing plan can be a valuable planning tool for any business.

- ■ Place. How are the goods going to be distributed and how are they to be sold? What outlets are being used? Are direct selling methods to be used or are agents being used perhaps working on commission?

Access to retail outlets can be a problem for some businesses. You need to demonstrate that you have given some thought to this and that you have secured retail outlets if the product is new.

4. PRODUCTION STRATEGY

If your business is concerned with manufacturing and production, a separate section should be devoted to the planning of production. If the business is concerned merely with expanding using existing production facilities, through perhaps obtaining new market outlets, then a separate production plan will not be necessary. However, you may need to plan for additional production facilities, new machinery, and increased capacity. You will need to identify the additional resources and capabilities that will be required for new production levels. Additional skilled staff may be required and recruitment policies should be explained.

For a new start-up business that requires production facilities then obviously the business plan will need to describe how these are to be obtained and how staff are to be recruited.

The assumptions described in this section will form the basis behind the projections in the expenses of the cashflow statements. There may be some research necessary in order to predict these forecasts accurately. You should not rely on your own estimates but obtain as far as possible quotations for ordering supplies and equipment that are required.

Timing

An important element of any manufacturing business is timing production to co-ordinate with sales orders and to match supply of materials with production capabilities and sales orders. This is the importance of integrating market predictions and sales back through the production process and ensuring that the supply of materials and components is of the quality required to ensure that your customers are satisfied with the quality of the product. It must be stressed that orders can be lost if insufficient attention is paid to quality in the production process and quality obtaining from suppliers. This can be a particular problem for a new (producing) firm which can be vulnerable if certain specifications have been laid down to suppliers with no guarantee that these are going to be met. If possible, although this may use up some resources, it is worth trying to get some prototypes made to check quality. Of course, this will be a particular problem where new technology or new production techniques are being employed, which is one of the reasons why financing new technology firms contains different and special issues from other types of start-ups.

Timing is important because resources and finance will be required before products are made, before sales are made and certainly well before income is received. This should be reflected in the cashflow statements. Any manufacturing and producing firm is certain to have a negative balance in the first part of the cashflow. It is better to plan properly for this, so that financial resources can either be set aside, if internal resources are available, or funding requirements can be made clear in the business plan

Action plans

To aid the planning process it is worth providing an action plan. The purpose is to map actions against time and the production process. This will allow you to plan different requirements into the production and marketing stages as they are required over time.

An action plan can be produced for any type of business and modified to produce a Gantt Chart, which maps out the sequential timing of decisions against production/sales levels and can serve as an action plan for the business.

5. SWOT ANALYSIS

A section on SWOT analysis involves the identification of strengths, weaknesses, opportunities, and threats for the business. There can be some dispute over how SWOT analysis can be presented and explained. To some extent, a SWOT analysis should consist of a series of short bullet points so that the reader can see quickly the main strengths and weaknesses of the business and the opportunity. However, the statements which consist of the bullet points should not be so short that they become perfunctory statements and the reader is left wanting and wishing for further explanation or elaboration. Again a balance has to be struck between the need to keep the statements short (and preferably punchy) and the need to provide an adequate statement that the reader or user of the business plan can understand and comprehend.

A long list of strengths and weaknesses is not necessary; the list should be relatively short, perhaps half-a-dozen bullet points under each heading. It is also better to be honest. A long list of strengths followed by a short list of weaknesses is more likely to raise suspicions from potential funders rather than impress them.

The SWOT analysis should 'fit' the business plan. If many strengths are shown but other aspects of the business plan are perhaps weak (such as limited analysis of market projections), then the SWOT analysis will look out of place in the context of the rest of the business plan.

There are few guidelines that can be given for the SWOT analysis. You as the entrepreneur(s) is/are the best person or people to write the SWOT analysis but, bearing in mind the points raised above, you should not be afraid to put down your strengths. These may include extensive experience in the industry, a reputation for quality, a high knowledge of working practices and employment conditions in the industry, existing contacts with potential customers, and knowledge of new techniques/technologies that can be applied to existing production processes.

A SWOT analysis will always remain subject to personal preferences and views. The reader of the business plan should be aware of this and will make some allowances for this. A different individual could interpret strengths and weaknesses in different ways. Unless a business plan is put together by an independent consultant, a SWOT analysis will remain a personal statement by the entrepreneur(s) of their view of the strengths, weaknesses of the business, and the opportunities provided by the business opportunity.

6. COMPETITION

The competition and a section dealing with competitive analysis will follow from the identification of threats in the SWOT analysis. The extent of knowledge on competitors will probably vary, but it should be possible to identify the major competitors and what their relative strengths are. It is also useful to identify what strategies they have used to establish their market position. For example, have they used market nicheing strategies? Or perhaps more aggressive market penetration strategies? Or have they established their position merely by reputation and word of mouth?

In this text, we have considered some of the reasons for the success of small firms in the 1980s and 1990s. Often the reason for the start-up of a new firm by an entrepreneur is that they have recognized a market niche in an industry that is not being catered for by existing (large) firms. A small firm/entrepreneur will have the flexibility to respond to new market opportunities and market niches. While it is likely that the competition may consist of well established firms, they may not have the flexibility to respond as quickly to new market opportunities and challenges.

The analysis of competition should match the market analysis that is presented in the business plan as has been discussed above. If you are predicting a relatively large market share, this will not fit with a competitor analysis which suggests that the major competitors are strong, well established, and that the market can be difficult to penetrate. This analysis should also fit the marketing strategy. A market nicheing strategy will probably aim for high quality services or products and likely outlets should have been identified that are willing to take your products or potential customers should have been identified if a service is being marketed.

You should also give some thought to potential competition. As opportunities develop, it could be that you may face competition either from additional entrepreneurs who start up or from retaliation from the existing competition. If the business plan is to be a valuable document over a three or five year planning period, then some thought must be given to future competition and the likely sources of that competition.

It is possible to provide contingency plans. However, given that the number of different possible scenarios is infinite, you will not be able to provide a contingency plan to cope with all possible eventualities, possible reactions, and strategies of the competition. All that can be done is to recognize that the outcomes predicted in the business plan can change and that the business plan should be used to monitor operations and then adjust predictions and/or strategy as circumstances change. As we will see later it is desirable to conduct a limited amount of sensitivity analysis that will demonstrate to potential funders that you have thought about different outcomes and the reaction of existing and potential competitors.

7. COMPETITIVE STRATEGY

In some ways this is the most important section of the business plan, since it should map out the strategy for the survival, development, and growth of your business. A strategy should be identified that will enable the business to meet the aims and objectives which will have been set out in the early part or sections of the business plan. The development of competitive strategy will be the natural outcome of the process of researching the market opportunity, the nature of the product or service, the SWOT analysis, and the competitive analysis. Porter (3) has provided a well known taxonomy of generic market strategies which are indicated below. It is likely that your strategy will fall into one of these three categories. Porter shows that competitive strategies are a response to the environment in which the business operates, in other words they are generic to the environment and the nature of competition faced by the business. Porter's three generic strategies are described below.

Cost leadership

Under this strategy, the emphasis is on maintaining a competitive edge through a cost advantage over competitors. It may, but does not necessarily, involve undercutting competitors on price and maintaining a competitive edge on price. Undercutting through price does contain disadvantages, it may lead to some form of price war and even if competitors are at a cost disadvantage they may be better placed to sustain losses that might be incurred through any price cutting war to gain customers. The advantage of cost leadership for entrepreneurs will lie in the generation of additional income that may result from cost reduction and which may be re-invested to provide new production techniques or products.

Differentiation

This strategy may follow from a need to diversify production or services. It should not be confused with the third (focus) strategy. It is a strategy that is more likely to apply to existing and well established producers where, perhaps, products have entered a maturity stage of their life cycle and there is a need to diversify production to maintain growth in the firm.

Focus

This third strategy is the one that is most likely to be adopted by new firm entrepreneurs. It recognizes that many market opportunities result from specialization. Small firms have the advantage that they can be flexible as well as specialized. The development of a focus strategy involves the identification of a market niche that has not been exploited by existing producers. The firm should be able to gain a reputation quickly for satisfying this market niche. Timing can be all important in identifying the correct time to launch and exploit the market opportunity. Thus there are market 'windows of opportunity' that appear at different times. Launching too early or too late can miss this opportunity.

Although Porter's categories have been very influential, they may be seen as a bit limiting. Kay (4) has produced a useful alternative analysis of competitive strategy that focuses on the importance of value-added that a firm can bring to the industry. The extent to which a firm will produce value added to its costs of production will determine its success. For example, in an analysis of the retail food industry Kay shows that the strategies adopted by Sainsbury and Tesco have been very successful at adding value to their operations through successful marketing operations. Kwik-Save has also been successful with a very different marketing strategy aiming to capture the low cost end of the market but still providing value-added to its operations. The poor market performer has been Asda, which has not been successful with its marketing strategies and has a low value added performance.

These analyses stress the importance of getting the strategy right for the type of market that you are in. There is no right or wrong strategy, but it must be appropriate for the business, the operation, the market, and the business development plan.

8. CRITICAL SUCCESS FACTORS

The identification of critical success factors is a useful section that should be included in the final business plan. It can serve as a useful summary and check of factors that have been identified in other sections of the business plan and is best placed towards the end of the business plan. Like the SWOT analysis it will tend to be a personal reflection on the most important factors that are going to be critical to the success of the business. Thus, again, it is impossible to be at all prescriptive about this section but you may like to think about the following factors:

1. What factors does the success of the business hinge upon? Are they factors concerned with gaining orders or are they concerned with securing quality from suppliers?
2. How important are the key personnel to the success of the business? If a key member of staff leaves, how will this affect the performance of the business? Can they be replaced?
3. How important is the recruitment strategy of the business? Does the success of the business depend on obtaining appropriate skilled staff?
4. Does the success of the strategy adopted depend on how competitors react?

It is worth considering each section of the business plan and identifying just one or two key factors from each section that will be critical to the performance of your firm and to its success. As an entrepreneur this will help you to identify key and critical success factors and at later stages to monitor performance. Having identified such factors you can adopt strategies that can ensure success or lead to alternative arrangements. For example, if a supplier is identified as a critical factor, you may wish to investigate alternative arrangements of ensuring supply.

9. CASHFLOW STATEMENT

The cashflow statement contains the projected income from sales and other sources and all the expenses concerned with the launch and operation of the business. It is best prepared on a computer spreadsheet package, although business planning software, mentioned before, will have its own spreadsheet and financial analysis built in.

The importance of the cashflow statement is that it shows the timing of income and expenses and should show all these figures for 12 monthly periods of up to three or perhaps five years, depending on the potential users of the business plan. It shows the liquidity of the business at any one time and reflects the need or otherwise to raise funds and credit. If the business plan is being prepared for a bank manager then it is unlikely that cashflow forecasts will be required beyond three years. If, on the other hand, it is being prepared for a venture capitalist then it is more likely that five years' cashflow forecasts will be required.

A *pro forma* cashflow statement is shown as an example in Figure 12.1 but the detail of the cashflow will obviously depend on the individual business. The notes given in the *pro forma* are referred to below:

1. Income will consist of sales, fees, and commission. It may include income from grants or loans. The timing of the receipt of this income should be as accurate as possible. A small adjustment to the timing of the income can affect the extent of any negative or positive net cashflow.
2. Total income just calculates the total for each month. On a spreadsheet this is easily calculated by inserting the appropriate formula to sum cells and then copying across different cells.
3. Expenses can either be summarized under different headings or shown individually, but they should identify all expenses from the operations of the business. They will include equipment, materials, computing equipment, staffing, car leasing, insurance, and promotional expenses. Again timing is important and should be as accurate as possible since a small adjustment will affect the extent of the positive or negative cashflow.
4. Staffing should include national insurance contributions, although NI payments can be shown separately.
5. It is important to consider and include items such as insurance. If you are a producer you will need products' liability, public liability and employers' liability insurance. If insurance is a relatively small part of sales, perhaps only 2 per cent, it can be paid in just one annual premium.
6. If the business is registered for VAT, then it will be entitled to a VAT rebate on VAT payments. These can be claimed every three months. Registering for VAT becomes mandatory over a threshold turnover of approximately £40 000, but registration is advisable at levels below this to claim VAT rebates.
7. Total expenses merely add up the expenses in each column and this is easily done on a spreadsheet.
8. Subtracting the total expenses from the total income shows the net cashflow for each month. A general point to consider is that you will want to take advantage of any credit. This will be reflected in the liquidity of the business as shown in the net cashflow.
9. The opening balance for the first month is normally shown as zero, although it is possible to have reserves (from previous operations) shown in the opening balance.
10. The closing balance adds the opening balance to the net cashflow. The closing balance is automatically carried forward to become the opening balance in the next month (period).

HYPOTHETICAL COMPANY YEAR 1

	JAN	FEB	MARCH	APRIL	MAY	JUNE	JULY	AUGUST	SEPT	OCTOBER	NOV	DECEMBER	TOTALS (11)
INCOME (1)													
SALES		3500	4000	5000	5500	5000	6000	3000	6500	6500	7000	10000	62000
FEES	2025	2025	2700	2025	2700	2700		1350	3375	2700	3375	2025	27000
GRANT													0
ENTERPRISE AGENCY	7000												7000
TOTAL INCOME (2)	9025	5525	6700	7025	8200	7700	6000	4350	9875	9200	10375	12025	96000
EXPENSES (3)													
MATERIALS	3500	3000	3000	3500	3000	3000	3500	3000	5000	4000	4000	3000	41500
EQUIPMENT													
MACHINERY	5000	5000	5000	5000									20000
COMPUTERS		3600											3600
PRINTER		1000											1000
VIDEO			750										750
TABLES			600										600
CHAIRS		600											600
BOOKCASES			300										300
WAGES (4)													0
PRODUCTION	2893.75	2315	2893.75	2315	2315	2315	2893.75	2315	2893.75	2315	2315	2315	30095
OFFICE	607.5	607.5	810	607.5	810	810		405	1012.5	810	1012.5	607.5	8100
HEAT AND LIGHT			1000			1000			800			1200	4000
RATES				1000						1000			2000
INSURANCE (5)				1500						1500			3000
TELEPHONE			200			200			150			250	800
CONSUMABLES													0
PRODUCTION	200	200	200	200	200	200		200	200	200	200	200	2200
OFFICE STATIONERY	300	100	100	100	100	100		100	100	100	100	100	1300
VAT (REBATE) (6)						-1575			-1500			-1500	-4575
TOTAL EXPENSES (7)	12501.25	16422.5	14853.75	14222.5	6425	6050	6393.75	6020	8656.25	9925	7627.5	6172.5	115270
NET CASHFLOW (8)	-3476.25	-10897.5	-8153.75	-7197.5	1775	1650	-393.75	-1670	1218.75	-725	2747.5	5852.5	-65345
OPENING BALANCE (9)	0	-3476.25	-14373.8	-22527.5	-29725	-27950	-26300	-26693.8	-28363.8	-27145	-27870	-25122.5	
CLOSING BALANCE (10)	-3476.25	-14373.8	-22527.5	-29725	-27950	-26300	-26693.8	-28363.8	-27145	-27870	-25122.5	-19270 (12)	

Figure 12.1 Cashflow forecast for a hypothetical company and *pro forma*

234

11. The totals are added horizontally. They need not be shown, but they are a useful check on calculations and can show the total income and expenses for the year.

12. The last closing balance for the year will become the opening balance for the next year and should be carried forward as in previous months.

13. If drawings are made by the owner/entrepreneur, perhaps as a sole trader, then these are best shown as part of the expenses concerned with the operation of the business. These are likely to be regular withdrawals and they should be shown monthly rather than as a total figure at the end of the year.

Note: The cashflow statement is not the same as profit and loss.

As stated before, the net cashflow reflects the liquidity of the business. The cashflow can show additional income, e.g., borrowings which are not part of the profit and loss account.

10. FORECASTED PROFIT AND LOSS ACCOUNT

It is advisable but not essential to forecast an end of year profit and loss account. This involves adding up all the trading income, subtracting cost of goods sold to get the trading profit and loss. General expenses for the year can be totalled, including depreciation subtracted from the trading profit to get the net profit.

11. FORECASTED BALANCE SHEET

A forecasted balance sheet is sometimes required, particularly by bank managers and this can be relatively easily calculated from the projections for the end of the year.

The balance sheet is a statement of assets and liabilities at any particular time period. As a planning tool it is not very useful, since it only provides a snapshot at any one time, but it seems to be required by bank managers (5).

A number of financial ratios can be calculated and included in terms of profitability and liquidity. It is not necessary to go into detail on the calculation and usefulness of these but standard business planning software will calculate these automatically.

12. SENSITIVITY ANALYSIS

The purpose of the sensitivity analysis is to provide a test of the susceptibility of the business to changes, or a test of the robustness of the business proposition to cope with unforeseen changes. We can assume that most of the expense forecasts will be accurate. Despite careful research income forecasts will still contain some uncertainty and the purpose of sensitivity analysis is to examine the consequences of changing some of the income forecasts on the net cashflow.

There is little point in developing any sensitivity analysis beyond the first year of operation, but it it is worth formulating for the first year what can be called an optimistic and a pessimistic scenario.

The optimistic scenario might increase sales and other income by 10 per cent. Expenses will need to be adjusted to allow for this, for example through increased cost of materials, and perhaps through increased salary costs.

The pessimistic scenario might decrease sales and other income by 10 per cent with appropriate adjustments of expenses.

WRITING THE BUSINESS PLAN

As indicated before, the business plan is best prepared on a computer package using a standard word processing package such as WORD PERFECT or WORD (for WINDOWS) combined with a spreadsheet package such as EXCEL or LOTUS (which if using a WINDOWS format can be imported into the final document) for preparing the cashflow. Alternatively, the business planning software that is now available will integrate a spreadsheet with a word processing package that contains the main sections of the business plan. PCs these days are relatively inexpensive, a small outlay will improve the quality and presentation of the final business plan and any intermediate feasibility study.

Some hints and guidelines are given below in terms of the actual writing and presentation of the final business plan:

1. The construction of the cashflow statement should be undertaken at a relatively early stage, perhaps after the analysis of the market research described in the previous chapter. This has the advantage of deciding what information and forecasts need to be justified and explained in the written parts of the business plan. It also allows you to consider whether you have done sufficient research and whether there are any additional expenses that need to be calculated.
2. It helps presentation if you use relatively wide margins, e.g., we would recommend at least 1 inch wide margins on either side and generous top and bottom margins. This avoids presenting too much information on one page and allows the potential user or funder to make notes.
3. Start each section on a fresh page. Again this improves presentation and enables the user to find sections quickly.
4. Avoid appendices where possible. If appendices are used to provide market research data, it can be difficult for the reader/user to refer to data while

reading the appropriate section in the business plan. Appendices may be used sparingly, e.g., to give CVs. These may be left out of some versions of the same business plan.

5. Do use illustrations, although do not overdo this. Comments have been made on the illustration of research data in the previous chapter. Illustrations are useful and can help the user assimilate data quickly. Ability to do this however, may depend on the sophistication of the software being used.

6. Do include a contents page at the beginning. This will enable the reader to locate different sections and navigate around the business plan document quickly.

7. Most word processing packages allow the inclusion of headers and footers. By allowing for generous top and bottom margins, this will allow either a header or footer to be inserted on each page of the business plan. This could be the name of the business which is used for the header or footer.

8. Do include some notes to the accounts, whether you are providing a cashflow statement only, or a more detailed set of accounts that may include profit and loss and a forecasted balance sheet. Even though assumptions will have been given in different sections in the business plan, it will still be necessary to provide some notes on certain figures in the cashflow to explain what additional assumptions have been made on the basis of calculation.

9. Do put contact names on the front or inside page of the business plan. Put copyright if you want to.

10. The business plan should not be too long, perhaps 30 pages including appendices is a rough maximum (or 10 000 words as a maximum). There is no ideal length, although there is little point in producing a very detailed plan if the only aim is to raise a small overdraft at the bank.

11. Bind the business plan securely (not stapled) and provide a cover that will stand up to some wear and tear. If you wish to you can go the expense of getting the business plan properly bound by a printer. However, we do not recommend this since you may wish to change certain sections or add pages. Generally this will provide you with less flexibility than a loosely ring-bound document, which will allow you to modify and produce different versions of the same business plan for different users and funders.

12. Finally, an over-used phrase is that the business plan should 'stack-up'. We would defy anyone to explain exactly what this phrase means but it is best expressed by saying, in principle, that different sections should integrate and support the findings. Assumptions should underpin the forecasts. If different sections are out of line this will be transmitted as an unbalanced plan. A strategy section that emphasizes small scale and quality should match other sections such as the market research and marketing strategy and the cashflow forecasts.

IMPLEMENTATION

As stressed above, the business plan should not become out of date as soon as the business starts operations. Before operation and trading the business plan is a document that can be read and used by a number of different people, perhaps other partners in the business, perhaps analysed by potential funders. It should itself enable planning of the launch and operation of the first stage of the business.

After start-up or launch of the new product/diversification, the business plan can be used to monitor performance against the projections in the business plan. It can be used to signal better (or worse) performance, dangers, and critical success factors. Timings can be crucial and, if properly planned for, production and marketing plans can be matched against business plan forecasts to give some guide to the performance of the business. Income and expense forecasts can be matched against real outcomes to give an indicator of performance. During the first year any change in performance can be matched against the sensitivity analysis carried out in the business plan and this will give some indication of the extent to which the business is out-performing or under-performing forecasts in the business plan.

It must be remembered that the business plan is a strategy document as much as anything else. It is not there merely to provide a financial forecast, but to provide the strategy for the survival, development, and growth of the business. If forecasts do prove to be substantially different from real outcomes, then the strategy will need to be reviewed and possibly changed and adapted to different circumstances.

Assuming that the business plan has been produced for at least three years, the business plan will need to be reviewed at the end of the first year. If there has been substantially different outcomes, it will be worth revising the business plan, perhaps by revising cashflow outcomes. Assuming that a spreadsheet has been used, this should be achieved relatively easily. The strategy and details provided in the business plan should still be appropriate and be used (perhaps with some modifications) for the remainder of the planning period. Forecasts should now be more accurate and more reliable. As the business plan is reviewed in subsequent years the advantages of forward planning should become apparent. The business plan should serve to guide planning throughout the life of the business.

FURTHER HINTS

1. Be confident in the presentation of the business plan. Careful research should increase confidence. Potential funders will need to be impressed by your own confidence and knowledge behind the forecasts that are in the business plan.

No matter how well the business plan is prepared, potential backers are still influenced by presentation.

2. Prepare for questions on the business plan. Is there anything missed out? If profit and loss is not presented, some rough calculations will give a potential backer an indication and may prepare for questions on this.

3. Do take the business plan to different agencies and backers and get their opinion on how it 'stacks up'.

4. Do not give up if you cannot raise funding at the first attempt. For example, our own research has shown that different bank mangers can have quite different interpretations of the same business plan, despite the advent of expert systems and credit scoring (2).

5. If you can afford it, get the comments of a qualified accountant to verify the contents of the business plan. Research has shown that bank managers are more (positively) influenced by business plans that have been authorized by accountants.

6. Be prepared to accept a long process of vetting if you are seeking funding from a venture capitalist. The due diligence procedure of a venture capitalist can take six months or more before a decision is made on whether to back a proposition.

7. A venture capitalist will also be looking for exit routes. If you are seeking this form of funding you will need to be prepared for the eventual Initial Public Offering (IPO) (share issue) of the business which is the normal exit route for a venture capitalist.

8. Try to find out what potential funders are looking for. Many agencies that might provide funding have very specific criteria, e.g., that you attend enterprise training sessions (if a new entrepreneur). Whether you need these or not, you will have to attend to qualify for the funding. There can be an assumption on the part of existing managers (in large firms) that they do not need enterprise training, yet the management of a start-up concern as a small firm needs different management skills from that of a large firm.

CONCLUSIONS

The research, design, and implementation of the business plan is part of the on-going planning process within any firm. If as a start-up entrepreneur you adopt planning policies that are based on sound research and careful consideration of strategy, this will have benefits throughout the life of the business. We have seen in a previous chapter that, during the 1980s, there were high birth rates of new small firms and entrepreneurs, but at the same time these were accompanied by high death rates. One of the reasons for these high death rates has been insufficient thought and time given to properly planning the strategy of the new firm.

We started this chapter by commenting that nowadays business plans are much more common and much more detailed than they used to be. Even only five years ago properly researched business plans were quite rare. One of the reasons for the growth in the use of business plans has been the spread of the agency movement and the requirement of banks (sometimes working in co-operation with agencies) for business plans if any funding is required. However, another reason is that it has become accepted that a carefully constructed business plan is important to the survival and successful performance of any business, whether large or small.

Business plans are very flexible. They can be used for both large and small firms, for start-ups or for expansion, for private or public sector organizations, and can be a few pages or a substantial document running to 10 000 words or more supported by appendices. Yet there is still no overall standard format by which any one individual business plan can be measured. It is because they are so varied and that they are relatively new (in evolution and use) that it is unlikely that there will be any standard produced in the near future. So how do we measure whether a business plan is of good quality? We are left with that over-used phrase that a good business plan should 'hang together'. We have indicated that what this really means is that the different sections should be inter-connected, that it should be underpinned by careful research, by knowledge of the market opportunity, and that the assumptions and research should underpin the financial forecasts.

Learning outcomes

At the end of this chapter you should be able to:

1. Construct the main sections of a business plan.
2. Describe the importance of strategic planning for the successful development of a business.
3. Appreciate the importance of careful research for the accuracy of forecasts in the business plan.
4. Construct a cashflow forecast from some income and expense assumptions.
5. Understand the advantages and limitations of (short) business plans for the adequate monitoring of business performance.
6. Appreciate the wide variety and flexibility of business plans and the need for a coherent national standard.

Suggested assignment: business plan

Note: This assignment should be coupled with the feasibility study assignment given at the end of the previous chapter which should be completed as precursor to the business plan.

1. Students are required to complete a business plan through the development of research work carried out for the feasibility study. The business plan should follow the guidelines given in this chapter and include sections on:

> Executive summary
> Introduction
> Market analysis and assumptions for cashflow
> SWOT analysis
> Competition analysis
> Competitive strategy
> Required resources with budget
> Cashflow forecast
> Profit and loss forecast if required by client
> Notes to the accounts
> Conclusions
> Appendices if required

The business plan will be produced by the students working in small groups and working as consultants for a client entrepreneur/firm. The completed written business plan will need to be of high quality, word processed and produced with a hard cover.

2. Students complete a final presentation to the entrepreneur/client.

REFERENCES

1. For example: BARROW, C. (1989) *The Small Business Guide*, BBC, London, or any of the commercial banks' own guides.

2. DEAKINS, D. and HUSSAIN, G. (1991) *Risk Assessment by Bank Managers*, Birmingham Polytechnic Business School, Birmingham.

3. PORTER, M. (1980) *Competitive Strategy: Techniques for Analysing Industries and Competitors*, Collier Macmillan.

4. KAY, J. (1993) 'Value-Added and Food Retailing', *Economics and Business Education*, vol. 1, no. 1.

5. FLETCHER, M. (1994) 'Bank Managers' Lending Decisions to Small Firms', Scottish Enterprise Foundation, University of Stirling, Stirling.

RECOMMENDED READING

BARROW, C. (1989) *The Small Business Guide*, BBC, London.

BARROW, C., BARROW, P., and BROWN, R. (1992) *The Business Plan Workbook*, 2nd edn, Kogan Page.

Index